Using Open Source Platforms for Business Intelligence

Using Open Source Platforms for Business Intelligence
Avoid Pitfalls and Maximize ROI

Lyndsay Wise

AMSTERDAM • BOSTON • HEIDELBERG • LONDON
NEW YORK • OXFORD • PARIS • SAN DIEGO
SAN FRANCISCO • SINGAPORE • SYDNEY • TOKYO
Morgan Kaufmann is an imprint of Elsevier

Acquiring Editor: Andrea Dierna
Development Editor: Robyn Day
Project Manager: Paul Gottehrer
Designer: Alisa Andreola

Morgan Kaufmann is an imprint of Elsevier
225 Wyman Street, Waltham, MA 02451, USA

Library of Congress Cataloging-in-Publication Data
Application submitted

British Library Cataloguing-in-Publication Data
A catalogue record for this book is available from the British Library

ISBN: 978-0-12-415811-5

For information on all MK publications
visit our website at http://store.elsevier.com

Printed and bound by CPI Group (UK) Ltd, Croydon, CR0 4YY
Transferred to digital print 2012

To Sam and Anne Wise

Contents

SECTION 3   BI STRATEGIES FOR SUCCESS – TYING IN OS ADOPTION WITH BI SUCCESS

SECTION 4   JUSTIFYING OSBI PROJECTS

Acknowledgments

I would like to thank the following people for their help, as it would not have been possible to complete this project without them. To Steve Dine, Dan Fitzpatrick, and Lindy Ryan for their patience and excellent feedback throughout the review process on this book. I would like to thank the following people and the companies they work for, for either helping to organize interviews and/or take the time to educate me further on specific products, open source outlooks, OSBI use, and general insights: Katie Hutchison, Jessica Swain, Greg Wood, Ketan Karia, Stefano Scamuzzo, Steve Sarsfield, Jill Hara, Susan Davis, Don DeLoach, Yves de Montcheuil, Mike Boyarski, Kim Leadley, Eduardo Paredes, Gerardo Macias, William McKnight, John Kearney, Zibby Keaton, Bruce Belvin, Rebecca Shomair, Kerstin Stephan, Holger Wegstein, and Benjamin Hohmann. In addition, there are several more companies that participated in case studies by sharing their experiences and outlook on open source deployments and their use of business intelligence — without their input it would not have been possible to provide insight into the real world applications of open source business intelligence. I would also like to thank Cindi Howson, Howard Dresner, David Loshin, Shawn Rogers, and Wayne Eckerson for sharing their experiences and advice unrestrictedly.

And lastly, I would like to thank Gail Wise, for providing advice, support and lending an ear throughout the writing and reviewing process.

Introduction and market overview

Introducing BI

Why is there a need for this book?

Many books exist that identify how to get the most out of analytics or how to develop an open source business intelligence (OSBI) solution based on specific development or solution requirements. The reality is that even though these books provide value within the niche they address, very little exists that provides an understanding of OSBI at the business level including:

1. What OSBI is and how its adoption can benefit organizations;
2. The general considerations required before embarking on an OSBI project and the potential challenges that exist;
3. How to justify an OSBI project from the business side (instead of from an IT development perspective); and
4. The tools required at the business decision-making level to make sure that your project is a success.

In a 2011 study of 163 companies by Project Management Solutions,[1] it was estimated that 37% of general projects are at risk of failure. Within IT related projects specifically, this number is much larger. In a 2010/2011 interview study by Geneca,[2] they found that 75% of participants lacked the confidence to achieve project success from the start, with 80% of professionals admitting that much of their time is spent on project rework. In essence, organizations are embarking on projects they may not be ready to tackle. Project failures, reworks, missing timelines, and going over budget are all signs of mismanagement, a lack of processes and best practices, and a misunderstanding of the requirements and end goal. Unfortunately, business intelligence (BI) is no different. And adding open source (OS) to the mix doesn't make things easier. In many cases, it is the opposite because of the promise of "free" and what that really means.

So, how will your organization ensure that you are in the 25% range of organizations confident and successful when implementing or expanding your OSBI environment? The reality is that there are no guarantees. But, being armed with information and an understanding of what tools you need to get there will help your business develop the proper approach to implementing an OSBI solution or, alternatively, deciding that it isn't right for your business. Either way, knowledge is power, and this knowledge has not existed in a cohesive guide to help business decision makers make sense out of business intelligence, OS, its overlaps, and how to make the right decision for the

---

[1]Project Management Solutions, http://www.pmsolutions.com/collateral/research/Strategies%20for%20Project%20Recovery%202011.pdf
[2]Geneca, http://calleam.com/WTPF/?page_id = 1445

organization as a whole. In the past, OS was a tool used by IT developers, but with the market slowly shifting towards self-service applications, business users require a greater understanding of how these solutions will benefit them by creating better visibility and higher productivity.

As an industry analyst and consultant working primarily with small and mid-sized businesses looking at implementing business intelligence solutions, I continue to see collaboration among c-level executives and IT directors when making technology and specifically, BI decisions. Because many IT developers like the promise of developing their own OS solutions for the business, many business decision makers hear the words "free software" and jump on the bandwagon. Without much else to go on, OSBI is selected. The hidden costs, extra time to develop, and other considerations seem to be outweighed by lack of initial software costs. Nowhere does the adage "free as in a puppy and not as in free beer" apply more directly than within a BI project. Business intelligence requires many separate components to make it work. Knowing how to put these together and understanding all of the areas where OS offerings may fit mean that deciding to implement OSBI requires more than a cursory understanding of the market.

The goal of this book, therefore, is to help you and others within your company make the right decisions when it comes to OS adoption. Is OSBI right for you? How is free software offset by development efforts and long-term maintenance? Is OSBI more strategic than traditional BI offerings? And how does OSBI differ from the broader business intelligence market landscape? All of these questions will be addressed while guiding you through the process of what it takes to successfully start and complete your BI initiatives. All of these questions so far are just the tip of the iceberg in terms of what needs to be asked when evaluating OS BI — or any BI project for that matter.

What to expect in this book

The overall goal of this book is to help you and your colleagues make the right BI-related software decisions. In order to do this, this book aims to address three key areas:

1. To provide an understanding of the OS market and OSBI specifically. This gives business decision makers a broader understanding of the OS market and its potential value to the business.
2. To identify what benefits, challenges, and efforts are required in OSBI development on a high level so that business decision makers will know what questions to ask.
3. To link the value proposition of BI with OS adoption — how to justify projects and make sure you have the resources you require to get the company from project initiation through BI development and delivery successfully.

Therefore, this book is broken into sections to provide easy access to your areas of interest. After reading through the sections it will be easy to go back to the areas that are of particular interest.

Section 1: Introduction and Market Overview provides an introduction of BI and why it cannot be overlooked. This section also provides an in-depth look at the OS market, BI OS, and the general options available. The importance of a general overview is not only to understand the market, but also to gain a broader perspective of how OSBI potentially meets the business requirements of your organization. In addition, because source code is provided for free, many solution providers tout that these are free solutions, when the reality is that development, maintenance, and additional hardware are costs that may be overlooked if decision makers do not understand the details involved within OS projects.

Section 2: A Deeper Look at Open Source BI goes a little deeper by providing a comparison of general OS and commercial OS offerings. This includes looking at the differences and the connotations of selecting one model over the other. This section also tackles the business benefits and challenges of OSBI and looks at why OSBI is becoming more of a contender within the realm of BI adoption. Because OS represents a niche area within the broader BI market, what it has to offer organizations is different from other business intelligence offerings. In addition, we will look at the increase in OS popularity and how it affects the BI market specifically and what it means for your organization should you choose to adopt OS.

Section 3: BI Strategies for Success — Tying in Open Source Adoption with BI Success discusses the types of companies that might benefit from OSBI adoption. Business decision makers require a broad understanding of the market to help identify how solutions compare with one another, whether OS or traditional solutions. This means defining the implications of adoption and use.

Section 4: Justifying OSBI Projects continues the theme from Section 3 by looking at how to sell an OSBI project to other business units by delving into the return on investment (ROI) and total cost of ownership (TCO) and by looking at ROI and TCO models that apply. This involves taking a step back and looking at what constitutes ROI and TCO within business intelligence projects and how they differ with OS specifically. This includes comparing options and looking at some of the differences in cost, internal resources required, and development and maintenance efforts. In essence, we take some of what we learned from Section 2 and transform it into practical next steps to evaluate potential OSBI offerings. Generally, ROI and TCO identification also enable stronger justification of project costs and initiation. Whether business or IT driven, project sponsors need to be able to justify their project costs and tie that to what they hope to achieve with their overall BI initiative. Justifying costs and project goals and tying that to increased visibility within the organization helps pave the way towards initial BI and expansions over time.

Section 5: Understanding the Technology Behind the Business Value takes a turn to identify some of the technical considerations in hopes of encouraging broader IT/business unit collaboration. Even though developers create the dashboards, analytics, and reporting, their main goal is to provide a strong data infrastructure. Because data integration, data management, and database design are the components that work towards building a strong BI infrastructure, they are impossible to overlook. Therefore, this section provides a high-level look at the general data integration requirements, what it means to work within an OS environment, what skillsets are required, potential challenges that exist, and some of the benefits of selecting OSBI. For business sponsors, this knowledge will increase the cohesion of IT/business unit relations and help business managers get a better understanding of all of the considerations and effort required to implement an OSBI offering.

Finally, *Section 6: Takeaways/Recommendations* puts all of the pieces together and provides some next steps and practical advice on how to get from software selection to implementation. Aside from the resources available through OS community participation, there are many resources that exist that businesses can take advantage of.

Now that we've looked at the purpose of this book and what it includes, let's get started! The first step is to separate ourselves from the topic of OS and to take a step back and look at business intelligence, what it is and why you need it. Once we understand its value independently, we can look at how the OS market has shifted some of the available offerings and the general expectations of organizations.

An introduction to BI

Overall, the software industry provides a broad range of solutions to meet the needs of companies, ranging from transactional and supply chain management to customer relationship management (CRM) and project planning. Organizations apply a wide variety of software throughout their companies to manage their daily operations. Unfortunately, many of these solutions are implemented independently of one another and use different infrastructures that do not easily integrate with one another. This makes it hard to understand customer lifecycles, identify broader supply chain or sales opportunities, or create a single view of information to enable better planning. Even though individual departments can generally get the general insights they need to develop the high-level metrics they require, the ability to integrate sales information with supply chain requirements or the ability to look at marketing campaigns and customer sentiment or product successes by geography may be nonexistent. Add to this the adoption of social media and continual data volume growth and using these channels to improve branding and to tie in sales and marketing initiatives and businesses may be hard-pressed to create a holistic view of performance.

Executives and business decision makers in this situation may be flying blind. In the past, executives were able to make their decisions and plan initiatives based on comparing printed static reports and conversations with business managers. This is no longer the case. A fast-paced competitive marketplace where customers (both businesses and consumers) can purchase products and services from anywhere in the world means that organizations can no longer overlook the use of analytics. Businesses require a way to centralize information assets from across the organization as well as access data from external data sources, such as through partner channels, suppliers, or on social media sites. Consolidating this data from disparate data sources leads to gained insights that are needed in order to remain competitive within a constantly changing competitive landscape.

Enter business intelligence. Figure 1-1 will provide an overview of how BI enables organizations to consolidate data from various sources, manage both data quality and business processes, and develop a series of analytics through interactive, front-end applications. Overall, traditional BI solutions have various layers but provide a way for systems that reside within disparate data sources to be integrated into a single database. The goal of this is twofold: One, to create a source of data storage and analysis that is separate from transactional data sources, and two, to enable historical data capture while limiting storage requirements that affect operational systems. Both of these combined provide the basis for a BI infrastructure. Once this infrastructure is put in place, organizations can develop the analytical layer to identify trends, manage performance, look at sales analytics, or develop thresholds as a way to alert employees of potential issues proactively. And nowadays, BI extends further into the realm of operational intelligence, where businesses look at monitoring the business in real time to adopt a more proactive approach to managing key performance indicators (KPIs) and overall performance.

Although considered by many as a software that supports operations, the reality is that much effort is required to develop and maintain a full BI infrastructure in-house. The diversity of solutions

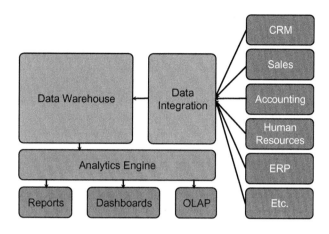

FIGURE 1-1

Traditional BI diagram — Identifying the design of BI solutions. © WiseAnalytics 2011.

available include both traditional BI environments and targeted solutions that are developed to satisfy a specific need or to address a defined business problem. Niche applications also exist that include industry-specific offerings or corporate performance management. But some of the most common BI applications include sales and marketing analytics, call center monitoring, and budgeting and forecasting. For instance, let's say a small retailer is trying to understand why sales for a particular product has dropped in 2 of their 24 stores but remained steady at the other locations. They might have to look at sales history to identify whether this is normal performance historically, whether circumstances have changed at those two locations, inventory, foot traffic, placement of items, and how these compare to the better performing locations. In order to gain this amount of visibility it becomes important to centralize varying sets of data. And what happens if weather played a factor? These two locations might be located in a dry and sunny region that has met with higher than average rainfall. In this instance, there might not be a need for customers to buy extra tanktops or sunglasses, providing a simple explanation for the drop in sales. Whether or not the answer is simple, the reality is that organizations require as much information as possible to better plan and manage their business.

In the beginning of all of this two disparate approaches to BI design became the de facto methods of development. On a high level, Bill Inmon,[3] known as the father of data warehousing, believed in the concept of building a centralized data warehouse with separate data marts[4] to address the needs of individual departments or reporting requirements, whereas Ralph Kimball,[5] known as the father of business intelligence, believed in the opposite approach — in essence, the importance of building individual data marts that reside within a broader data warehouse infrastructure.[6] Over time, these

---

[3]For more general information on Bill Inmon you can refer to Wikipedia: http://en.wikipedia.org/wiki/Bill_Inmon

[4]A data mart can almost be defined as a mini data warehouse. Essentially, a data mart is a subset of the information you would want stored in a data warehouse and usually represents a set of information required for reporting or analysis within a specific business unit — i.e., a repository of specified information. For more information, you can refer to: http://searchsqlserver.techtarget.com/definition/data-mart

[5]For more general information on Ralph Kimball you can refer to: http://en.wikipedia.org/wiki/Ralph_Kimball

[6]http://www.nagesh.com/publications/technology/173-inmon-vs-kimball-an-analysis.html

approaches have guided companies on how to build their BI strategies. And many have followed these two approaches. At the same time, due to the maturity of the market, other organizations do not follow either one of these structures but rely on vendors or consultants to make choices for them. Overall, the right strategy for your company might not be the same for another company.

In addition to the types of applications, BI's delivery and development also differ based on varying models within the industry. These include software as a service (SaaS) or cloud offerings, best of breed deployments, and OS. No matter what type of deployment, tying BI to business value and specific goals helps organizations develop a successful initiative independent of how BI is developed internally. However, the type of deployment also requires consideration because different choices will affect implementation times, development efforts, overall costs, and required resources for ongoing development and support. This is why an in-depth look at OS BI and what it has to offer becomes important. With vendor consolidation and acquisitions, new entrants, and changes in trends and features and functions, a static look at BI remains impossible. The chart below provides a general understanding of various solution types and how they fit within the overall market enables both technical and business decision makers to make the right choices for their company.

BI Delivery Type Breakdown.

BI Type	Definition	Solution Parameters
Traditional	Business intelligence is installed and developed at the customer site, with the general purpose of reporting and analytics using historical data sets.	Organizations can use one BI component or many. This may include a data warehouse, interactive reports, analytics, and/or dashboards to provide a diverse access point to information analysis.
Software as a Service	BI offerings or components that are hosted by the solution provider and offered as a service to organizations through online access.	Expands all areas of BI – with data warehouse solutions being called DaaS or data as a service; most offerings providing dashboards and analytics are targeted to specific industries or business areas.
Cloud	Similar to SaaS based on the fact that solutions/data are hosted externally to the organization. In many cases, organizations develop and maintain their own BI applications.	Many organizations choose to have portions of their data housed within a public or private cloud. BI vendors are beginning to provide this option to their customers.
Operational	Similar to traditional BI in terms of delivery but focuses on real-time or continuous business visibility.	Operational BI (OBI) requires a specific infrastructure that enables continual data updates to feed into front-end applications.
Open Source	Similar to traditional BI delivery and development but uses free source code as the basis for development.	Both community (free) and commercial versions exist and span all components of a BI environment.

Even with all of this being said, in some cases the term business intelligence can be a huge misnomer. Organizations search for ways to enhance data visibility and to increase their decision-making ability through the use of technology. The promise of BI has always been to address process bottlenecks, create a single version of the truth, and use transactional and other forms of information to drive corporate decision making while increasing profits and lowering costs. BI strives to do this by using analytic databases and interactive analytics to link business processes with consolidated organizational data. However, without the proper guidelines and project planning, initiatives might be doomed to failure. One of the best ways to get the most out of BI is to align BI use to organizational goals and overall operations.

Sometimes this can be easier said than done. One of the most important aspects outside of defining the business goals involves identifying the type of BI to be used. This choice means looking at whether an organization will implement a full BI solution, consider a best-of-breed alternative, look at SaaS, or customize an analytics environment through the use of OS. Once an organization determines this, they can narrow their search to the solutions that meet these needs. Although the other delivery methods are outside the scope of this book, your company may still want to consider a mix of solutions. Therefore, it makes sense to look at how business intelligence and OS intersect.

The components of business intelligence

Before we expand to look at the OS market, let's look a little deeper at how business intelligence pieces fit together by taking a closer look at Figure 1-1 above. The data warehouse represents where all of the information for later use is stored. Figure 1-2 shows this on a high level. The data marts so valued by both Inmon and Kimball are what make up the whole of the data warehouse. While information can be stored within the data warehouse even if it isn't being used within a specific data mart, the way in which data is captured, stored, and processed is outside the scope of this book as the aim here is to give you a very broad understanding of BI and how each component fits within a bigger whole. What Figure 1-2 does show, however, is that data can be stored multiple times within the data warehouse to address different data functions.

On the one hand, this leads to more secure access to data, whereas on the other hand, there is much more redundancy. It is important to note at this point in the discussion that both Inmon's and Kimball's approaches to data warehouse design and development are more old school, in the sense that as technology has advanced, organizations can now virtualize their data or run queries in memory, eliminating the need for robust data mart development. However, for the purposes of this book, a general BI overview will provide enough of the basics for an understanding of the OSBI marketplace.

The next component is data integration. Data integration and how it works could be a book on its own,[7] as there are many areas within data integration such as ensuring the quality of the

---

[7]And here are some of them if you'd like to explore the topic further: http://www.amazon.com/s/ref=nb_sb_ss_c_1_16?
url=search-alias%3Dstripbooks&field-keywords=data+integration&sprefix=data+integration%2Caps%2C157

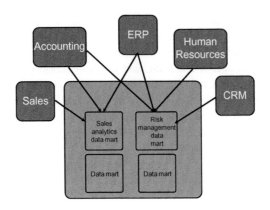

FIGURE 1-2

Understanding the data warehouse. © WiseAnalytics 2011.

information being stored or making sure that data is transformed and can be accessed within a reporting application in the most efficient way. When looking at the simplest form of data integration for BI, we refer to ETL, or extract, transform, and load, which does essentially what it says. Information is extracted from a data source. This can be from an Enterprise Resource Planning (ERP), packaged software to help organizations run the transactional side of their business, or CRM application, other transactional systems, or from Salesforce.com, QuickBooks, etc. Once the data is extracted, transformations occur so that when it is loaded within the data warehouse, it will be within a format that reflects the analytics required. Another common way in which data is loaded is using Extract Load and Transform (ELT), instead of the transformations happening before being loaded into a data warehouse, they occur afterwards.

Figure 1-3 represents a simplified look at what either one of these scenarios might look like. From left to right, the first data extract represents the ELT vision whereby data is loaded into the data warehouse as is. In many cases, the information required within specific tables are extracted and joined so that they can be populated within the data warehouse. Therefore, either Entry #1 or Entry #2 is possible, and depends upon the model chosen.[8]

Once the data is stored within the data warehouse, it can be manipulated — hence the next component being the analytics engine. This is the part that is most difficult to explain because of the fact that some solutions provide analytics within the front-end tools, while in other solutions all of this happens within the data warehouse. For companies doing all of their data transformations within the data warehouse itself, many times the number crunching and algorithms being applied will occur at the same time, with the report or front-end data analysis tool simply providing the results of these inquiries. Other BI offerings enable robust calculations within their

---

[8]Here is just one of the many online resources explaining the differences: http://www.dataacademy.com/files/ETL-vs-ELT-White-Paper.pdf. To identify which option best meets your needs, you might want to start with an online search with parameters "ELT vs. ETL."

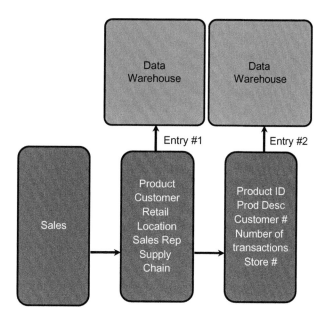

FIGURE 1-3

Data integration activities. © WiseAnalytics 2011.

toolsets. In some cases organizations leverage one or the other, while in others they leverage both. Hence, the whole discussion of analytics can become quite complicated.

The important thing to remember within all of this, though, is that the information consumed within reports and dashboards is often different than the way it would be if seen within its original table. For instance, let's say an organization wants to identify its internal sales performance leaders. This might mean looking at sales by rep, which stores or regions they are responsible for, how often do they up-sell, cross-sell, or re-sell to the same customer, and what products or services they are responsible for. To create proper analysis of performance, extra calculations are required. Within many reporting environments, the calculations are developed during report development. However, if an algorithm needs to be repeated many times, then it may be applied during the transformation phase (provided more complex data integration processes are being applied), meaning that it can be hard for business users to backtrack and identify what the original data looks like.

Overall, the ability to access diverse data sets, consolidate large amounts of information, perform analyses, and visualize this information in an easy-to-consume way is a key value to BI adoption. This is partially why various options exist. On a high level, reports can be provided to business users at different levels. As Figure 1-4 shows, many reports now come with the ability to identify high performance and problem areas through stoplight coloring. Dashboards provide a deeper level of interaction through the use of charts, graphs, geospatial access, and multiple other types of visualizations. Online Analytical Processing (OLAP), enables multi-dimensional analysis and is generally relegated to more advanced use as it enables multi-dimensional analysis. On a simple level, a business analyst can look at trends over time and drill through data while looking at

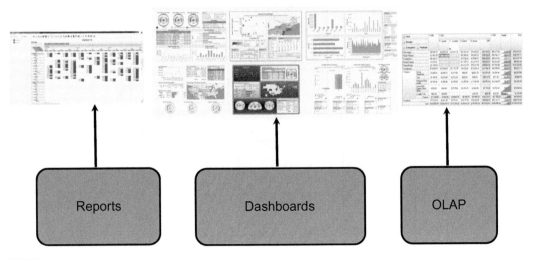

FIGURE 1-4

Front-end BI access points. © WiseAnalytics 2011.

different timeframes and how they compare or by looking at specific features of the data, such as product codes or geographic region.[9]

The important thing to remember on the whole is that BI should be used to support your business and analytics requirements. This means using technology to suit your needs and not having to fit your business processes into how the solution works. Therefore, if rolling out a solution at the management level, having a self-service model that enables easy to access reports or dashboards with the ability to drill through and identify potential causes or who is responsible for specific processes is important. If using BI as an analytics tool only, with end user use being relegated to more technical business and data analysts, then the ability to interact with the data and to create new joins and analytics may be more important than providing high-level information.

There is a term floating around the market place called "self-service." The problem is that this term differs based on which vendor is discussing it. The importance of self-service is that solution providers are trying to expand BI use by creating easy-to-use applications. This ease of use should reflect who is using the solution. Just as different business users have different roles within the organization, the way they use BI will be different. Ease of use should reflect this. Understanding how BI works and how the components fit together can help empower you to make the right choices for your organization.

---

[9] The visual images were taken from:

1. Reports: http://www.google.ca/imgres?
   start=91&hl=en&sa=X&biw=1370&bih=1060&tbm=isch&prmd=imvns&tbnid=pBwEUeNyxVmHZM:&imgrefurl=
   http://www.freedownloadmanager.org/download/reporting_software/&docid=BVxVjjIvu-PYHM&itg=1&imgurl=
   http://www.xcubesoftware.com/Visualyzer1PNG&w=1919&h=1040&ei=UVNmT9GOG-bV0QGpn4H-Bw&zoom=1
   &iact=hc&vpx=509&vpy=158&dur=2046&hovh=165&hovw=305&tx=144&ty=111&sig=108172123316056972975
   &page=4&tbnh=108&tbnw=200&ndsp=36&ved=1t:429,r:8,s:91
2. Dashboards: http://www.dashboardfree.com/
3. OLAP: http://www.softplatz.net/shots/38280-src.gif

OS overview

Why understanding OS matters

Chapter 1 looked at BI, what it is, how it works, and a little about why it is important for your organization to consider it. If you've already looked at it, or have been using it, then you might be wondering what OS is and how it applies to BI. After all, the promise of free software can be a strong driver for many organizations. In general though, the search for the right BI solution takes time and much study. Even organizations with mature BI environments that have used this technology for years tend to reevaluate their current solutions every few years as they expand their BI use. With advancements in database technologies, increasing storage, broader applications of analytics, and lower price points, old data warehouses no longer provide optimal BI analytics support. The same can be said for front-end analytics and reporting applications that only meet the needs of a subset of end users and that have limited functionality and interactivity in comparison with newer application options. Consequently, market shifts that exist within OS or broader technologies make evaluating the role of technology and current IT infrastructure within any company essential to maintaining competitive advantage and data visibility. For BI this is especially true because the whole goal of its use is to enhance overall decision making.

Because OSBI can be considered a newer entrant to the overall BI landscape, organizations should develop an understanding of the broader OS market, framework, and why it matters to be able to better understand the differences in licensing, costs, methodology, and development. In general, many traditional software models are shifting to provide organizations with more flexibility in the areas of maintenance, licensing, and development. We can see this as many BI offerings develop complementary cloud solutions, which include subscription licensing to let customers pay on a monthly or yearly basis. Although OS solutions do include commercial offerings that resemble traditional BI offerings somewhat, their overall premise and methodology differ from other software options. This makes it difficult to compare OS against traditional BI offerings unless there is a strong understanding of how OSBI and general OS solutions work. The way to do this requires moving beyond free source code and internal development efforts towards looking at the broader applications of OS, its community driven approach, and how it has evolved over time.

Therefore, before delving into OSBI, looking at how OS can be applied within organizations, and the various trends in the marketplace associated with its use, it is important to take a step back and look at OS more broadly. In many cases, businesses jump into BI or apply new types of technologies without evaluating the benefits and challenges in relation to their company specifically. Many of the companies I've spoken with over the years will state honestly that they have selected their BI solution because a former colleague of theirs or one of their friends working for another organization implemented X solution. Although most BI offerings can be broadly applied within most companies, this is not the way to go about optimizing business visibility. Having a general understanding of technologies and financial considerations gives decision makers an entry point to a broader understanding. This means that a deep background is still required to make informed BI and technology decisions. With the number of solution offerings available, the evaluation of BI can become overwhelming. Developing an understanding of solution type, key differentiations, solution capabilities, and value proposition of each means that companies can consider OS alongside traditional BI options and evaluate both on an even playing field. In addition, with the increase in BI decisions coming from areas of the company external to IT, understanding OS and specific BI offerings becomes more important than ever.

Taking this further, OS actually reflects both a philosophy and set of methodologies. Some organizations are more apt to adopt the same premises and outlook in relation to their software development. Therefore, in some cases, OSBI may not be adopted because of the desire to have access to free source code, but rather because companies like the idea of working with open technologies and not being limited to proprietary software. Organizations with this type of outlook are ripe for OS adoption. Other businesses may apply their own set of standards or may be tightly linked to proprietary software and hardware infrastructures. As OS adoption starts to expand, many organizations are beginning to integrate OS projects with proprietary applications to get the most out of a mix of customized and off-the-shelf solutions. The implication for BI solutions is that companies may be more likely to consider OSBI due to their comfort with other projects that are based on previous OS initiatives.

As long as organizations understand all of their BI options from both a business and technology perspective they will be better able to make the right BI decisions, with the goal being to implement the best possible solution for the business. And this means going beyond what is recommended by friends or former colleagues. With the emergence of commercial OS options, which are most similar to traditional BI solutions, the playing field is leveled because OSBI now crosses into the realm of both traditional OS options and provides more direct competition within the broader BI market. Therefore, the real goal of this chapter is to provide readers with a greater perspective of OS environments that can help companies move beyond a general understanding of the background of how OS solutions relate to OSBI and towards being an active partner with IT developers in relation to development requirements and software selection.

A historical look at the broader OS market

Open source is not just a set of solutions sold or marketed by vendors. The adoption of OS actually reflects an outlook and set of methodologies that fall outside the realm of proprietary software development. The fight between proprietary and open software with access to free source code continues to exist and even thrive despite the decades of each developing their own niche products to deliver within organizations. How and why businesses choose to apply technology and select either proprietary or OS may or may not reflect the philosophy behind free software adoption. Let's look at a broad and general history of OS and use it as an entry point as well as a first step to understanding the background of OSBI and its evolution towards broader adoption.

Initially, developers created software that was applied in a limited way within organizations. For instance, many CRM or ERP solutions were built internally to meet individual needs. In other cases, proprietary solutions were selected for key operational solutions such as ERP with supporting solutions being developed in-house. A good example is reporting, whereby many organizations needed to create their own way of integrating multiple data types to try to get the most out of information, hence the importance placed on Excel. As time went on, as price points started to come down, and as businesses started expanding in relation to the use of personal computers, it was assumed that most knowledge workers did not require access to the source code behind the applications being used. This enabled broader use across the organization and ensured that only developers or those with in-depth knowledge could play around with the solution. Couple this with the fact that many organizations wanted to create and control their own methods and processes and proprietary software was born.

To understand OS more completely, it is first important to look more deeply at what proprietary offerings are. Overall, it can be said that proprietary solution providers have the main goal of making profits. This is done through the control of intellectual property. A pretty straightforward definition is provided by pcmag.com: "proprietary software is owned by a single organization or software."[1] This differs greatly from the world of OS. Proprietary solutions have the goal of controlling intellectual property, but free software has a different market outlook. Open source is based on the goal of sharing and trying to enhance applications through collaborative efforts without being limited by challenges of trying to control intellectual property. Consequently, a rift was created within the software community.[2]

So how did OS develop into an area that is looked at by many companies and widely adopted? And why does the market need this diversity? The GNU General Public License (GPL) is a body that was created with the goal of peer production and collaboration through the ability to share free software, while preserving the rights of the user and not the creator.[3] In essence, the key difference between this outlook and that of proprietary offerings is whose rights are protected. In his article, "Why Software Should Not Have Owners,"[4] Richard Stallman, activist of free software and founder of the GNU Project, discusses the philosophy of providing developers with free software. Stallman looks at the concept of freedom and its importance in relation to information and the difference between OS and free software. But this distinction causes extra confusion; after all, in Chapter 1, one of the determinations of OS was the fact that it is free. Basically, the ethical idea behind free software is that it is software that gives the user freedom — freedom to create, among other things. The premise behind OS is that the ability to use source code for free hopefully leads to the best possible solution with a continuous focus on improvement.

While both are similar in outlook, they also differ. Within the camp of OSBI, although some developers may feel attached to the concept of free software, the reality is that most BI-related OS

---

[1]http://www.pcmag.com/encyclopedia_term/0,2542,t=proprietary+software&i=49869,00.asp

[2]Developed by the Northwest Regional Educational Laboratory, Portland, Oregon. http://www.netc.org/openoptions/background/history.html#overview

[3]Developed by the Northwest Regional Educational Laboratory, Portland, Oregon. http://www.netc.org/opneoptions/background/history.htm/#overview

[4]Richard Stallman. http://www.gnu.org/philosophy/why-free.html

projects, from the developer perspective, are based on the premise of developing solutions with the goal of continuous improvement and developing the best possible BI. There is a focus on community development or vendors enhancing solutions based on use and customer feedback. Either way, although different in outlook, the output is similar. Both provide access to software offerings and/or source code without the confinements associated with proprietary solutions.

The BI market adds extra confusion to this explanation because there is a continuing focus on commercializing offerings, creating a two-tiered approach to solutions and a shift away from Stallman's outlook related to the provision of free software access. Basically, the market falls into various categories, one of which is commercial OS. Commercial OSBI offerings resemble traditional BI solutions but are based on OS development by taking OSBI one step further and creating an out-of-the-box OSBI solution with additional features. The implications are that many OSBI vendors are developing profit models based on capabilities and not simply services. These differences will be discussed in Chapter 3 when we explore the convergence of OS with BI.

The increasing focus on commercial OS, however, pushes the boundaries of the concepts behind OS availability and its general philosophy. After all, commercializing open software begs the question of whether these offerings can still be called OS, if OS is based on free software that protects the rights of the users instead of the creators. And in reality, the creators in this sense end up being the solution providers and not the developers themselves. Even though community versions still exist, both types of solutions might differ greatly even though they are technically the same market offering.

On the other hand, because the general BI market is becoming more saturated and solutions are becoming less differentiated due to enhancements in technology, there is a slow shift towards value added services, with organizations looking for diversity in their product offerings. As OSBI continues to move in this direction in order to compete with mainstream BI options, its focus on commercial offerings, while taking advantage of ingrained training and support, will continue. As this trend continues, both types of delivery options will continue to exist, but many vendors will expand their focus in the direction of profit-based BI offerings while continuing to develop solutions with OS as the framework, although a move away from the philosophy of free software and OS seems to be antithetical to OSBI. However, by combining both philosophies, organizations can choose their comfort level with OSBI and grow in their adoption over time. For instance, some organizations want to try software before they choose to buy it. In this case, community first with an expansion to commercial might be the way to go. Other organizations want to take advantage of the concepts of OS and the perception of lower price points but still use more traditional software, which also makes commercial offerings a good choice. There are also many companies that have diehard fans of OS, with IT developers selecting OS even when price is not a consideration.

As you can see, the concept of OS has far-reaching consequences for broader software adoption, especially when looking at its effects on BI. When breaking OS down to its bare bones, the reality is that free software proponents do not feel that a corporation, in essence, should control the intellectual property associated with software development and take away the autonomy and flexibility of development and use. This next section will take this further to look at why many organizations are looking at OSBI as a valid alternative to more traditional types of BI deployments. Although initial thoughts might center on the reality of free software, the appeal is actually much broader. And even though the next section focuses on the positive aspects associated with why organizations are attracted to OS, future chapters and individual sections will discuss real-life examples of adoption, what worked, the challenges, and why some companies might want to steer clear of its use.

The general appeal of OS

Many of the benefits of OS are the same, irrespective of whether discussing a BI endeavor specifically or one outside the realm of BI. Even though developers like the concepts surrounding OS due to the free source code and flexibility of development that does not exist within a proprietary environment, project sponsors still require buy-in to move away from traditional software offerings.[5] Even for organizations familiar with OS environments, the transition towards using OS for BI requires extra justification based on the fact that OSBI still remains outside of the realm of traditional software offerings for many.

The following list looks at some of the benefits of OS and the positive aspects associated with applying an OS framework as part of a BI initiative. Therefore, even though the benefits mentioned below reflect OS in general, more specific examples and applications will relate to OSBI specifically to provide some insight into how and/or why similar organizations might be interested in OS adoption.

Community: OS communities are the basis behind OS success. Online communities decide the success or failure of any OS solution due to the fact that the rate of development is affected by the amount of interaction. For instance, even for vendors that control development, community interactivity helps them determine their product roadmap. The general purpose of the community is to interact with others in relation to common projects and to collaborate with others on similar initiatives. Additionally, community involvement provides developers with access to information, resources, and a way to contribute knowledge and expertise outside the confines of the organization. This is done by adding source code to the community portal, answering questions, and working on specific development projects. In some cases, community involvement and the availability to participate will differ depending on the OS environment and/or solution provider.

Collaboration: Collaboration within OS is really an extension of the community. One of the main benefits outside of the ability to coordinate development efforts among multiple companies is the development cycle of OS solutions. Due to the sheer numbers of developers involved within OS projects, or at least providing feedback, bug fixes and updates to products are provided more quickly. Because of this, there is a broader focus on continual improvement and quicker updates to commercial software offerings as well.

---

[5]Just a quick note on development flexibility. Free source code essentially gives programmers a skeleton of a BI solution. Essentially, developers can download software from the Web, which installs easily and can be customized to the liking of the business. Even though this will be discussed at length further in this book, it is important to note early on that many developers are drawn to the independence of being able to customize solutions and develop custom applications without the confinements of proprietary software.

IT developer flexibility: Each organization differs in terms of their specific business, how it is run, and the interaction of disparate business units. Even working within similar industries and having like corporate structures does not ensure the same metrics identification or overall business vision and goals. Open source enables broader flexibility in relation to the development of targeted solutions. Proprietary software limits the ability to customize, change, and enhance offerings. While many organizations choose to make changes outside the parameters of what a proprietary offering will allow, support for these changes are nonexistent. Therefore, if a developer "breaks" a solution, they will have to fix it independently, even though the organization is most likely paying for software support. Within OS, the sky is the limit, with encouragement from both solution providers and other developers to experiment, fix problems, and share discoveries. In addition, more flexibility exists in relation to applying business requirements and enhancements over time.

Organization ownership: One of the debates between proprietary and OS models is intellectual property and solution ownership, as already discussed. Proprietary models base their raison d'être on making money and controlling defined solution offerings (which is why aspects such as support are limited to what is being controlled by the vendor). This limits the ownership of any one solution, as organizations are tied in to service agreements and support that limits what a business can do in terms of really making the solution their own and optimizing solution architecture based on their needs as opposed to how the proprietary solution is designed. Open source is almost the opposite. Source code is provided for free — in most cases — with the intention of encouraging creativity and individuality. Consequently, both the organization and the developer ownership of projects and solutions can only be fully realized through the adoption of these solutions.

Building targeted/unique solutions: As mentioned, due to unique organization-wide requirements, many companies prefer to develop their own solutions in-house. Off-the-shelf offerings generally adhere to the 80/20 rule in which almost 80% of the functionality will meet the business requirements upon initial implementation. The additional 20% requires customization. Even with most of the features and functions aligned to business goals, the reality is that many companies still get benefits from taking the time to do it themselves, depending on what the final end goal is. OS provides the basics as opposed to building a full solution in-house and couples that with the additional goals identified above.

Continuous development: In many cases, the continuous development environment enables OS solutions to enhance their offerings with software releases that occur more often that other types of software offerings. Most vendors schedule regular development cycles to provide enhancements to their customers, OS has the added advantage of access to a greater number of developers with more diverse skill sets who constantly testing and developing within their own environments.

Commercial OS for BI: The six benefits above lead to many OS solution providers developing commercial software that can compete with traditional BI offerings while integrating the general benefits associated with broader OS environments. For organizations not sure about whether OS is for them, there is still the possibility of adapting the OS model within a traditional offering through the adoption of commercial OS, essentially taking a mix of the best of both worlds. Although not true OS anymore, in the sense of its original altruistic intent, commercial OSBI is still built using OS solutions and provides more out-of-the-box functionality.

The OS market specifically

Even though a part of BI and the focus of this book, OS actually lives independently and has its own niche within the software market, as discussed. OS solutions exist within every software market, from front-end operational, transactional, and operational systems to complex database development environments. BI represents a subset of available offerings.

For many years OS has been a movement of its own, providing IT developer access through online community involvement and broad collaboration on multiple projects. With communities and broad OS projects, some developers now prefer to create their own solutions as opposed to implementing standard commercial offerings. Once a company starts to build its own applications, adding on may seem like the natural course of action. The same is true when looking at BI projects. Organizations used to OS naturally flock to BI offerings that provide the same flexibility while using open standards.

Due to the success of general OS technologies, access to documentation, and community support, some IT departments look to OS for many of their operations and transactional solutions. With BI being the next step to broader data and business visibility, organizations used to OS are more likely to embrace the opportunity to expand their OS environment by adding a BI framework.

Until a few years ago, the adoption of OSBI was used in this fashion. Organizations not familiar with OS were rarely aware of the availability of OSBI offerings. Due to general OSBI success, solution providers decided to educate the broader BI marketplace in hopes of expanding their market share. Consequently, companies that may not have looked at OSBI as an alternative or as a contender now look at OSBI as a way to gain competitive advantage within their respective industries. Due to this increasing interest, OS solution providers felt they could capitalize on this demand by expanding their offerings by providing a two-tiered approach to OSBI. The first being the type discussed — free access to source code. The second being a commercial offering that mimics traditional BI offerings by providing native access to additional features not available in the community versions. This shift has led to OSBI solutions becoming direct competition for traditional vendors as companies start to evaluate types of solutions side by side.

As discussed, the commercial OS market opens OSBI up to the broader BI marketplace. For businesses without strong IT infrastructures or developers looking to create BI solutions from scratch, commercial OS provides a way to get the benefits of OS coupled with traditional software models. Because of the strong community focus of OS solutions, the development cycle tends to be quicker, as internal R&D departments can take advantage of community involvement to identify bugs, trends in requests, and collaborative work. The constant focus on collaboration and enhancements make OSBI solutions attractive to organizations that look at BI as a way to remain ahead of the curve by using technology to drive business.

Personal thoughts about OS expansion

Even though this last section sounds like I am a great proponent of OSBI, the reality is that I don't believe that it is the right solution for all organizations. Throughout this book, starting in Section 2, I will introduce various organizations involved in OS projects as well as some consultants and discuss their OSBI experiences. These will shed light on the benefits and challenges of such implementations. But I do not want to give the impression that I encourage OS adoption. In fact, although I think that some companies do and will benefit greatly from its adoption, in other cases I feel that organizations should select a more traditional approach to BI use. Overall, the end choice is yours, but hopefully by the end of this book you will have the tools you need to make the right strategic choices for your business, both short term and longer term.

The convergence of OS and BI

OSBI gaining popularity

In the beginning, OSBI remained an area outside of mainstream BI.[1] Companies adopting BI within the realm of OS were mainly those familiar with OS methodology and practices and incorporated these frameworks within their IT platforms. In most cases, adoption was driven from IT departments or within niche industries looking at solutions with lower price points. The comfort and knowledge of BI practices more broadly remained small at best, meaning that many organizations were limited in their ability to get the most out of the OSBI technologies available. In addition, much of the development effort stayed focused on IT-centered initiatives, making business unit input secondary to IT-driven initiatives. After all, without a deep understanding of technology or the value of OS, communication between IT departments and varying business units remains limited, and the ability of business decision makers to provide valuable input is less than ideal. We'll discuss this more when looking at selling BI in Chapter 10.

On the other side of the coin, OSBI vendors have focused their efforts on integrating their solutions within other OS offerings, such as reporting with databases, etc. This means that their visibility remains within OS circles, online communities, and through trade shows dedicated to showcasing OS technologies.[2] In the past, this limited OSBI's reach and overall understanding within the world of BI. Many companies considering BI remained unaware of OS options and in some cases, its existence altogether. In other cases, organizations felt that free source code would not be of value or would require too much work to develop something effective within the organization. After all, for businesses that place value on the mighty dollar, anything free can lead to a perception of lack of worth. And even though OS is not free due to the development efforts and overall maintenance required, the lack of budget required for additional software potentially leaves a sour taste in some decision makers' mouths.

Because of these factors and many more, most of the understanding that existed in relation to OSBI remained limited to those with OS development experience, leaving many business units in

---

[1] When I first started attending TDWI (The Data Warehouse Institute) conferences almost 7 years ago, OSBI vendors were nowhere to be seen. They started popping up just over 5 years ago and during one interview I was told that it was a strategic move and that at OS conferences they were asked, "what is BI?", whereas at TDWI, they were getting questions related to OS, including, "what is it?".

[2] Some of these include: http://oss2012.org/, http://www.oscon.com/oscon2012, http://www.opensourceconference.nl/771, http://www.opensourceworldconference.com/en, with others being specific to universities, types of OS applications, etc.

the dark about OS outside of knowing the name of the reporting solution they were using. Although requirements may be gathered and business rules input provided by the business, without end user or business stakeholder understanding, some of the technical requirements or other aspects of OS might be misunderstood. For instance, implementing an interactive reporting solution on top of an organization's operations systems might involve developing a series of parameterized reports that reflect a limited set of data tables or that are based on predefined timeframes dependent on overall IT dependencies within other business functions. To move to the next level, however, the business requires an understanding of what is possible as well as what lies outside the possibility of OSBI's capabilities, if anything. The goal being to align corporate and business goals with BI project expectations.

In the past, this advanced understanding may not have been as important. But within the past few years, OSBI vendors have become much more entrenched within the broader BI marketplace. They are better known, market their unique outlook, and have several well-known customer reference points to draw from. Because of all of this, organizations can no longer feign ignorance. In some instances organizations evaluate OS and traditional BI side by side based on features and functionality, while in other cases companies place OS as a high priority to save money on software expenditures. Add to this the increase in expectations concerning collaboration, self-service BI, and other market trends, and the importance of IT and business units working together cannot be overlooked. Luckily, with the increasing popularity of OSBI within mainstream BI channels, this becomes possible. Granted, much of this newfound understanding of OSBI within many organizations really is based on the efforts made by OSBI vendors and their goal of becoming a competitive factor within the BI marketplace.

Although still a large part of OS collaboration, the transition to becoming a competitive factor within BI has implications for both vendors and organizations alike, as discussed in the following.

Vendors: Solution providers now focus on targeting two audiences and customizing their marketing efforts based on either OS-only or BI-specific campaigns. These are the developer community on the one hand and organizations looking at BI implementations on the other. This push towards broader customer bases means general customer expansion as well as new offerings. For instance, commercial OS is becoming quite popular within BI circles as it combines the benefits of an off-the-shelf solution with OS methodology. In addition, it widens adoption of OSBI to include business units and implementations independent of IT-development-only initiatives.

Organizations: Companies evaluating BI solutions now have additional offerings to consider. In some cases, organizations do not want proprietary software that is difficult to integrate with existing data sources, or to pay the maintenance fees associated with large-scale deployments. These businesses also have the option of implementing a community version and then upgrading to commercial use if desired. Even though other solution providers offer free trials or versions of software, limitations normally exist. Development efforts might be more extensive, but the investment made pays off automatically if the organization is satisfied with the designed solution.

Increasingly the push towards commercial OS and marketing campaigns that increase general awareness of OSBI solutions leads to businesses evaluating OSBI solutions alongside traditional BI solutions. Now, after many years of having BI within the organization but being limited by out-of-date technologies, some companies are looking to rip and replace their traditional BI infrastructures and use OS solutions instead. Due to market changes and technological advancements, BI offerings are also different than they used to be. More interactivity and flexibility exist both in relation to front-end solutions and delivery methods. OS is beginning to compete more broadly on this level by continually taking advantage of its community involvement.

The expansion of OS offerings and positioning

The position of OSBI within the broader market landscape is slowly shifting to cover the expanse of the general BI marketplace in terms of capabilities provided. In addition, the market breaks down further to include free software, commercial offerings, and BI in the cloud, among others. Whereas several years ago OSBI remained an option outside of mainstream BI, now OSBI is becoming a valid alternative to traditional BI offerings. In general, the OSBI solution landscape is broken down as follows:

- free source code to be used at will;
- free OS with additional services; and
- adoption of commercial OSBI options.

Organizations generally choose to apply one of these models once they select OSBI. General adoption and availability, in turn, leads to vendor expansion and broader availability of solutions. Although some OSBI offerings are still focused on free source code access, many have shifted towards commercial offerings in the hopes of becoming direct competitors within the realm of traditional BI solutions. *Section 2: A Deeper Look at Open Source BI* delves into commercial OS and its implications to the broader marketplace. Consequently, OSBI adoption is moving along the spectrum from general IT developer adoption through full BI implementations. Some organizations move throughout the phases identified above, while others look to commercial offerings as a first step to implementing BI or as a reevaluation of their BI environment. Either way, all provide logical entry points or expansions into OSBI.

Free source code and the IT development efforts associated with developing independent BI applications represent a bulk of OSBI initiatives. Many organizations still select OSBI source code as a base for their BI initiatives. While taking part in community endeavors, internal creation and deployment of analytics remains the extension of tweaking the source code to meet the business requirements of the organization without having to evaluate and select traditional software. Although still subject to the cost of development, many of these organizations feel that this alternative provides them with free software because of the fact that they do not pay for software or licensing and are not limited by proprietary software limitations.

In some cases, IT developers want more defined support when implementing an OS solution. Therefore, the addition of training manuals and general documentation or paid support complements the OSBI development environment. Some OS solution providers consider a customer as anyone who purchases anything. Therefore, when evaluating a solution provider based on customer base and viability, it becomes important to identify general customers versus full solution or commercial customers and get an explanation from the OS vendor as to how they break down their customer base. Either way, the fact remains that OSBI vendors offer varying levels of services and support for their customers. Organizations looking to remain independent of commercial software use can still utilize documentation and support services without compromising on independent development efforts.

Finally, some businesses prefer to adopt BI using traditional models. For these companies, project sponsorship and overall development efforts may or may not reside within IT departments. These organizations are beginning to evaluate commercial OS alongside their traditional BI counterparts. One OSBI vendor actually confided in me that a large number of their opportunities are coming from organizations that are disillusioned with their traditional implementations. And in essence, commercial OS provides similar benefits and overall models as a traditional BI offering. However, they may couple more flexibility due to being aligned with an OS model.

The unique fit of OSBI and its effects on the broader market landscape

As identified above, OSBI represents one type of deployment model within the realm of BI. In addition, both OS and commercial OS represent a niche market within the BI space that has opened up this broader market to businesses that may have felt that BI was out of their reach. With the focus on free software and by becoming a key consideration of many businesses, other solution providers have started providing free trials and versions of their software to give companies the opportunity to try BI without making blind investments. As traditional BI vendors expand the way they provide their solutions to customers and as OS becomes a more viable option, companies start to look at both types of offerings on an even playing field, leading to the likelihood of OSBI acceptance on a broader level.

Organizations can select any of these models and develop a successful BI framework to meet the BI requirements of their company. This actually makes it more complicated for companies trying to figure out what model will work best within their organization and what the real differences are between various offerings. After all, if many solutions can be accessed for free, what are the real differences? Overall, most free offerings made available by traditional vendors are limited by the number of users, how many data sources can be accessed, or delivery (i.e., desktop only). This shift in the marketplace, even with these limitations, is great for organizations because it puts greater power into the hands of end users by increasing overall diversity. By pushing the boundaries of what BI has to offer, other solution providers end up being forced to expand their offerings to compete with broader models of deployment. In the long-term this means that OSBI can also help push the limits of traditional BI solutions and become an integral part of the broader BI marketplace.

Breakdown of OSBI technology

Now is a good time to turn our attention towards the types of offerings available within OSBI. Overall, BI solutions are similar in terms of types of available offerings, whether traditional BI or OS. However, in order to understand the potential of OS, it becomes important to break down the market into digestible chunks by understanding the technologies and how they fit together to provide real business value, even though the concept of value is broad and not always concrete because not all organizations can associate financial benefits to their BI deployments. The ability to define value in terms of business visibility becomes an essential part of any BI software evaluation. The proper way to do this requires stepping back from current industry knowledge and looking at the available solutions from a new perspective.

This section shifts focus from the market and looks at a breakdown of technologies. What is available within OS and how do organizations know what they need within the stack? Answering these two questions alone can help businesses position their needs within the market and choose relevant solutions accordingly. In some cases this may be only evaluating OS technology, while in others this means determining how OSBI offerings match up to broader market offerings.

Each area of technology or solution type discussed below represents a piece of the full BI pie. Even with the desire to deploy a full BI framework, organizations still have the choice to pick and choose what solutions they use and which ones are within the arena of OS. Generally, adapters exist that help with disparate solution integration and enable businesses to pick and choose preferred solutions that meet the targeted business needs of the organization.

The general BI landscape is broken down into the following components, which are discussed in more detail below: data warehousing, analytics, reporting, dashboards, data integration, and embedded analytics. Since we've discussed these in Chapter 1, it doesn't make sense to go over them here. So, for the breakdown provided below, we are going to focus specifically on how these components relate to the world of open source to help you understand how the BI and open source overlap.

Data warehousing

The data warehouse has always provided the back-end infrastructure portion of any BI project. And in many cases, it represents the easiest adoption of OS. This is due to the fact that any data warehousing initiative requires developer effort. Whether using consulting services for an implementation or developing a data warehouse in-house, the amount of effort required to fine-tune and maintain the data warehouse leads to an expectation of effort required. After all, even companies now leaning towards implementing a data warehouse appliance realize that a specific amount of effort and skillset will be required to maintain it over time. This type of expectation means that organizations looking at gaining new or targeted skills where much ongoing effort is required are more likely to be open to adopting an OS platform. Although still required to purchase hardware, with a free software component the organization has full control over how they develop and manage their solution, and all of this without having to worry about proprietary roadblocks.

This lack of restrictions enables IT developers to become more creative and design solutions that meet the needs of the organization beyond that of an out-of-the-box data warehouse. In terms of available options for businesses, two forms of OS data warehouse offerings exist, as follows.

OS data warehouses

Some OS technologies, such as MySQL and RedHat, can be customized to serve as data warehouses. Many organizations adopt these database technologies to store their operational data outside of a traditional MSFT SQL, IBM, SAP, or Oracle shop. These developers are actually able to transfer their knowledge from database optimization to data warehouse creation. This in turn becomes cost effective to the organization because no new resources are required to develop the new data warehouse. And for environments where this is not the case, businesses can take advantage of multiple IT staff having transferrable skills that can be used across IT initiatives.

OS database technologies are not initially optimized for data warehouse use and may require specific development functions to enable crossover functionality. Each database requires unique customization and potentially different skillsets, meaning that data warehouse goal alignment with realistic expectations becomes essential for a successful data warehouse project. In terms of software selection, OS database vendors will generally be in a position to have potential data warehousing capabilities even though they fall outside of the traditional data warehousing market.

Solutions that use OS databases for date warehouse optimization

Many data warehousing solutions are taking advantage of OS technology as a way to develop analytics platforms while remaining competitive in terms of overall pricing. SAND and Infobright are two examples of vendors that use OS as their system of choice. The key benefit for organizations, aside from optimized OS data warehousing performance, remains lower overall price points. Because development efforts are based on free software, proprietary costs do not apply. Generally, these offerings compete within both the traditional data warehouse and appliance markets.

In some cases, businesses don't realize the technologies within the back end of these solutions and select them based on their best of breed functionality (as each data warehousing solution has their niche applications). For other organizations, the use of OS databases provides a huge benefit. Either way, the ability to incorporate OS applications into broader offerings benefits organizations and vendors alike.

Analytics

The goal of analytics for most organizations differs in many aspects but also overlaps in the sense that businesses apply analytics to broaden visibility into performance and the ability to plan more effectively. Applications are broad and can be applied across any business unit and can apply to any business need. Some OS vendors such as Jaspersoft or Pentaho offer these feature sets and are known as BI solution providers.

Within any analytics application that is built in-house, development requirements are high. For businesses that develop analytics independent of an out-of-the-box solution, the reality remains that, whether mainstream or OS, the efforts involved to streamline requirements remain similar. Many organizations are looking at targeted analytics due to an increasing variety of available offerings because they provide a high percentage of the required functionality out of the box. Others choose to develop their own applications in-house. Either way, OS use for analytics can be a good step towards detailed and targeted solutions.

Most OS solutions that provide analytics do so as part of a broader BI solution. For organizations considering analytics as a standalone to fit with existing applications, each solution should be evaluated separately to identify required skillsets and which analytics require customization. Generally, high-level analytics are available with detailed functionality requiring customization. However, the extent of customization and development differs per solution, which would be the same with any commercial software offering.

Reporting and dashboards

Reporting has always been a key aspect of BI. Organizations look to their reports to identify performance, trends, and discrepancies in financials. The reality though, is that to remain competitive, reports are no longer enough. Now interactive reporting with drill-through capabilities is essential. Many organizations and solution providers alike combine reports with charts, graphs, and other dashboard visualizations. With this being said, reporting still remains a separate area that most OSBI vendors focus on to provide customers with high levels of interactivity. In addition, because of spreadsheets and the inability to maintain a single access point to data across organizations, reporting enables a single access point to data as well as its maintenance.

Now, with interactive drag-and-drop development environments, report creation becomes an easy access point to BI-related information. In many cases, the first access point to BI or an organization-wide reporting solution. Jaspersoft is known for its strong reporting solutions, with the rest developing high-end reporting solutions to compete with Jaspersoft's reporting environment. Due to this focus on features and functionality sets, most OSBI offerings can provide similar reporting functions as other BI vendors.

Dashboards are a little bit different. In essence, dashboards are still the newest entry to BI components. Based on the fact that dashboards are created using a set of visualizations that provide metrics and performance indicators to executives and business managers, they provide increased levels of ease of use. This enables broader BI adoption. In addition, due to their recent place within the BI market landscape, the development environment remains similar to the wider market, with development efforts being similar across the board at the visualization layer.

The main issue with dashboard design, development, and the efforts involved in getting the information represented properly remains within the data layer. Each solution, whether OS or traditional, involves a data integration layer required to load and stream the data effectively. This requirement remains the same whether data is captured within a data warehouse or not. The differences involve the processes required to load and maintain data quality over time.

Data integration

Outside of Talend and Javlin (CloverETL), data integration suites within the OS world that focus on BI specifically are hard to come by. These solutions, however, provide general integration features with easy to set up processes to capture and load the relevant data sources. Commercial versions generally offer more robust functionality, but for simple projects these solutions are easy to use, unlike other more complicated offerings. The challenge for businesses remains identifying the data integration requirements and matching them with the developer efforts and skills required. After all, at the community level, many of these solutions lack the sophistication of other solutions available in the market. Overall, though, data integration initiatives require large effort no matter what the solution choice. Therefore, an in-depth cost-benefit analysis should be completed to determine the benefits of OS versus more traditional or larger scale integration efforts. Considerations include the number of data sources, the amount of transformation, business rule complexity, ease of integration, and the list goes on. For many organizations, the choice of back-end solutions takes more effort than their front-end counterparts due to the complexities that exist within integration activities.

Embedded analytics

The R Project is a good example of embedded analytics and a statistical analysis solution that provides advanced statistical analysis within an OS framework. R is one of the software choices that many BI vendors use to embed within their offerings or to provide adapters to connect to in order to enable statistical and predictive analytics capabilities. Not many solutions exist with advanced analytics capabilities within OS, but those that do are very powerful and are used for higher education and research functions. With more demand for increased complexity, the use of R continues to increase and to become more commonplace within OS projects and traditional BI implementations alike.

General considerations for organizations

Even though it might be too soon to identify whether your business would benefit from OSBI, here are some initial considerations:

- Identify the model that fits best within the organization. For instance, which of the three levels of OS would be the best fit?[3] If an organization is already familiar with OS, then developing a full BI solution on its own might be realistic. The other end of the spectrum might be a business looking for alternatives to what it is currently using, but not comfortable with independent development. In this case, short list criteria will involve non-OS solution providers, making the selection process more difficult due to the large number of potential competitors.
- Look at what benefits of OS meet the business requirements. Whether access to a community, developing a fully targeted solution, collaborating with other organizations, or the like, different aspects of OSBI will appeal to different organizations as well as project stakeholders. The ability to hone in on and match benefits with the investment made in the project will help organizations get more out of their OS initiative. In addition, now that business units are becoming more involved in the software development process, inclusion in OS ideology can help attain and maintain stakeholder and end user buy-in.
- Evaluate overall costs and deployment models. Although not yet discussed at length, looking at the costs related to new hardware, software, licensing, support, and maintenance help limit the scope of software selection due to budget constraints. OSBI offerings may have similar models but will still differ in terms of costs and efforts depending upon the end goals of the organization. With businesses looking at developing and maintaining the solution independently of the software provider, costs associated with development and maintenance may still match traditional software offerings depending on what the company hopes to achieve.
- Identify the general challenges of OS. Based on the benefits, organizations can deduce some of the potential challenges. Instead of only looking at what can go right, it is also important to take a step back and identify what might go wrong. For instance, organizations that develop an OSBI solution in-house are stuck with IT as the go-to group for changes or additions to BI. Based on

---

[3](1) Free source code to be used at will, (2) free OS with additional services, or (3) adoption of commercial OS BI options.

the responsibilities of IT, fast turnaround times might not be realistic all of the time. How this affects business decision making will differ depending on the role of BI and its applications.

Overall, a broad overview of OSBI, its evolution from fringe BI to general use, some of its uses, benefits, etc., provides the basis for the rest of this book. By setting the stage and providing a first glimpse at available solutions and how developers and others within the organization can apply OSBI, businesses can identify whether OSBI might be the right fit, in addition to getting a first glimpse at some of the key vendors within the OSBI market. Now we move on to look at the OSBI market.

By looking at some of these considerations early on, you can build a framework that you can take with you and use throughout the book. For instance, what if your organization already has some OS? Or what if you are limited by specific technical requirements such as native Oracle integration? These questions and others will affect the end result of whether OS is viable and, if so, which model.

A look at the OSBI market

Introduction

The lines between OS and BI are blurring as OS solution providers begin to expand into commercial offerings and more organizations look at OSBI as a valid alternative to traditional software. We'll explore the differences between commercial OSBI and community options later, but for now let's build on what we've discussed so far. Even though OSBI represents its own market, organizations require an equally strong understanding of successful implementation strategies for BI in addition to the inner workings of OS to be successful. Therefore, although this chapter focuses on drivers affecting OS adoption, it also looks at why OS solutions are becoming a more popular addition to an organization's IT infrastructure (at least in some cases).

In the past, most OSBI information reflected the need for IT developer understanding. Solutions were adopted and maintained within IT departments. In some cases, business users were aware of OS use, while in others the name of the software used was the only recognition of whether or not OS was in use. As BI becomes more self-service and business-user focused, more business units are becoming project sponsors and driving multiple IT-related projects. Therefore, their knowledge-base of potential software requirements is becoming more dynamic and targeted on the specific benefits provided through BI adoption.

When looking at BI specifically, overall adoption of solutions has created a broader awareness of what is available in the marketplace. As this market broadens, business unit sponsors are becoming more involved in BI initiatives. Unfortunately, even with this new involvement, many solutions are elusive to business users beyond their BI interaction after implementation. Even with all of the resources that exist, it is still difficult for organizations to understand how each product differentiates itself within the broader marketplace. A good example is a company that I worked with about a year ago that was looking specifically for a hosted (or Software as a Service, SaaS) BI solution. After the requirement-gathering phase, I developed a short list, focusing on SaaS BI vendors only. The project sponsor then told me that she was surprised I didn't mention a specific vendor. She felt that vendor would be a perfect fit. The only problem was that this vendor did not and still does not provide a hosted option and was limited by platform and integration capabilities. What this example illustrates is the fact that even though a plethora of information exists, organizations do not find it easy to sift through the market and identify which solutions best meet their organization's specific needs.

To break through the barriers of BI complexities, business leaders require a broader understanding of what is available and how it can be applied within the organization. Overall, the best way to do this in relation to OSBI offerings is to look at the evolution of the market, the whys behind its expansion, and what is available now. This analysis extends beyond general drivers and more towards providing a broader understanding of the OS market and how OSBI has evolved into its own niche area within the broader BI landscape. This is exactly what this chapter does. It provides an in-depth look at OSBI and the various components that are required to make it a reality. In addition, you will gain some perspective relating to the implications of OSBI, both in relation to organization adoption and broader market penetration.

The OSBI market — a general overview

To understand OS and BI solutions specifically, it becomes essential to take a step back and look at OSBI from two perspectives. The first being within OS itself, and the second by looking at how OSBI has become a general contender for organizations evaluating and adopting BI. In essence, this takes what we've specifically looked at in Chapters 1 and 2 and brings it to the next level. After all, both perspectives affect OSBI in terms of market strategy and overall use. Whether within the OS space or as an extension of BI applications, both markets are slowly shifting to accommodate for greater flexibility in use and maintenance.

In the first case, OSBI remains part of a framework that offers free source code to developers. With a focus on using free source code to enable community development and collaborations, OSBI's goal is to provide the best software by having many people work on its development. Although not free for the purpose of being free in and of itself or for the altruistic reasons behind being free as in solutions provided by the free software movement, cost-free software (where most of the community OSBI offerings fit) lessens the costs associated with software adoption. This makes it easier for organizations looking for lower-cost solutions to still take advantage of BI even if they don't have a large BI budget. And even though BI is starting to become an essential aspect of any company's business vision and performance management, until more recently, it remained a nice to have application with limited ability to calculate ROI.

In the second case, commercial OS enables OSBI offerings to mimic traditional BI and provide similar value propositions while remaining unique at the same time. The expansion of technology and the lower cost of ownership of BI overall provides a market space that demands flexibility. Whether in the guise of SaaS, predictive or advanced analytics, dashboards, or more data storage and complex queries with quicker delivery times, end-user expectations have changed. Companies want quick implementation times, lower software costs, flexible licensing and support, and the feeling that they are valued and that their business problems are understood. Because OSBI offerings base their premise on building the best possible applications, they are well poised to expand into the traditional BI marketplace by pushing the limits of those same vendors they are slowly trying to displace. Even if some of these offerings don't match the breadth of available capabilities, their presence within the market provides organizations with greater overall flexibility.

These represent the two main drivers that lead to the continual expansion of adoption among organizations looking for OSBI. It also provides a great introduction into the whys and hows of OSBI's transition to mainstream BI.

A look at a transitioning market

The strides that OSBI solution providers have made within the past few years are quite broad. It takes more than marketing efforts to increase the importance of a subset of solutions within any given market and OSBI offerings have definitely stepped up to the plate to provide customers with added value. The ability to expand the value proposition from free software for IT developers towards organization-wide and departmental deployments means that solutions provide value outside of the costs (or lack of costs) associated with OS offerings. And although the perception of "free" is enough for some decision makers to move towards an OS model, the reality is that based on newer low-cost models, software costs alone do not provide actual insights into whether a solution will be lower in costs several years down the line. This debate about whether community models are really "free" will be discussed in greater detail later on in this book.

Beyond costs, though, other aspects of software solutions will be defined as a value add based on the specific needs of the organization. This value add and how to define its value will differ for varying companies, but the changing BI landscape and vendor offerings available mean that OS solutions now compare to traditional offerings while still providing a unique value proposition. For instance, companies looking to embed analytics into their ERP or CRM solutions may want a set of software that can be easily embedded within these solutions without having to worry about proprietary roadblocks. Alternatively, business units may want professional services based on vendor industry expertise. In addition, certain organizations look for long-term viability or a specific set of features. In some cases, organizations want a number of these aspects combined and expect it out of vendors due to the number of market players. In each case, organizations will look at a variety of features, integration, etc., and in some of these cases OS will be a contender.

Whereas years ago OSBI could not compete on many of the levels that businesses rely on to make their solution choice, now most can meet any of the criteria identified above. Also, the BI industry encounters waves of acquisitions based on technology that leave the vendor landscape with mega vendors offering everything and best of breed providers enabling enhanced functionality within the broader BI spectrum. This causes a general expansion within the mainstream BI marketplace. For OSBI, this means providing solutions that meet the full spectrum of BI offerings while maintaining the integrity of being independent. This levels the playing field and helps create an environment whereby more competition exists for mega vendors. And due to the emergence of OSBI as a mainstream market contender, organizations are beginning to expect free offerings from all types of solution providers across the BI and performance management spectrum. Consequently, there is also a shift the other way, whereby traditional BI vendors provide free trial solutions or limited access to their software offerings. This limits the value of free software access and expands the benefits of access to source code and development flexibility.

Traditional OS communities

Overall, general OS provides a different value system attached to software design than traditional solution offerings. In some cases free source code is enough for IT departments to jump at the chance to create unique and customized applications. In other cases developers are drawn to the community and the freedom associated with OS environments. Although OSBI does not always follow the same outlook as free software, some available offerings still target community OS as their key market strategy. Others are moving towards commercial offerings as a main transition in the provision of their solutions, with the goal of appealing to the mainstream BI marketplace. Either way, the value proposition of community development remains a key driver of OS expansion.

As mentioned, one of the benefits discussed in relation to OS is the availability of free software. The reality, and what we've also mentioned, is that there is no such thing as free software. Organizations need to identify the costs associated with any software implementation, especially within an environment touting "free." Although the source code might be available without initial cost, the time involved to develop solutions, the additional hardware required, and potential new resources needed to maintain the solution means that long-term pricing might be higher. The benefit of cost in the case of both community and commercial OS is based on lower-cost development due to an OS back-end. As we look at the types of offerings later in this chapter, the concept of OS used as a base of a broader solution will be discussed at length. And an in-depth look at all of the costs associated with an OS project will be evaluated throughout the pages of this book. This way, it will be easier for you to identify whether OS really does provide your company a lower-cost alternative to BI deployment.

Adopting OSBI

The convenience of OSBI has been a key driver in broader adoption. Organizations are moving towards ease of use in terms of end-user adoption as well as skills required for development. For instance, the diversity of offerings and newer focus on commercial solutions means that products are developed with interaction in mind both in terms of easier developer environments as well as ease of use. Both of these help enhance overall experience, leading to broader use and overall adoption. Generally, businesses look for quick fixes to their business pains and BI has become that quick fix. The type of BI adopted within companies, however, differs greatly among organizations. Whether due to industry expertise, solution roadmaps, or the like, OS adoption has increased to the point where leading vendors can no longer ignore its market presence.

The question that needs to be asked is what has led to this overwhelming adoption of OSBI offerings within mainstream BI? Although only a subset of reasons, the following provide good insight into the increasing demand for these solutions.

> **Lower development costs.** This actually has two aspects. The first is the ability to integrate OS code into commercial software, leading to the no-cost association for proprietary-related development. The second is the fact that with so much community involvement and overall collaboration, issues can be worked out proactively based on wider knowledge sets so that development efforts are less than they would be in comparison with traditional initiatives. Either way, part of justifying BI costs includes the people hours required to create the solution. For instance, it may pay for a company to pay more for software if that software provides out-of-the-box capabilities that limit the amount of customization required as opposed to using free software and spending months and multiple resources to get the solution up and running. So

even though other solutions may be less expensive in the beginning, the overall solution costs may actually be more in the long-term despite the lower initial price point.

Broader deployment methods. Outside of the addition of cloud computing, the effects of diversity in deployment have had more of an indirect effect when looking at the OSBI market. Organizations can now select how they want to deploy BI. Choices include desktop, Web, hosted or as a service, and in the cloud. This relates to increased flexibility and autonomy, which transfers the power into the hands of business and technical users. In the past, BI offerings were controlled by solution providers selling their products without focusing on the intrinsic value provided to the customer. Now, many solutions are customer facing and are developed and deployed with the customer's business needs in mind. OS fits nicely into this category because of the intrinsic flexibility associated with varying options. However, it is important to note the fact that for community offerings, IT developers still remain the main access point to OSBI adoption. Obviously, with additional types of deployment available, businesses are able to pick and choose what serves them best. The same can be said within OSBI. IT developers have always been able to create customized solutions without the limitations of traditional software offerings. Add to this cloud computing options and commercial availability and OSBI expands to broader flexibility that compares with broader deployment overall.

Proprietary no longer. When solution availability was limited and the market was less mature, many organizations flocked to proprietary offerings due to lack of selection and perceived viability. With few large scale BI vendors and viable industry solutions to choose from, enterprise organizations were stuck implementing large scale BI infrastructures based on integration with other proprietary offerings. When BI was limited to robust data warehousing, ad-hoc reporting, and multi-dimensional analysis, organizations had one way to go to develop a consistent and effective BI environment. Due to technological advancements, vendors that may not have been able to compete within the market now provide prominent offerings within the BI marketplace. And although many businesses still look towards proprietary solutions, the reality is that most companies want technologies that can be easily integrated within a diverse framework. Proprietary offerings do not easily allow for this. On the other hand, OS does. The goal of OS is to be flexible and open to integration with a variety of platforms. And with customer expectations looking at open platforms, OSBI becomes a more lucrative choice for some businesses.

Customer value needs to be first. As mentioned above, most proprietary solutions are based on the premise that businesses need what they are selling in the way they are selling it. What this fails to take into account is that software should be developed and marketed with the goal of providing business value to organizations and using technology as a complement to business processes. Unfortunately, the history of BI represents a backwards approach to customer value and service. Some mega vendors consistently fall into the trap of entitlement by presenting their solutions in such a way that reflects exclusivity. For instance, although many customers will say they select solutions based on market share and viability, actual satisfaction levels and positive customer sentiment may potentially be lower with these vendors due to perceptions of lack of value in relation to high licensing and maintenance costs. Luckily, newer approaches to BI take into account the principles of social media and focusing on customer interaction and job support. The goal of BI should be as an agent of change and information visibility by empowering users with the ability to dissect what is occurring within their company and their partner (including supplier, customer, etc.) channels. Although heavily focused on developers, OS solutions have always been community-driven, in essence making them customer centric — even if not in the way we mean in reference to being business-user focused. With commercial applications becoming commonplace, the customer centrism continues with broader market offerings.

Technology advancements – the "wow" factor. In many cases, original BI based itself on reporting and a back-end data warehouse. The term BI definitely did not reflect the ability to gain intelligence through data analysis. Outside of reports and historical trends, the general payoff within these solutions was low with high price points. Also, the technology behind BI was limited due to storage size, query performance, and integration. Organizations with large datasets or advanced analytics requirements were severely limited in how they could apply BI within their organization. Now these roadblocks no longer exist. Big data, advanced analytics, in-memory, and the like are buzzwords that reflect how businesses are developing and managing their information management platforms. Now the term BI actually reflects the business value it provides. In addition, both vendors and organizations take advantage of OS offerings, specifically within the realm of back-end data management. Multiple data warehouse vendors develop their platforms using OS technology, enabling broader development and lower customer price points. This in turn broadens company comfort with OS solutions more generally and within BI specifically. Overall, though, one of the main reasons for broader BI adoption is the fact that technology now does what organizations want — the ability to perform complex queries on terabytes of data with completion in seconds exists, which is becoming the norm. In comparison with historical data warehouse structures, this truly provides a wow factor because organizations can actually achieve results that were impossible just 3 to 5 years ago.

Low TCO/high ROI. Technological advancements and flexibility drive BI market demand. With data storage and in-memory capabilities costing less than in the past, developing strong data warehousing infrastructures has become quite possible. Add to this access points like Google Analytics and analytics have become more commoditized in the minds of organizations. After all, if it's possible to access Web stats and perform analyses for free online, why shouldn't the same be said for other solutions that provide similar functions? Based on this fact as well as the fact that companies can now more broadly control their BI experience through self-service deployments, the demand extends towards the deployment of offerings that have quick implementation times with lower costs of maintenance. Whether this means lower initial software costs or less customization over time, businesses want to be able to tie their BI investment to concrete TCO and ROI calculations. This might mean something different to different businesses. To most, ROI is measured in cost. However, in other cases, companies value increased insight, autonomy, and increased actions of employees, etc. When looking at OS specifically, these solutions are generally less expensive to deploy. With built-in, free community support, ongoing costs can be lower than other traditional BI offerings. In terms of total cost of ownership (TCO), this speaks volumes.

Expectations of free. Whether through free trials, free desktop versions, or the ability to consume reports free of charge, the notion of free is only a couple of years old. Beforehand only OSBI was free, with most other solutions costing an arm and a leg (or close). Although not all OSBI drivers are derived from OS offerings, as shown in the preceding points, business expectations regarding access to free software is 100% OS-oriented. A few years ago when OSBI gained credibility in the marketplace, businesses began to wonder why they should pay for something when they could get general access to BI without paying for software. Consequently, now the possibility exists to try solutions at differing levels and access points for free. In addition, in the marketplace, the goal is broader adoption and increased market share. With free solutions this is possible and very probable in terms of widespread adoption. Add to this the availability of integrated applications that help businesses get access to various types of information and analytics quickly, and companies are increasing their "free" software expectations.

Future focused. The market is future focused, with development and marketing efforts addressing trends that may or may not take off in the long run. The BI marketplace is constantly discussing the prospects surrounding trends that have not seen wide adoption. Unstructured data is one good example. Over the years it has been touted on and off as an area that would gain wider adoption, but it still only applies to a limited number of BI deployments. On the bright side for companies adopting BI, this focus works to their benefit through research and development efforts that are continuously focused on integrating forward-looking technologies into market offerings. A good example is the proliferation of mobile BI. Vendors have been offering multiple levels of mobile access for many years. However, a few years ago adoption levels were very low and use was limited. Now with mobile devices representing a main way of communication, businesses are using phones and tablets to do business. This trend will only continue well into the future. And many other examples exist. No matter what, the ability to continue developing solutions ahead of the curve lets companies take advantage of technology once they are ready.

Why OS?

These new demand areas help answer the question of why businesses are starting to look at OSBI as a valid alternative to traditional BI. Free software is becoming more common within both BI and with broader adoption of free software downloads from the Web or through app stores. Either way, the concept of free is becoming much broader and affects both businesses and consumers. Between free software downloads, app store downloads, and the like, the market is slowly changing to embrace free offerings. Whether this means the eventual end of unique OS differentiation remains to be seen. But what will occur is massive adoption of analytics that are tied directly to business performance on a broader scale because price no longer remains an obstacle.

After all, many ERP and CRM applications now have analytics embedded within their offerings. This leads to a question surrounding the fact that if organizations can access analytics within an application, why would they want to develop a broader BI initiative when access to these analytics is free? Realistically, the fact remains that the value created through overall information visibility across the organization will always trump any benefits received from limited data visibility within a single application.

How each of these components relates to OS and the provision of free software is simple. The first identifies the fact that free software is gaining credibility within the overall marketplace, making OSBI an easier sell among executives that are tied to proprietary software offerings. The second addresses the increasing importance of metrics management and analytics to further operations. With analytics becoming a general feature set within broader applications, decision makers are beginning to expect these features as an inherent part of their computer interaction. Both of these aspects lead to OS adoption, whether directly or indirectly.

Taking this one step further means looking at the definition of OS and free software and identifying why its expansion has become so relevant within organizations. Providing software free of charge creates an interesting dynamic within the analytics space. Will these applications commoditize BI overall? Maybe, but probably not. Even so, what they will do is provide all organizations and consumers with the ability to gain insights quickly. Whether this means identifying product performance or trends in music consumption, analytics are becoming a common way to interact with information and online content.

Looking at BI specifically, with the number of BI solutions available, organizations may wonder why OS should be an option. After all, aside from the lower costs of commercial OS in relation to traditional offerings, what are the real differences? In some cases the availability of free source code may not be a benefit due to a lack of internal resources and/or skills to provide all of the development efforts required. Other organizations are using alternate versions of free software to further their business efforts and are open to the concept of expanding their use of OS.

With many factors going into the changes surrounding OS adoption, the barriers to entry involving lack of knowledge or IT development infrastructure to deploy solutions are no longer restricting adoption. For companies without supporting BI infrastructures, commercial OS solutions exist that can help them get on track and take advantage of free solutions. The differences between community- and commercial-based OS will be discussed in the next chapter with an overview of the differences between vendor offerings and the various outlooks vendors have on their commercial products and services.

OSBI transition and the expansion of OSBI into BI

As explained, the OSBI market has shifted within the last couple of years. Aside from becoming a reputable player in the BI space, vendor products and service offerings have expanded to provide similar value as their newer competitors within the broader BI marketplace. Consequently, OSBI vendors are no longer looking at themselves as a separate entity. Now, OSBI solution providers market their offerings as direct competitors to traditional BI offerings and, in some cases, as an alternative to other BI solutions. The success of this strategy can be shown within businesses that have actually decided to rip and replace their previous BI infrastructure to adopt an OSBI platform. Although not yet mainstream, this strategy's popularity has grown considerably with OSBI's general popularity.

Direct drivers leading to OSBI expansion previously discussed include market demands for more diversity, free software availability, and lower price points with quicker implementation times. Although all drivers have created a market shift, these are ones that have started with OS offerings and expanded into more broad OSBI offerings. Both organizations new to BI and those with mature infrastructures are starting to demand more flexibility in development, deployment, and licensing. All of these lead to organizations looking at the features and functionality that OS does best. This in turn creates not only market demand for OSBI, but also an opportunity for vendors.

OSBI vendors have been taking advantage of these market changes to become mainstream and viable BI options for companies. A shift in marketing strategy means that OSBI solution providers are now found in the same places as broader market players. For instance, instead of only partaking in OS-related trade shows, OSBI vendors can be found at BI and data warehousing conferences and online within BI-related channels. This expansion of visibility provides business and IT decision makers with more access to these types of solutions and increases the likelihood of general consideration and software evaluation. And because more businesses are aware of OSBI, evaluation and adoption rates are expanding. Consequently, the transition of OSBI to general adoption has been quite accepted within the broader market.

Even with all of these benefits of OSBI offerings and widespread adoption being discussed, the reality remains that not all organizations are open to the concept of OSBI solutions. Despite the lack of flexibility associated with proprietary offerings, many organizations feel more secure and have already invested a lot of time and money to maintain and expand their proprietary environments. For these companies, the promise of OS may not exist. This means that vendors need to move beyond traditional methods of marketing to prove their worth to these types of organizations. The reality remains that even with OS becoming more widely adopted, there will always be companies that prefer to control their data assets and expand upon their proprietary infrastructures.

For the rest of the market, traditional OSBI offerings are not the only free choice. The expansion of traditional BI offerings to include free desktop or limited access versions may be a viable alternative to OS in general, as already discussed. Although these solution types aim at providing similar OS value, their solutions were developed and maintained through commercial deployment models. Now that these vendors are shifting focus and trying to expand their market share, organizations can consider them part of the free software craze. Because of this focus on free, and with the availability of newer distribution channels, it can be assumed that in the coming years the way in which OS is distributed may change and include other types of free solution offerings as well.

Realistically, all of this leads to increasing OSBI adoption within mainstream BI applications and organization infrastructures. As OS offerings become more similar to traditional BI but still retain a general differentiating value, their unique value proposition and place in the market will remain. However, due to the increase in other forms of free software, their role within the BI market will change. Once a general understanding of OSBI within the BI market exists, it becomes possible to look at where OSBI fits within the broader OS market.

OSBI within the OS market

So what does this mean for BI within the OS market on a broader scale? Up until now, most of this book has centered on how OSBI solutions have slowly expanded into the traditional BI market. This has been accomplished by looking at the history of OSBI and the business drivers and industry trends that enable broader OSBI adoption. But what about where OSBI fits within broader OS? After all, the OS community has been very active for years, working outside the traditional software landscape to develop targeted business applications across industries and software types. Looking at this aspect of OS can help you determine whether some broader areas of adoption might apply to your business or BI strategy.

Within these categories, BI represents one area of OS. Looking at OS more broadly means identifying the fact that most, if not all, software has OS options. BI is not a new player in this arena. In fact, developers have been able to adopt OS solutions on a broad scale to include CRM, ERP, supply chain management, database development, etc. For some organizations this means having IT development teams design and deploy a wide range of OS solutions that are now passed off as homegrown business applications.

One of the benefits of this approach remains that many OS offerings partner with one another to provide overall business-driven applications versus a best of breed or piecemeal approach. In all areas of software, vendors partner with each other to ensure that customers can apply various technologies and integrate solutions with minimal hassle. Traditional software providers develop application program interfaces (APIs) to make this transition easier for companies. OS is no different. Partnerships create an arena whereby database, analytics, and integration vendors can partner to provide a full end-to-end BI solution. And in some situations, partnerships exist to apply analytics on top of operational solutions to provide added insights to daily operations. Either way, OSBI provides extended value to both BI functions as well as transactional insights.

Where OSBI solutions will/should be in the future

Applying this more broadly means understanding that the BI market constantly shifts to take into account broader and newer technology. The OSBI arena matches these advancements step by step and has the added advantage of community and broad collaboration to further development efforts. As social networking takes hold and people expect higher levels of interaction both inside and outside of business, the ability to take part in software development and release cycle efforts will be a greater advantage as companies demand more autonomy within their BI offerings.

On the other hand, many OSBI offerings are transitioning towards commercialized software. After all, these companies need to identify revenue-generating models and many do so by developing a two-tiered approach to OS. With this being the case, how will OSBI maintain its unique value proposition within the broader BI marketplace? And how will the broader BI market be affected by the influx of free solution offerings? Overall, the influence of OSBI cannot be understated. Because of changes within the general software market and new flexibility, more free applications will come into existence, with the line between free and commercial becoming blurry. The ability to fund projects becomes important for future development, but based on the increasing adoption and utilization of free, vendors need to develop commercial offerings that double as value-added services as opposed to having broader features and functionality. How OS vendors accomplish this remains to be seen.

With the push towards free solutions and analytics applications, the concept of OS blurs because these other solutions market themselves differently. After all, when everything becomes free, where does the value exist? This will be the true turning point for OSBI offerings. The push for OS has become so great within BI that free software offerings are starting to become second nature to organizations in relation to their expectations. Consequently, more free offerings will exist, but the framework of what OS means within the BI arena will also change to take into account these offerings and the expansion of OSBI offerings to include commercial software and broader service availability.

Implications for businesses

The expansion of the OSBI market increases an organization's flexibility to develop and to deploy BI offerings that best suit its business needs without software cost constraints. Consequently, more businesses are adopting OS without waiting for IT developer initiatives. Because BI is becoming more end-user and business focused, this trend of business level sponsorship will continue making OS ease of use a priority. In addition, all of the drivers and market overview directly apply to businesses by pointing out implications of adoption. These include:

- Organizations taking advantage of free software: With the market providing more free solutions, businesses will increase OSBI adoption while the market shifts and free software availability broadens.
- Commercial software without the high costs: Whether specifically OSBI or software that embeds OS solutions within, as OS vendors continue to provide broader features and greater ease of use, the demand for these benefits to go mainstream will continue. Organizations will begin to expect these same benefits within the broader BI landscape and, to remain competitive, vendors will have to keep up.
- Community support and project collaboration: Social media takes collaboration to the next level. OSBI remains in the lead in terms of community involvement and interaction. Businesses can now become more involved in the development efforts and use and be able to benchmark their success against others.
- The need for in-house developers and resources: One thing organizations need to remember about OS adoption is the fact that more internal development may be required and that free software does not mean free. Time to develop and maintenance over time are areas that might increase cost exponentially.

A deeper look at OSBI

The increasing popularity of OS

More organizations are becoming aware of OSBI options and more are looking at OSBI as a valid alternative to traditional software offerings. The markets are converging and the lines between OS and BI are becoming blurred as OS solution providers expand into commercial offerings. The differences between commercial OSBI and community options will be discussed at length in Chapter 5. For the purposes of this chapter, we are building on what we've learned so far. In essence, we are moving beyond what OS and BI are towards the implications of adoption and why OSBI is becoming more important in general. Even though OSBI represents its own market, the reality is that to ensure a successful implementation, organizations require an equally strong understanding of successful implementation strategies for BI specifically, in addition to the inner workings of OS. Therefore, although this chapter focuses on drivers affecting OS adoption, it also looks at why OS solutions are becoming a more popular addition to an organization's IT infrastructure (at least in some cases).

A look at BI drivers

BI is becoming commonplace within organizations. Most large enterprises have some level of reporting and analytics to identify key metrics and drive performance and planning. Newer entrants to the market and diverse deployment methods[1] are now making it possible for small and mid-sized businesses (SMBs) to adopt robust BI solutions that address the same business pains being faced by their enterprise counterparts. Add to this broader availability of traditional BI solutions at lower price points and it becomes possible for BI to reach more people and provide broader-reaching business benefits. The reason mid-market availability is so important is because by opening up the market to SMBs, all organizations can take advantage of what BI has to offer, based on size, structure, budgets, etc., and find solutions that meet these varying requirements.

In addition to market expansion, over the past several years, BI has gone from a multi-dimensional analysis and reporting solution for the select few to an organization-wide solution used to drive business success. Its overall importance within companies keeps growing in relation to C-level executive priority and broad adoption.[2] Add to this the increase in cloud computing, big data, virtualization, and expanding OS options, and businesses are now in the position to apply BI

---

[1]For instance, those discussed in Chapter 1, including SaaS or cloud-based offerings.

[2]In Gartner's study, *Amplify the Enterprise: the 2012 CIO Agenda*, Analytics and BI rate number one on what is important to CIOs minds. This study interviewed over 2300 CIOs. http://bi-software.blogspot.ca/2012/02/gartner-study-shows-bi-importance.html, with the actual report being found at: http://www.gartner.com/id=1901814.

in the way it was originally intended. In essence, they are actually using technology to help enhance the business decision-making process and not only as a tool to look at historical trends.

Although BI was always poised as a set of tools and applications aimed at better business decision-making, historically this was almost impossible. Limitations in processing, data latency, storage, query speed, and predictive and advanced analytics created an environment whereby BI was partially a chore. Now that solution goals are aligned with technological advancements, organizations can actually achieve a centralized data repository that enables advanced analytics that drive business insights, higher levels of efficiencies, and better decision-making capabilities.

OS is no different. Now that organizations can take advantage of up-to-date technology that can meet the business needs of companies, organizations can take a step back and identify what products have to offer. With an increasing focus on social media, OSBI becomes a natural fit due to its focus on community and collaborative development. Developers work together on projects, share ideas, and look for ways to continuously improve their development efforts and overall product design. Going one step further is the identification of factors that make OSBI a contender within broad BI adoptions. Aside from better technology and lower entry price points OSBI has unique factors that lead to its broader adoption and in some cases, evaluation in exclusion of traditional BI models.

Let's look at some of these factors with a focus on comparing pricing, features, licensing models, maintenance, and extensibility. In addition, we'll also look at some broader issues affecting the increase in OSBI popularity, including integration considerations and broader deployment methods such as SaaS and cloud-based computing. Finally, the following sections consider the relationship between increasing adoption of social media and online community involvement and how it translates to OS interest and consideration.

Price comparability

Although price points differ based on products and services offered, OSBI generally compares well to traditional pricing models. But before looking at OSBI specifically, it becomes important to take a step back and look at the overhaul BI has undergone in relation to pricing and general BI entry points. Until a few years ago, most BI pricing was outside of the scope of many businesses. A set of proprietary solutions provided businesses with robust BI solutions with high price points. The alternative existed in little known community OS offerings that were outside the radar of most organizations. Many of the larger players charged a fee for software, about 20% yearly for maintenance and support, as well as an additional license fee for each user. Some vendors also have different pricing structures for the type of user, for example, report developer versus end user, or based on CPU. The point is, all of this can get pretty pricey.

Although not the only reason for the shift of pricing and solutions moving downstream to target a broader market by changing pricing models or by offering more for less, one of the reasons OS has become more important within the debates about BI accessibility is its price points, especially the general focus on either free software or subscription-based models, which are also the same for many SaaS providers.

As mentioned, now OSBI offerings are becoming more mainstream. OS solutions used to be marketed within OS communities but not within BI market events or the typical online channels.[3] Because of this their price benefits were rarely seen as anything but a set of free source code that required a lot of development effort. The advent of commercial OS and the broadening of OSBI marketing efforts have made OS more accessible. Proprietary software comes at a price — high R&D costs, limited integration, and intellectual property associated with large-scale solution providers. These factors drive prices up. BI on the whole, however, is slowly becoming more cost effective based on some of the following industry trends:

1. New entrants to the market, both SaaS and SMB-targeted offerings, provide solutions with the goal of making them accessible to a broader range of organizations. For organizations unable to spend $100,000 or more on a BI solution, they are able to subscribe to a service or implement BI for less by paying monthly or yearly subscription fees. In some cases this means solutions are targeted to specific departments or vertical markets. In other cases, leading solution providers develop SMB-targeted solutions at lower price points with a subset of functionality to enable people who wouldn't normally have the opportunity to apply a full BI suite within their organization. The bottom line is that this model enables BI to be a fixed cost (providing usage doesn't expand[4]).

2. The data warehousing market has started to expand. There are more diverse offerings that include appliances, which are combined software/hardware offerings, and data as a service (like SaaS but for data warehousing purposes specifically). In addition to all of this, some data warehouse solutions are built using OS database technology as the back-end. The benefits to customers is the ability to implement a data warehouse at a lower price point based on the fact that OS code is considered more of a commodity. And because of this, companies are able to implement a data warehousing solution for less than traditional data warehousing offerings. Overall, data warehousing solutions highlight lower market price points and increasing BI adoption. Cheaper storage, quicker query times, and commodity hardware leads to broader offerings for less. This in turn leads to more businesses able to develop strong data warehousing infrastructures without breaking the bank.

3. With the increasing popularity of OSBI, the idea of free software becomes an expectation. Many customers expect some level of free. Consequently, solution providers now offer free trials or limited personal versions of their software for free. Most of these "free" solutions do not provide organization-wide BI deployments without some add-on or payment requirement. Others do provide full features and functionality but only to a certain number of end users. We discussed this a bit in the previous chapter, but the reality is that free offerings tend to be useful for individual users or small groups, but most are too limited to provide value on a departmental or organization-wide level. Either way, BI becomes a smaller version of what it should be within the organization. The plus side is that businesses can now access a variety of solutions to identify which one best meets the company's needs. Even though no such thing as free really exists due to development and maintenance costs, OS provides the closest thing when looking at software costs alone.

---

[3]For instance, some of the main online resources for BI-related content are BeyeNetwork (now under TechTarget) and Information-Management.

[4]Some subscription models are priced based on number of users or the amount of data being stored. Therefore, what is initially affordable may become less so over time if data requirements or adoption grow exponentially.

All of the points mentioned above create lower price points within the BI industry and for organizations looking at BI for the first time or thinking of expanding their overall use. The BI market is seeing a shift in more solutions that are providing more value per dollar. When looking at OSBI specifically, the ability to provide free software has driven the market towards the free software trial versions defined above. Consequently, OSBI remains comparable and in some cases has lower price points overall.

Features and functions

All BI vendors place effort in enhancing their product offerings and constantly strive to increase their overall functionality. With research and development aimed at making analytics more efficient, increasing ease of use, and taking advantage of new technology to enhance BI delivery, vendors have gotten to the point that most solution offerings are similar in terms of features and functionality provided. The real differences exist within the value-added services that are offered. Now vendors require key differentiators that are based on industry-specific functionality, niche analytics, implementation times, and the additional services provided.

BI solutions used to be able to differentiate themselves based on levels of interactivity, drill-through capabilities, and the like. Add to this various levels of integration with multiple data sources and organizations were semi-limited in the types of solutions they could choose. Now that these roadblocks no longer exist as much, organizations can look beyond traditional solutions and can compare offerings that traditionally would not be seen in the same short-list evaluations. This increases company flexibility and places the responsibility on the vendor to sell the value of their product. In relation to overall features and functions, OS solutions are able to take advantage of both internal and external R&D efforts.

With the additional external input to development activities, OSBI helps push the boundaries by having more than internal R&D to focus on enhancing the available feature sets because of all of the community feedback and involvement. Consequently, this fact alone helps drive the broader market by creating higher customer expectations. Now that OSBI represents a subset of the overall BI marketplace, competitors need to step up to the plate by increasing their focus on development efforts and making sure that their customer needs are taken into account. In essence, technology is now at a level where the promise of BI can be realized. BI solutions are no longer limited by lack of technology, storage, or processing power. Because of this, BI is being driven to the next level based on the availability of a wide range of features that can be provided out of the box.

Licensing models and the issues surrounding them

Traditional software models involve high costs over time. Not only do companies pay for initial software, hardware, and implementation services, but there is an understanding that maintenance, support, and licensing will account for an average of 20% of total software costs on an ongoing basis. Until recently, most organizations accepted this as fact and budgeted accordingly in relation to ongoing software costs over time for an average of 3 to 5 years. Vendors were able to change pricing for licensing or charge astronomical fees for end-user or data storage expansion. Consequently, many businesses were left wondering whether their BI use really provided the desired ROI.

In the last couple of years this has changed dramatically. Some of the discussion earlier in this chapter directly touched on the changes taking effect in relation to licensing models, giving OSBI an advantage in the race to provide value to businesses in relation to licensing models. For instance, some of the reasons behind OSBI adoption, such as community, collaboration, design flexibility, etc., create an environment that requires an alternative licensing model. This leads to alternatives in licensing and the way in which OS vendors choose to interact with both their community and their customers.

In general, there is no way businesses adopting OS and vendors developing solutions based on free source code would be able to implement the same type of licensing as proprietary BI offerings. It would be virtually impossible to restrict access to a limited number of users or application use. In addition, looking at CPU or data volumes also falls outside of the scope of vendor control due to the independent nature of BI development efforts. Both of these licensing guidelines restrict end-user creativity.

Based on these factors, OSBI vendors require a different method on which to base their licensing models. Depending on the solution, varying licenses will exist. Outside of purchasing documentation or training, access to support and commercial solutions ends up falling within more traditional licensing costs in the form of a subscription.

Looking at subscription licenses independently of individual offerings

Subscription-based licensing provides organizations with greater flexibility. The concept behind subscription fees is that customers pay yearly or monthly fees to access solutions, as in the case of SaaS offerings, or to receive support services and other benefits provided within an OS environment. Either way, a move towards subscription fees whether for licensing specifically or for general software access and use presents a break from the traditional BI payment pattern. For organizations that may not have enterprise budgets, the ability to pay a known yearly or monthly fee and know exactly what they are getting allows them to budget appropriately and provide cost benefit analyses to justify their BI use.

For vendors, subscription fees provide a regular revenue stream and create a product offering that resembles a service. Due to the increasing similarities between solutions in terms of features and functions, solution provider key differentiators are becoming the value-added services offered. Whether in the guise of professional services, subject matter expertise, or customer support, subscriptions go a long way in creating an environment focused on value added. Subscription licensing is becoming more common because many vendors are starting to move towards more flexible business models. On the other side, organizations that buy software and pay for support on an ongoing basis invest a large amount of time and effort to integrate new software within their existing IT framework. Consequently, these companies may be less likely to change their BI software due to the perceived efforts involved. With subscription models, this is not so. Organizations pay for software use, meaning if they become unsatisfied with the solution, they stop paying. What this leads to in many cases is an extra focus on providing high levels of customer service because a key goal becomes to maintain high levels of customer renewal.

Maintenance

Software maintenance represents an extension of licensing. Organizations pay for user licenses and demand a certain level of support to meet their needs. However, this level of support encompasses many aspects of value-added services. Traditional BI offerings tend to develop licensing models that include end users and servers but exclude additional maintenance and support. With OSBI, on the other hand, subscriptions generally include maintenance.

Maintenance on its own is no reason for organizations to start flocking towards OS options. However, the importance solution providers place on continued development and their focus on customer satisfaction puts them at an advantage in relation to traditional BI vendors and has led to increasing popularity. Traditionally, because of astronomical support fees, solution maintenance has come at a cost. With newer entrants to the market and more diverse pricing, organizations with mature BI environments are starting to feel taken advantage of. With BI starting to become more commoditized based on the use of Google analytics and the availability of free trial versions of software, traditional licensing, support, and maintenance models no longer work. Businesses are looking for added value and key differentiators based on an increasing focus on providing customer value.

Looking at maintenance specifically and the ability to quickly address bug fixes, provide new releases with regularity, and align product updates with customer desires. For instance, many vendors base their development efforts on customer goals. This may include integration with specific databases or the ability to apply various types of which makes OSBI solutions more likely to be considered within organizations looking at the longer-term benefits of BI solution offerings. The list is endless. In some cases, this focus may create a solution that only meets the needs of a specific industry or business issue, but in other cases, it helps vendors develop better product lines and keeps them in tune with what is happening among their customer base.

Nowhere is this truer than within the realm of OS. Other BI solution providers may partner with customers to provide industry-specific solutions or may solicit customer advice, but OS solutions are built on collaboration and customer involvement. Obviously, this is a generalization, because there are different ways, as discussed in Chapter 6, capitalizing on something that doesn't refer specifically to monetizing might be a better word as end users aren't really monetizing their use. As a general example, though, with regard to OS development, there are many instances where bug fixes are made by community members. Developers look for ways to constantly improve upon feature sets and work together to make sure the solution constantly gets better. Vendors add to this by setting aside R&D budgets to take community endeavors and make them a part of the final solution. Being a cyclical process means that the maintenance process is never-ending. And although not so different from traditional solution providers, the advantage lies in community involvement and massive collaboration from developers that are constantly interacting with solutions and providing enhancements for end users within their organizations.

The increasing popularity of OSBI and the specific benefits that exist through the adoption of OS remain obvious when looking at maintenance specifically. As shown above, OS solutions provide the most efficient maintenance of BI vendors due to their structure and community focus. In addition, this creates more competition in relation to overall solution maintenance.

Extensibility

Many organizations have been using BI for many years. With advancements in what businesses can do and the value BI now provides, there are constant initiatives that look at expanding internal use and maintaining overall business value. This drives increasing BI adoption for all types of BI in general. In some cases, companies expand their current offering and add features and upgrade to newer versions, while in others, businesses are looking towards newer offerings that include dynamic interactions and more flexibility. Overall, the ability to expand BI functionality, overall use, and business applications make BI more valuable to the organization.

With broader trends, including agile BI, self-service access, and embedded analytics, companies are looking for solutions that can grow with expanded use and support multiple applications internally. When organizations used to evaluate BI offerings, there was a focus on large proprietary solutions that provided specific analytics or BI interactions. Now businesses want solutions that can meet their expanding needs over time. In some cases this means adding more end users, being applied across additional business units, or supporting initiatives that provide more information to customers, partners, or suppliers.

Open technology and integration

As businesses become more complicated and require more visibility into disparate data that resides both inside and outside of the organization, integration becomes a key factor in implementation activities. Integration activities can take the bulk of time within any BI project. The ability to consolidate data into a single source and create a holistic view of what is occurring both inside and outside of the organization creates a high value proposition for the delivery of any BI solution. In addition, businesses are starting to add unstructured and semi-structured data while looking at social media trends and integrating these new forms of analytics within their BI use. With the added complications of adding a variety of data sources, the more commoditized a set of data sources is the better in terms of general integration activities.

Open technology and the premise behind OS solutions involve the provision of free source code. As an extension, this means being able to provide front-end solutions that easily integrate with databases on the back-end. Solutions are generally easier to integrate within an OS environment, making BI expansions and diverse implementations provide a quicker time to value.

Sometimes organizations overlook the importance of data integration activities because BI sells itself on the ease of use and broader availability of dashboards and interactivity. Even though this is a great entry point to BI adoption, organizations sometimes overlook the importance of the data behind the analytics because dashboards pass themselves off as a front-end access point to BI without discussing the effort required to create a strong dashboard.

Organizations can't overlook data integration activities such as extract, transform, and load (ETL), data quality, and overall data management tasks. When looking at OSBI overall, one of the most important aspects of any BI project is the ability to take into account integration efforts and ensure strong levels of data quality over time. Luckily, the market can now handle strong data integration infrastructures with OS and lower cost options. These newer options open the market to help create full-scale BI solutions irrespective of whether organizations choose a best of breed offering or one that includes all aspects of what BI has to offer.

BI in the cloud and SaaS offerings

Another BI driver involves solutions offered as a service and offerings that can be housed external to the organization. Although not directly related to OSBI, the reality is that both OS and SaaS have changed the market landscape enough to create a better vantage point for organizations looking at BI solutions. Both of these are key drivers to the increasing success and broadening of BI adoption. Some of the reasons include less infrastructure required, the ability for vendors to provide BI as a service, and price drops to lower BI entry points. In addition, the increasing availability and flexibility of SaaS enables broader adoption of BI in the cloud, whereby the solution is housed in a similar fashion as a SaaS model but can be accessed as a service or developed and deployed internally.

Traditionally BI implementations involve hardware, software, and integration considerations that can increase the general scope and budget of BI projects. SaaS and cloud-based offerings lessen the load by taking out the additional internal infrastructure requirements. For organizations, less internal infrastructure leads to lower costs and less maintenance. This in turn makes BI's value proposition rise because it becomes easier to sell to decision makers and end users alike. In addition, as BI becomes easier to use and to maintain, the way in which it is applied within companies changes. Organizations can now move beyond limited end users or targeted analytics towards meeting the needs of multiple departments and business issues.

BI as a service has enabled companies to push the boundaries due to shifting expectations. With BI delivery available offsite, companies are no longer concerned about servers and integration, and development activities. They can focus on solving business issues and leave the heavy lifting to service providers. And although not necessarily the case in cloud-based deployments, developers are beginning to see the benefits of hosting data in the cloud.

Aside from external development and less internal infrastructure considerations, a services-based model makes SaaS a key BI driver. For OSBI solutions, this means looking at the value they can provide to customers in addition to features, functions, and free source code. And because the market is being driven by new services-related offerings and OSBI focuses extensively on community involvement, this transition is probably easier with OSBI solutions.

The final reason SaaS and cloud-based BI solutions are strong drivers towards BI adoption is the fact that offerings are generally easier to use and less expensive to deploy. Although most organizations look beyond price to identify the right solution for them, the lowering of price points enable a broader range of organizations to consider BI. These are many of the same companies that will now look at OS options as a potential option based on flexibility in design, lower price points, and a focus on providing high levels of service.

Collaboration and social networks

The focus areas of OS such as collaboration, customer involvement, and the development and maintenance of online communities reflect the current trends of BI and end-user computer interaction. The popularity of Twitter, Facebook, MySpace, LinkedIn, and the like create an environment whereby many types of computer users and people with varying levels of comfort interacting with technology can play on an even playing field. As people broaden their horizons by using the Internet to learn about different cultures, keep in touch with friends and acquaintances, increase social awareness, or shop, their demands grow. They are now used to getting information easily without having to wait for feedback from an external source, and are also able to customize their interaction and look and feel. And because of this, many people want to expand this interaction to include the way they use computers at work.

Businesses are now starting to accommodate these changes. In some organizations collaboration between departments is expanding, computer use is becoming more user-friendly, and virtual organizations and business relationships are becoming the norm. With all of these changes occurring, the ways in which people do business also has to expand to make sure that companies remain competitive and provide an environment targeted to ease of use and high levels of interactivity. Traditional business applications do not provide the level of functionality needed to remain competitive and the reason is simple. Historically, applications were created based on tasks that people did to get their jobs done. And in many cases, this meant employees had to follow a set of procedures that required a high level of training and low ease of use. With all of the advancements and the shift towards online communities and social networking, application development now has to change to accommodate end users by becoming intuitive and complementary to how they do business and interact with technology. This differs from the traditional way in which people had to adapt to technology.

Vendors, on the other hand, are working on enhancing solutions to include chat functions, notes, alerts, voting, and sharing capabilities, and all of this with the goal of deploying solutions that meet the needs of businesses and providing competitive advantage while shifting towards the "technology adapting to people" model. Unfortunately this is easier said than done in many cases. Software providers may be early adopters of new technologies in relation to taking advantage of feature and functionality sets. When it comes to reengineering solutions to mimic social media environments, however, that is a different story. In these instances, the effort and cost involved in a full solution redesign remains astronomical.

For BI, many vendors have already incorporated the interactive features highlighted above. Few have gone the extra mile to create truly interactive applications that are based on end-user interactivity. The closest exists in the form of dashboards to varying degrees. However, many solution providers are now integrating the ability to identify customer behavior based on Facebook profiles, likes, etc. This is the first step towards organizations really being able to take social media analytics to the next level. At this point in the game, some of these solutions are more prevalent within the traditional BI market as opposed to within OS, but eventually we can assume that this will change to reflect overall changes and adoption of social analytics.

Whether or not OSBI vendors have developed their software with the premise of social networking in mind, the fact remains that their platform is based on this concept due to the collaborative nature of this technology, with the next step being analytics on top of community involvement. Although still facing the same challenges as traditional BI vendors in terms of designing solutions that meet these changing needs, OS outlook supports collaboration and social network integration. Before communities were mainstream tools to communicate across geographic boundaries, they existed within the confines of OS.

The ability for OSBI to move into the competitive realm of traditional BI is partially due to it being ahead of the curve in relation to developer interaction and interactivity. Even if this doesn't always translate to more advanced solution offerings, the fact remains that online communities and large-scale collaboration is second nature within many OS environments. With the push towards commercial OS offerings, the next level is accomplished through the creation of interactive development environments and a focus on agile BI to give end users the ability to change their environment as desired.

Putting it all together

All of these drivers are leading to broader adoption and deployments. BI in any capacity and with any type of implementation is now possible. With OSBI also enabling broader use through commercial offerings, organizations can take advantage of the type of BI they want without limitations. OS, SaaS, and newer entrants have leveled the playing field due to lower price points. With more robust data integration offerings and less expensive data storage, more businesses can apply advanced analytics while maintaining current IT infrastructures. Overall, a combination of factors applies to any organization's adoption of OSBI, with those discussed above leading the way to more overall business value.

The differences between general OS and commercial offerings

Understanding different OS models

BI represents its own unique market when looking at how OS offerings are structured and brought to market. Before discussing the specific differences between commercial and community offerings, it is important to take a step back and look at the market breakdown to understand the uniqueness of this market. In previous chapters we looked at the market on a broad level, but now we turn and look at the specifics that expand beyond OS in general to decipher what OSBI models exist. For instance, how are these solutions developed? How are they managed? Why do some vendors feel the need to transition towards commercial offerings while others stay true to the central tenets surrounding what OS really means? Answering these questions in advance provides greater insights into why there has been a push towards commercial offerings and how this push may affect your likelihood of adoption, the options available, and how to benefit most from OS in general.

The problem with categorizing OSBI vendors into commercial or community providers is great. Within OSBI, each solution provider seems to have its own model and own ways of defining what commercial means, the scope of its community offerings, and how it centers its market presence. What I mean by this is that some vendors look towards the community to help them develop offerings, others develop solutions internally but listen to end-user feedback for the development of additional functionality, while others use their OS offerings as a tool to engage clients in projects. These differences might not be a factor in which solution you select, but they may affect development cycles, roadmap, support, and the like. Therefore, it is still important to understand the diversity of this market as a backdrop to the commercial OSBI market. So, let's look at the different ways in which OSBI offerings come to fruition.

Internal development

In these situations, vendors develop their solutions independently of the community. In essence, aside from the provision of free source code to organizations, the development cycle is not very different from that of traditional software vendors. In most cases, these solution providers have their own group of developers who focus on software development and may use additional resources from partners, etc. They may involve the community or get feedback from customers to identify the focus of new capabilities or bug fix efforts and target their development efforts based on the projects they are working on.

SpagoBI, an Italian-based OSBI provider, actually represents a good example of how the concept of internal development works. Although not fitting the traditional definition of a vendor because their solution was initially developed to support their consulting practice, they base their software development on projects that they are working on and develop these solutions internally with internal developer and partner network help. SpagoBI also develops their solutions in conjunction with an internal roadmap they define while focusing mainly on developing solutions that best meet their customers' needs. According to Stefano Scamuzzo, SpagoBI International Manager, SpagoBI only provides customers with "a single version of OS software which is totally free, and strongly believe the most important component of a BI solution is the project and not the product." Therefore, instead of focusing on community participation, they target customer engagements as a way of expanding their solution availability.

SpagoBI's internal development shows how BI providers within this category are able to provide a strong community interface so that external developers and other companies can communicate and have their questions answered, but where general community members are considered guests as opposed to active participants within the development cycle. This is not to say that developers do not have a say, as it is possible to be accepted into the development community, but it should be noted that no one community member has more development say than any other.

Although the example provided is a front-end BI offering, in many cases this type of development is limited to database and data focused vendors, in the sense that solutions are developed by the vendor and managed by them. For instance, Ingres, which considers itself an OS vendor, provides customers with free access to the database environment they develop but not to the actual source code.

Community collaboration

Other vendors take a different approach and look towards the community to help develop and refine their toolsets and solutions. In most cases, OS development follows this model, where an initial shell of an offering may have been created or where multiple entities come together to create or work on solutions. IBM[1] is a good example of a proprietary solution provider that is involved in many OS projects and that designates resources to OS development. Their commitment to OS development is clearly stated on its website and actually identifies some of the reasons why OS is an important type of software to bring to the market. IBM states that they are "an industry leader helping governments move toward greater openness and innovation. IBM's commitment and perspective on intellectual property, open standards, and open source software emerges from our experience in the marketplace and, equally important, from the direction in which we see information technology taking the larger society."[2] OS vendors also participate in OS projects, such as Jaspersoft and its involvement on several committees and within many communities such as SourceForge, the world's largest OS development website.[3]

Obviously, not all OS projects have dedicated vendor resources, but IBM's involvement helps highlight the importance placed on the development of free software and support for OS on a broad

---

[1]http://www.ibm.com/developerworks/university/opensource/
[2]http://www-03.ibm.com/linux/ossstds/
[3]http://www.jaspersoft.com/jaspersoft-community-involvement

level. Within BI specifically, many communities have thousands of members with contributions occurring daily. This high level of interactivity enables changes and improvements to be made more quickly than by some traditional BI vendors. This level of interactivity, however, does not ensure the depth or breadth of these additions, only the fact that they happen more often.

OS as a consulting tool

The third type of development involves solution providers like SpagoBI that develop OS offerings around consulting engagements. Some others are like SpagoBI in terms of only providing projects for their solution offerings. Consulting practices such as StrateBI[4] offer analytical solutions but also provide training and consulting for other forms of OSBI adoption and are not limited to one solution.

Although no single type of development is better than the other, each provides an entry point to OSBI that may not have previously existed for organizations in the past. For instance, consulting fees can be astronomical when looking to third-party resources for requirement gathering, software selection, and implementation. Paying only for project work and not for software may lessen the overall cost of adoption. Community development also allows IT developers to adopt software for free, but internal IT developers are responsible for BI development, which can take months and months to get up and running efficiently. With developer-led development, organizations can select either approach (the use of consultants or not) and the outcome will be similar to the approaches above.

Looking at community and commercial OS models

As you can tell, no single model of OS development exists within the realm of OS. Unfortunately, this is even more the case when looking at community versus commercial offerings. OSBI vendors have developed their own types of commercial offerings to take advantage of the marketplace and the sales opportunities that exist. Even though the lack of cohesion can complicate things, we can still try to define this market space, making it easier to understand the differences between both types of offerings.

The concept behind commercial OS is the provision of additional services, support, training, off-the-shelf software, and the like for a cost. Many OSBI vendors offer commercial software solutions in addition to their more general community versions. Within the BI market landscape, this creates a two-tiered view of OS. The first being free access to source code and community development and the second being a professional and more robust version of the offering for a fee. Both represent different outlooks, with adoption potentially being affected by the BI requirements of the organization. Depending on the business needs and requirements, internal IT resources, and familiarity with OS development, one model might bring more value than the other. This section aims to break down why you would select one over the other.

Because commercial and community OS versions offer unique value to businesses, organizations need to understand the differences of each. Without being able to validate the unique

---

[4]http://www.stratebi.com/en/stpivot

propositions of each, it becomes impossible to justify commercial adoption or provide the value of implementing a commercial solution. After all, the potential to use free source code and to develop the additional feature sets that mimic commercial offerings may be possible with intense development efforts. Once businesses justify the costs versus the benefits of this type of effort (developing TCO and ROI evaluation models will be discussed in a future chapter), if no added value exists, then it might make sense to look no further than free offerings. The reality, though, remains that commercial offerings, both in relation to OS and traditional BI solutions, will always be the way in which a large part of BI developments are selected. With OS becoming more popular and widespread, its use becomes more of a competitive factor within the broader market.

The easiest way to decipher the differences between both delivery models is to note that most community versions are downloadable from the Web. Once the solution is in place, IT developers can create their own BI offerings. In most cases, this requires in-depth knowledge of the platform and how to navigate through it. This includes data integration, linking tables, developing front-end applications, tweaking features, etc. Commercial versions of OSBI are usually based on the free versions with more features with an easier-to-use interface, making it easier to get up and running more quickly. In addition, many of the capabilities found within the commercial version represent more of the trends-related market features. For instance, advanced analytics, support for more data sources, and higher levels of interactivity are just some of the features that are more likely to be built in to a commercial offering.

Some questions that arise include: If source code is available for free, what makes any commercial offering a valuable alternative? Do commercial OSBI offerings provide added value to organizations looking for BI solutions? And how? These questions, and others, provide the framework required to dissect the differences between both models and to evaluate commercial solution offerings against traditional BI players. After all, selecting OS and developing unique BI applications differ from evaluating commercial software products and implementing an out-of-the-box BI offering.

With the emergence of commercial OSBI offerings, these vendors are on a more level playing field with their traditional BI counterparts. This, in turn, expands their potential audience and customer base. The real goal of these companies is to increase revenues and overall profits, and hopefully not ruin the integrity of the community solution while in the process. The question comes back to, how do these vendors sell the value of their commercialization of free software alternatives? One of the ways is to provide more of a differentiation of the software options. So, let's look further at what these models actually are.

OSBI models

Across the various OS solutions several models of commercial OSBI exist. All are based on the same premise mentioned — building up profits and developing a revenue stream. The reason I've said this a few times already is to state the fact that OS is more of an outlook in terms of providing access to non-proprietary and open access to free software. Once this vendor outlook expands to include the commercialization of software, it becomes more difficult for vendors to pretend to follow the altruistic approach to software development and delivery.

On the other hand, the types of resources placed on a commercial development process means that there is the potential to compete with the broader BI marketplace. After all, community development provides many benefits and a customer-centric approach to software development, but revenues are still required to take this one step further towards advanced development efforts and effective and wide-spread marketing campaigns to increase general adoption.

With this being said, certain commercial models lend themselves more to broader solution offerings, while others base themselves on fees for services. Both these types of vendor programs will be discussed at length below. The important fact to know is that the type of model selected reflects the end goal of the vendor. As many traditional BI vendors develop free solutions, many OS vendors are moving in the opposite direction. And although they will continue to offer free source code to their customers and potential customers, the real goal will be to develop a strong commercial model to build a solution that provides added value. This expansion leads to broader market competition because of the increase of solution offerings on the market due to the use of commercial OS as an alternative to traditional software.

Now that we've looked at the differences of community and commercial offerings on a high level, let's delve deeper into the four areas that exist within the OSBI landscape.

Community – truly free

Community OS has always been the *de facto* standard of free software. Because we have discussed OSBI in detail and will continue to do so throughout this book, this section will be brief because many of the aspects and considerations of free software will be provided throughout the book. However, looking at community OS as a business strategy actually relates to the other types of commercial offerings as well because all OS includes a strong community component, many community involvement in many cases a way to gain visibility into a potential commercial customer base. In essence, community development and collaboration drives these solutions towards both broader community development as well as broader expansion into the commercial market. Consequently, even as vendors move more and more towards commercial offerings, community will always be important. This importance relates to the fact that aside from customer requests, the main development efforts that occur – at least within community environments that encourage open development – will continue to take place through online collaboration, either in the form of personal or company projects or general enhancements.

Therefore, the vendors that focus mostly on community OS require ways to generate revenue. But these might focus on other OS models or be a combination without a direct strategy targeting commercial business practices. With pull marketing becoming the key way organizations attract customers – i.e., through online presence, social networking, and providing expertise to customers – community OS ends up being a natural way to attract customers in a way that does not force sales or appear to be a hard sell. In essence, by being known as experts and partners within the industry, perceived value of services increase and help drive OSBI adoption and potential eventual commercial OS use. Generally, if and/or when companies choose to move forward with a purchase, many look at a separate purchase as a way in.

Free software with separate purchases

Selling training, documentation, and support may be the most common model and usage of commercial OS. Even before the advent of commercial offerings and a two-tiered approach to OSBI, many solution providers offered these products and services for a price. Based on required skillsets and development projects, IT developers may or may not have all of the skills necessary to develop targeted solutions. Alternatively, they may want to lessen the learning curve or get better ideas about how to optimize their BI environments. For each organization buying extra products and/or services, the requirements or desired level of commercial involvement will differ. IT developers need to identify what works best for them. Is documentation enough? Does the BI project require an additional and formalized support structure? Or does the company want to build a specific set of expertise in relation to OSBI development and maintenance?

In general, documentation represents the how-to of any solution. With source code customization, having access to a guide becomes more important than with traditional solutions. Consequently, many businesses that choose to go the OS route actually purchase documentation to have a reference point moving forward. The good thing about OSBI documentation is its continual expansion and the ability for developers to have constant access to updates in features, functionality, and technology adoption. With the continual changes within BI, unless a person takes an active role in being kept up to date, it remains next to impossible to keep up to date with all of the changes.

Training represents another aspect of services that organizations may take advantage of. Traditionally, training within OS offerings remains within the realm of becoming well versed within the development environment with the goal of developing targeted expertise. In terms of OS solutions, it is normally possible to find the skillsets desired, but internal resources looking at OSBI for the first time may require some updates to their skills. No matter what the reasoning, because many OS vendors rely on their services as their main revenue stream, training can be very comprehensive.

Within traditional BI proprietary environments, many organizations complain about the costs of support and maintenance over time. In many cases, licensing fees are constantly being raised, support structures are changing, and the "value added" aspects of a solution are more difficult to discern, making it more likely for an organization to select a different model. Because community OSBI solutions do not charge for software, the initial costs are lower, with support generally being provided based on a yearly or monthly subscription fee. These support costs are also traditionally lower than proprietary offerings, making adoption of formalized support options easier to sell to the business.

This is why many organizations subscribe to this type of OSBI. They have the freedom to develop unique applications while utilizing the expertise of the vendor for support and other services without having them involved in the project. This keeps organization autonomy intact. Even if many solutions require similar feature sets for like business units, the reality remains that some companies prefer to develop and to maintain their own solutions in-house and like what OS represents. However, additional support or documentation may bring these businesses to the next level in terms of their OS adoption and use.

Commercial offerings

Similar to traditional BI offerings, commercial OS refers to solutions built using OS technology but sold and maintained using the traditional software sales and licensing models. As mentioned earlier, OSBI vendors have a two-tiered approach, with their commercial offerings being a more robust offering in comparison with their free counterpart. In some cases, organizations could develop the same feature sets with a lot of work. In most cases, it pays to go commercial to save the time in these instances. With that being said, organizations still need to evaluate on their own which model will pay off more for their BI initiative(s). Depending on whether the features included in the commercial version actually meet the "need to haves" of the organization, one option may be more feasible than the other.

Solutions with extra features that provide a value add are generally comparable to other commercial BI offerings. The goal of solution providers is to provide a competitive advantage to customers through adoption, with the benefits generally being lower price points and more dynamic development cycles. In addition, although community solutions are supported, the adoption of commercial solutions provides an environment whereby issues are more likely to get solved faster due to the adoption of a paid-for model. These are areas that appeal to many small and mid-sized organizations that are starting to adopt BI in droves. Larger enterprises are also looking at ways to create more value out of their current BI environments. Depending on what they have done in the past, part of this might involve the addition of OS.

Overall, the development of commercial OSBI solutions is a natural progression based on the increase in overall OSBI adoption, brand recognition, and the increasing importance placed on BI in relation to gaining business visibility. This overall market shift means that organizations are now more likely to consider OS solutions alongside traditional BI offerings. With this being the case, it stands to reason that vendors would develop comparable out-of-the-box offerings that are user friendly and that can be driven from the business side as opposed to remaining within the realm of IT development.

The services approach

The final OSBI commercial model is represented by the services approach. The services approach means that software is provided free of charge with the commercial aspects being the services provided. Services generally relate to professional services and the consultancy involvement within the project. For every BI project, organizations require proper business and systems requirements, technical needs identification, integration, etc. to develop the shell of a successful BI project. All of the aspects that surround the software component involve potential services that can be provided by a third-party source. Some vendors provide free software as a complement to their professional services.

In these instances, the services represent the project management, requirements gathering, implementation, customization, testing, and the list goes on. For organizations considering vendor professional services or external consultants, the ability to get software for free lessens the overall costs of BI projects. By combining a services approach to OSBI, vendors are maintaining the integrity of free software while increasing the value of successful BI adoption and the value of intellectual property and expertise.

Looking at the community/commercial focus in the broader market

It is interesting to note that as more OS vendors work towards developing commercial offerings, the demand for free access to solutions is on the rise. In my opinion, this is partially due to the fact that OS is becoming more mainstream within the BI marketplace. Organizations now want to be able to try a solution before buying it or applying it departmentally or organization wide. More and more, vendors are meeting this need by offering free trials, free downloads, and limited free versions of their software for specific use. Vendors feel that by providing free access to their software, potential customers are more likely to buy full-solution offerings providing they can test out the solution in advance, as well as increase the number of people familiar with their software on a technical level. These free applications may be limited in feature sets, deployment methods, or users. No matter what parameters, the fact remains that many organizations now expect some sort of free to be associated with their BI implementations. Add to this the fact that OS consistently improves upon its offerings and drives community involvement to build better solutions with the goal of keeping up with industry trends, and most traditional BI vendors try to develop comparable offerings.

Market competition creates an environment where vendors will follow one another and try to provide customers with comparable features and functions out of the box. The same holds true for OSBI vendors expanding into the realm of traditional or commercial BI. Without the ability to enhance profits and develop targeted marketing campaigns, the ability to compete on an even playing field with traditional BI vendors in relation to their sales and marketing efforts remains unbalanced. Moving from free to commercial levels this playing field on many levels.

Vendors are now able to provide benefits on both fronts; commercial-level products and services on the one hand and free source code availability on the other. This makes it possible to remain competitive within the marketplace, both in terms of marketing activities and software development. With this transition into the broader market, many OS vendors are acting in a way that looks like they are heading against the curve. As traditional vendors develop free versions of software, OS offerings are moving in the other direction. OS vendors are looking for ways to monetize their products by developing two levels of software availability while maintaining their commitment to their community. This explains the goal of commercial OS and general BI visibility. Even with this being said, it should be noted that there are other vendors that will continue to access community OSBI as a way to build customer BI environments or as the bare bones for broader solution offerings, as is the case for many data warehouse offerings.

Even though up until now the focus has been on the financial benefits of commercial OSBI development, the reality is that this limits the overall value BI can bring to an organization. There exists a definite value proposition in implementing a ready-to-use and targeted solution within the organization. OS vendors can provide their community and commercial customers with more value by focusing on enhancing their features and functions. With greater profitability, more resources exist leading to the ability to develop better applications on a greater level. Add to this the benefits of being a part of the OSBI community and customers can combine the advantages of OS and a commercial offering.

Many vendors are turning their focus on developing their commercial offerings. Whether this is beneficial to commercial or community customers remains to be seen. Different companies will have different outlooks on which model benefits them. And even within organizations themselves, opinions will differ. A good example is that many IT developers prefer to develop systems independently without being constrained by a ready-made solution. Business users may feel differently. Many want the perceived safety of an out-of-the-box solution with traditional support. Luckily, OSBI vendors can meet both types of needs. For instance, government and higher education are industries that are likely to compare OS alongside traditional BI solutions because they want to limit spending. For instance, in one case, a university's library is using Jaspersoft for its reporting needs to help manage an interlibrary loan system and gain visibility into how it is performing across various universities. Part of its decision was based on being able to access reporting for free. And with several internal developers, the extra time that it took to develop the reporting solution was not seen as negative due to the cost savings.

When looking at commercial development in relation to industry trends and solution adoption, OS vendors can be said to be moving against the grain. Even though they've helped push the trend of free solution offerings, they have also made a play for the exact opposite by building profit-based models to increase their overall market penetration. Taking this one step further, the focus on a new level of OSBI commercial offerings also leads to a new level of services. Many of these services relate to a new level of support and maintenance. Many organizations are already subscribers of OSBI vendor support, but with the added commercial offerings, formalized support has become a larger part of the benefit of choosing a commercial BI package.

The rest of this chapter explores the development of commercial OS at a deeper level with the goal of demystifying the differentiations between various OSBI commercial outlooks.

The drivers of commercial OS for BI

As discussed, the transition from free has led to the emergence of commercial OS offerings. Many OS vendors have been around for a while, but they struggle to develop the right commercial model for themselves. In some cases, vendors decide to remain free, as is the case with those basing their software delivery on BI projects and not on software, while others continue to transition towards a commercial model that competes directly with traditional BI vendors. For instance, the better-known OSBI vendors, mainly Jaspersoft and Pentaho. Either way, specific drivers exist that have led to the expansion of OSBI offerings into the realm of commercial solutions. As mentioned, the drive for profitability represents a main push towards commercial OS. But there are others. They include the increasing need for customization and support, broadening acceptance and adoption of OS, and project collaboration.

Free source code enables broad customization. As businesses start to develop their own targeted applications, the levels of customization and support grow. Organizations look for ways to increase their competitive advantage through the development of targeted applications. And although the levels of customization may change, the importance of support continues to increase over time. Community support is one level, but formal support represents a general requirement as many large organizations desire a formalized support structure to maintain their IT environments. Consequently, in some cases OSBI vendor revenue comes from leveraging their support options.

The increase in adoption and acceptance of OSBI leads to broader opportunity. Vendors take advantage by developing a two-tiered set of offerings. Different organizations have diverse business pains that lead to the need for BI, whether performance visibility, financial planning, marketing effectiveness, and the like. Add to this the fact that companies have different approaches to software development and some will prefer commercial over community. This provides opportunities for vendors and organizations alike. Today what companies want are quick implementation times, short time to value, lower costs, and the list goes on. Vendors take advantage of these opportunities and one way to do so is to provide commercial offerings to the companies that would most benefit from them. Because OS solutions provide these benefits, organizations begin to expect them but may not be comfortable with community OS environments. This is where the ability to take advantage of the benefits but not the perceived risks of OSBI exists. It should be noted, however, that any BI or broader IT project has risk built in, and organizations with strong IT development in-house may see not having full control over their development environment as a risk.

Collaboration is also a popular trend within BI. OSBI solutions have prided themselves on community participation and collaboration. Because of this, vendors can take advantage of their ability to provide strong interaction and community involvement to sell the importance of a higher level of collaboration. As BI adoption expands and as BI use matures, organizations look for better collaboration capabilities within their BI environments. OSBI vendors can take advantage of this with both types of offerings because a collaborative community environment is one of the key elements of their overall framework.

The bottom line

Breaking out OSBI into either a community or commercial offering is not enough. Within the community arena some players develop solutions internally, while others look towards broader community participation. Commercial offerings also differ, and while some vendors focus on training, documentation, and support, others are developing two types of solutions that continue to diverge as time goes on. Whether the implications of this are that community and commercial solution focuses continue to diverge remains to be seen. Overall, the important thing to remember is that when you are looking at adopting a commercial version of software, it's important to make sure the vendor(s) you evaluate provide a transparent definition of what commercial means to them.

Business benefits and challenges of OS for BI

Many of the items we'll be discussing in this chapter we've already mentioned very briefly — lower implementation costs, higher levels of collaboration, etc. The considerations discussed so far provide a great start to defining why organizations should or should not consider OSBI offerings and which types of solutions might best meet the daily challenges of the business. This chapter takes things one step further. Although project sponsorship can come from different areas within the organization, the increasing role of commercial offerings, self-service BI, and broader access to analytics makes business involvement in BI projects more pronounced.

The increase in business involvement actually changes the way in which projects are justified within organizations. In the past, business units may or may not have been involved in project sponsorship. Projects were generally controlled by IT or driven by them. So, infrastructures were designed with internal efficiencies in mind. For instance, projects addressed questions such as, what is the best way to capture transactional data and not affect daily business operations? Or, how can the data warehouse be tweaked to optimize query performance or support intra-daily data updates? Obviously, these factors depended on the BI infrastructure itself, but they also highlight the traditional IT-centricity of any BI deployment.

What this shows is that even if solutions are developed for business users, the main focus remains within the realm of IT. OSBI is no different. With strong IT developer efforts being involved in OSBI, organizations sometimes focus on the IT side of things without the realization that end-user requirements are the most important element of a BI deployment. OSBI provides a lot of opportunity for unique and robust BI applications and the ability for IT developers to manage the process. The value of BI, however, remains in the hands of the business. With BI environments becoming more mature, and with commercial OSBI offerings becoming widely adopted, the mental shift towards business-centric applications is now a reality.

Slowly, the focus of projects is shifting to reflect increasing business involvement. This new involvement includes sponsorship and projects centered on addressing business problems. In essence, it is taking OSBI to the next level by changing the focus from IT development only towards a more inclusive approach. And although this all sounds theoretical in nature, vendors are actually developing their BI platforms to be more interactive and user friendly at the end-user (or business) level. The shift away from being technology driven means that the way solutions are evaluated and justified within the organization is no longer only related to cost of hardware, software, and support. Companies are now looking at the business factors and how they address the performance challenges being faced.

When looking at business challenges, these changes in BI focus leads to a change in the way BI is managed. It is no longer enough to provide a value assessment of technology, infrastructure, or what a solution can do. Organizations are now looking for business benefits that attach themselves to overall ROI but that also extend beyond traditional cost-benefit analyses. Overall, the way in which decision makers are evaluating BI has changed.

How business and IT approach BI

A new reality exists in terms of how organizations approach a technology-related project. As businesses start to transition towards more business-centric BI applications, shifts occur in technology focus. And since business units are more concerned with solving business problems than with IT architecture, a slight shift exists in relation to how organizations make their software selection decisions. This highlights the difference in outlooks between departments. What this means in layman's terms is that IT wants to make sure that all of the pieces fit, that data integration processes are efficient, that data warehouses are optimized for quick performance, and the list goes on. Business units want to make sure they are meeting their strategic goals, increasing profits, making their customers happy, etc. Obviously, the best approach is to merge this worldview. Unfortunately, both groups have their own languages and ways of doing things. Adding to this is the fact that disparate departments also have different focuses. Finance might worry about ensuring compliance and mitigating risk, whereas supply chain wants to make sure that products get to where they need to be on time, and sales and marketing want to ensure product visibility and increasing overall sales.

The reality within most organizations, however, is that there remains a lack of collaboration between disparate business units. IT developers continue to work independently and involve business users in limited intervals in order to develop end-user applications that meet the general needs of the business but that do not necessarily provide strategic value. OSBI offerings have been notorious for this type of BI development. Because of the structure of OS offerings, most of the effort involved has remained the responsibility of IT. But with commercial OS offerings, companies are realizing that more collaboration is required. The reason for this is because IT developers are the key participants of community OS applications, whereas vendors try to develop commercial offerings with business users in mind.

Overall, collaboration represents the ideal situation within any BI development. Organizations require both IT to create the shell of a solution with a strong back-end and the business to define the rules and interactions required to make it useful. Useful might mean different things to different people, but the reality remains that only a collaborative effort can achieve the long-term goals of any organization.

Saying this is easy, but why does this really matter? With collaboration, both IT and the business will get value out of BI. If not, then projects driven by IT developers will most likely lack essential business components. Organizations consistently complain about delivery times and updates taking too long, of not being understood by IT, or of getting access to the right information after the fact. All of these things lead back to a lack of collaboration. Yes, IT may be overworked, and development activities may be intricate and time consuming, but the value of these activities eludes the business side of the organization because of the rift that exists between the two.

The following comic strip highlights perfectly the way in which many solutions are developed and deployed, with a lack of understanding among varying stakeholders. I came across it when I worked as a business systems analyst and at the time it did a really good job of expressing my frustrations of being the bridge between IT developers and business managers. The business managers had requirements related to the types of metrics they needed, and IT had restrictions based on the technology being used. As the comic strip shows, business users express themselves based on the context of their jobs and experiences. Business analysts and consultants look at requirements as a hybrid, with the goal of bridging the gaps between what businesses need and the requirements that IT needs to develop the best possible solution. On the other hand, IT looks at everything from a technology perspective. This includes what steps are required to produce the desired features and functions, new data sources, tables, or fields required, how they are joined together, and the list goes on. Making sure these three roles actually see eye-to-eye is as difficult as reflected by this comic strip.[1]

So, where IT looks at integration, resource management, deployment, testing, etc., business looks at how to get value out of information. Whether it's getting a "single version" of the information architecture, a broader look at strategic planning, sales insights, or more, generally business users are not focused on the technology side of BI projects. The business goals of IT projects normally relate to becoming more efficient, cost effective, and providing an increase in visibility.

---

[1]http://www.projectcartoon.com/cartoon/3

Essentially, in terms of outlook, this means that IT and business units live on different planets. And although positive on a broad spectrum, it only ends up that way when collaborative efforts are made to work together. The good part is that certain overlaps exist between both. One of the common elements between both is the cost associated with development. Both business units and IT departments are limited by the financial resources available. Therefore, the more both work together, the greater the chance of getting more done for less.

The relationship between business and IT

As discussed, in many cases the relationship between business and IT remains antagonistic. Some business units understand their role and purpose within the overall structure of their organization, including how they interact with IT. For instance, accounting and finance understand that they manage the cash flow of the company, sales drive profits/revenue, and marketing helps build branding and drives sales, etc. With IT this is not as simple. On its own, IT does not provide added revenue to the company. IT maintains an infrastructure that allows the rest of the organization to complete their processes effectively. But, the bottom line is that one cannot function without the other.

In today's world, if IT did not exist, neither would organizations. At the same time, without the business to drive revenues and form an infrastructure, there would be no need for IT. Consequently, the relationship between both should be complementary. With the industry focus on collaboration, more organizations are working towards the creation of cohesion in relation to their BI projects. Whether this will have a broader effect on organizations remains to be seen, but OSBI provides a good start for businesses looking at transitioning towards a more collaborative approach to building a BI infrastructure. An in-depth look at commercial versus community OS options provides a detailed account of the market transition towards a more end-user focused BI outlook.

Hopefully, with commercial OS and the traditional involvement of IT developers through OSBI development, business and IT units will be able to increase their level of collaboration.

Are benefits and challenges different or similar for business and IT worldviews?

The discussion related to how business and IT interacts leads to questions surrounding whether or not the two overlap. And if so, how? Although a little outside the scope of looking at business benefits from a business perspective, understanding how both overlap becomes important to build a case for driving BI projects from a business perspective. Whether business units or IT, there are key overlaps that help both see things from a similar perspective. The main ones being related to cost savings and revenue increases. Although different for both in terms of how this is achieved, the end goal remain the same.

After all, key goals of any organization are to make profits, stay competitive, become more efficient, etc., as discussed. And even though these specific points might remain the same, unfortunately this does not extend to how business units and IT departments need to address key decision makers and sell the value of BI. For business units, cost represents one aspect, with other benefits such as increased productivity, information visibility, and better ease of use being a way for organizations to sell the value proposition of BI applications.

This section looks at these benefits in terms of OSBI consumption and development and the benefits of choosing OS from the business perspective. With commercial offerings this becomes easier to justify because many business decision makers are familiar with traditional BI offerings or have at least conducted initial research. But even filled with this knowledge, understanding how traditionally technical benefits actually reflect business needs helps business decision makers by giving them more opportunity to sell OSBI to the broader organization.

A look at OSBI benefits

OSBI benefits from a business perspective do not change greatly from broader software benefits. The differences are reflected within the outlook of business users and business decision makers. With this being said, even business departments and project stakeholders require an understanding of how the technical side of BI works, not for high-level technical details but to gain an understanding of how data and OSBI more generally fit within a business framework. For instance, business insights are only as valuable as the information available. Because BI is largely based on capturing disparate data, understanding the technical implications, even at a high level, remains important for defining business strategy and the business value of BI.

All of this discussion surrounding business and IT cohesion relates to OSBI in the following ways:

- Any software project requires both types of involvement to achieve the best possible solution. With OSBI this is even more so. Community editions require a high level of IT developer involvement. To achieve a high level of interactivity and end-user value, business involvement is also essential.
- The more interaction between the two the better! Although already discussed at length, what hasn't been talked about is the ability to offset costs. Generally, varying cost centers will sponsor BI projects. With additional collaboration across the organization, departments can share costs by sharing resources, allocating server space, or sharing project sponsorships and budget allocations towards software projects.
- Lack of stakeholder involvement can take away from potential benefits and create broader challenges in the long run. The comic strip above actually highlights the challenges involved when a lack of collaboration and proper communication exist. Each iteration of a deliverable that doesn't provide benefit has to be redeveloped and updated in hopes of getting it right, leading to longer development costs and longer time to value.

With all of the crossover between business and IT considerations, what benefits for businesses actually exist within an OSBI deployment, irrespective of commercial or community deployment? The following benefits provide insight into what businesses need to consider and how some more technical considerations actually benefit end users, not only IT.

Quick deployment times

BI can be implemented within an organization in more than one way. In some cases, business units choose to implement BI independently of other departments and IT involvement. In others, a company-wide approach is taken. A good example of departmental BI remains the increasing popularity of SaaS to provide departmental analytics. Until recently the most commonly applied SaaS-based analytics were solutions applied on top of Salesforce.com. Because Salesforce.com is an operational application, companies monitoring their sales and CRM-related functions need a way to track information and initiatives over time. BI, with the ability to house historical data and develop analytics that take into account trends over time, increases the value of Salesforce.com data. This BI application generally is limited to a departmental function.

A company-wide approach, on the other hand, takes into account more diverse data access, metrics, and strategic goals that include the design of the overall solution. Add security considerations, added complexities, and the like, and organization-wide solutions require much more information to get up and running. This added complexity exists whether considering commercial or community OSBI versions.

However, as discussed, the inclusion of IT support remains essential to business success — at least in the long run. If this is the case, then how does OSBI account for quicker deployment times in relation to traditional BI implementations? And is this even possible? The reality is that no BI initiative is simple. Each requires full-blown requirement gathering, business rule identification, and technical requirement gathering to turn it all into valuable insights through data capture and analytics.

The OSBI fact remains that whether commercial or community solutions, IT developers and other IT staff are required to help with both types of implementations. Obviously the amount of involvement differs with each. In addition, normally IT involvement includes acting as a go-between with the vendor to collect the technical requirement and to interact with the community. Although considered time consuming, the reality is that this creates an environment whereby implementations can be completed more smoothly.

For instance, the reason behind looking to outside sources to manage BI initiatives partly relates to long implementation times that create roadblocks to process improvements. After all, when businesses are looking for something new, many times it is because something doesn't work or they cannot access the required information in the way they need. This drives the desire to have immediate access to information and necessitates the need for quicker deployment times. Therefore, business sponsors don't want to wait in line until their project comes up or have to deal with IT resources working on multiple projects.

In terms of the value of getting solutions up and running more quickly, OSBI offerings have a fairly good track record in comparison to some traditional players that require a lot of initial preparation. William McKnight, President of the McKnight Consulting Group,[2] with experience in both traditional and OS implementations, states it best about working with OS. "I'm going to be able to get an OS tool up and running for the client more quickly, but then we'll probably run into a few more hiccups. But quick is very important these days, with the client's patience playing a key role. If we have to get a tool up and running tomorrow and need to hit the ground running, we can download an OS tool today and be up and running tomorrow." Because of community involvement, non-proprietary development environments, and the like, many OSBI implementations are accomplished more quickly than with other types of BI implementations. This highlights the concept of quick time to value in one sense by being able to download software and build out applications quickly. But as McKnight says candidly, this does not mean that the ride will be a smooth one. As

---

[2]http://www.mcknightcg.com

stated, in many cases, this initial time to value offsets additional development efforts that will be required to optimize the actual BI application.

Internal development efforts can better align with business goals

With strong collaborative efforts, OSBI enables greater potential for successful development (as discussed in detail in relation to IT and business collaboration). However, this means the potential is there, if done right, but it should not be an expected outcome. In addition to the fact that many OSBI offerings develop solutions based on community feedback, OS prides itself on providing access to source code and broad development. Although driven by IT, these initiatives and collaborative development efforts actually focus on providing analytics solutions to business users. The fact that this occurs on a broad level means that development efforts seem to be tied more directly to business success. After all, IT collaboration includes gaining insights from other organizations with similar business problems.

With commercial OS the result is the same, but with more focus on out-of-the-box offerings with a broader set of features and functionality. Generally, this also transforms into less efforts required on the IT side. From the broader business perspective and OSBI value, development is more focused on business in comparison with other types of BI delivery models. Based on community availability, customer input, and commercial OS outlooks, software development efforts are broader than other available vendor offerings. As a side note, there are other vendors that also pride themselves on this type of development and product delivery. In some cases, they do match OSBI offerings in this sense, but on a high level that compares all traditional offerings with that of OSBI availability, this isn't the case.

Customization options

Whether or not all of the feature sets required by businesses are automatically available, over time companies will need to customize and change what their solution does and how they interact with it. Businesses require high levels of customization, meaning that the more customization available, the better. Because of the access to OS source code, more customization options are available. And in many cases, companies build applications from scratch based on high levels of customization. In addition, the ability to customize without the restrictions of proprietary software can provide companies with the ability to look outside the box.

With commercial OSBI, internal IT developers have a lot of flexibility to customize offerings as well. Many of the required feature sets within commercial offerings have already been completed, because most vendors create their commercial offerings to satisfy their customers. With this being said, it doesn't mean your company won't have customization options if you select a traditional offering. This isn't the case but, as mentioned, only a certain amount of customization will be supported. For some organizations this works just as well or even better. For the proponents of OS, not so much. Therefore, even though it can be said that most solutions provide a high level of customization, OS generally goes one step further based on its purpose and design.[3] And for businesses that prefer internal development, OS allows them to customize more broadly. Otherwise,

---

[3]This refers to the purpose of OS discussed in Chapter 2 — free and open software without the restrictions of proprietary use.

commercial options take the desires of multiple companies (as mentioned in the section above) and develop solutions based on end-user goals.

What all of this leads to are better self-service capabilities. Organizations are starting to want greater autonomy and control over how they interact with BI on the business side. Enabling end-users access to customize their own solutions and interactions enables broader customization and gives business users more freedom, with less emphasis on IT development. Irrespective of OS or traditional BI offerings, eventual customization in the hands of end users will become more commonplace.

Subscriptions

Although yearly subscriptions are not always cheap, the reality is that this type of pricing enables organizations to get exactly what they pay for. For instance, companies may be charged based on the number of end users, amount of data stored, complexity of queries, number of services, servers, and the list goes on (which leads to our next point below − flexibility). Generally, organizations also have access to upgrades, bug fixes, and community support. Subscriptions take the place of initial software costs and yearly maintenance and support. Basically, organizations get the use of everything for a single yearly cost.

In terms of business benefits, justifying costs to executives may be easier based on the fact that companies can provide a formalized breakdown of yearly costs without having to worry about additional expenses. Vendors provide detailed analysis of their cost breakdowns, enabling businesses to broaden their understanding of the benefits BI use will provide them. Also, some organizations tie themselves in to contracts for multiple years, enabling them to create a BI environment with fixed costs over a period of time. Although subscription fees may increase over time, this helps organizations manage their BI costs and potential usage over time.

On a practical level, many businesses want to deploy BI more broadly than in the past, but costs of large-scale BI offerings inhibit this potential. A lot of subscriptions provide the ability to broaden adoption because most organizations can allocate yearly funds towards BI maintenance and support. Although subscriptions differ from this type of traditional access, companies get access to software, maintenance, and support, for one cost.

OS framework

One of the most interesting aspects of OS is its focus on providing companies with access to source code and free expression. Without the restrictions proprietary solutions place on adoption, integration, and use, organizations can develop the best possible applications of BI. Proprietary offerings generally only allow customization provided by the vendor, which limits the ability to create solutions that can be used the way the end user wants. And most vendors do base their products on that model.

The OS framework takes a different approach to intellectual property and access to technology by enabling companies to develop what they want when they want. As people get more used to free apps and general ease of use, this secondary model will become much more important and valuable within the realm of business. In addition, companies are starting to debate these thoughts internally and demand more flexibility, with some organizations becoming drawn to open platforms because of the added freedom and flexibility associated with solutions that are not limited by proprietary-based rules. Overall, businesses are starting to expect free. This becomes obvious with the advent of free BI offerings, trials, and the like. With OS, companies are taking this one step further towards broader flexibility and creativity within BI use.

In terms of the real benefit to business, an open platform provides lower costs of development because the protected qualities of proprietary offerings do not exist. Add to this both commercial and community flexibility in design, deployment, and pricing and the business benefits of OS become more obvious.

Business benefits — a wrap-up

What all of these factors have in common are quicker deployment times, more defined business interactions, customization capabilities, and flexibility. The bottom line is (if done right) cost and time savings are obvious within an OS project. Whether commercial or community, the levels of interaction and support cannot compare with traditional BI offerings because of the framework on which they are built. Companies can choose to have their offerings provided or develop targeted BI applications in-house without the limitations associated with proprietary software.

Overall, all BI requires investment, but businesses can rely on either internal development staff or commercial offerings within OSBI projects, leading to greater flexibility. Add to this the potential to deploy in the cloud, and solutions are providing a broader delivery platform, leading to more business options. Not only are companies dead set on providing lower-cost alternatives to save time and money for their BI projects, they also want to know that they call the shots. With proprietary offerings, companies are stuck with what vendors can provide. And although in some cases these same limitations exist within OSBI solutions, organizations can also rely on their own resources to create what they need in terms of business value and information insight.

Obviously all of this overlaps with IT requirements, but by matching the two, business units get more benefits from OSBI. The importance of understanding the interrelationship of data, how OSBI saves times and money, and broader BI options help business decision makers make the best choices for their companies. And none of these decisions or general knowledge base should be limited to technical staff. For business units to get the most out of BI, they require insights into the solutions that expand beyond business considerations.

In addition to the benefits and general factors that affect business, organizations should look at the business challenges of OSBI as well. Once both are identified, it makes sense to conduct a cost-benefit analysis to take into account whether OSBI works and, if so, which model and how to adopt it. The following details some of the main challenges involved in selecting and implementing OSBI from a business perspective.

A look at OSBI challenges

As with all benefits, challenges exist. Depending on the outlook, organizations may feel that some of the benefits actually represent challenges. Not all companies are open to taking source code and optimizing it or alternatively, adopting an open framework through commercial OS that is based on community development and not based on proprietary development. However, even for businesses that are open to OSBI solutions or that want to sell the benefits of these offerings to final decision makers, definite challenges of OSBI exist. On the other hand, some organizations are tied into contracts with vendors or already like their existing relationships with mega-vendors such as Oracle or IBM and want to expand use through broader adoption.

The following sections identify specific OSBI challenges that organizations should evaluate and consider to determine whether a proper fit exists. In many cases OS does offer benefits to the business and can bring BI use to the next level. But, for organizations that already have many proprietary offerings or that limit themselves to specific platforms, OS offerings might not be the best way to achieve successful BI.

Development efforts, long-term costs, and BI and IT collaboration have been discussed as benefits in some respects, but they also represent broader challenges to OSBI adoption. Organizations should weigh each of these as both and identify whether they present themselves as challenges or benefits for the organization. No current guides exist to define which outlook any organization will take. And even if they did, it would be impossible to apply OS generalities to each organization effectively.

Development efforts

As mentioned, commercial OS offerings can enable implementations in less time for some companies. In addition, commercial OS offerings provide solutions that are similar to other BI solutions out of the box. Overall, it is pretty safe to say that commercial OS mimics traditional software offerings in many ways, and therefore has similar internal efforts required in order to get systems up and running. As time goes on, these similarities will probably increase. Therefore, in most cases development efforts will be equal within any BI project. And although differences do exist depending on integration and customization, they are not big enough to be a key differentiation, as many BI solutions are becoming quicker to implement in terms of time and effort required.

Community solutions are different because they require a lot of IT developer interaction. So, even though, as McKnight says, they can help companies get off the ground running, this is only at a simple level. Optimizing solutions can take more time than with traditional BI offerings and this offset in time needs to be evaluated. Does extra time to optimize a solution really provide the additional value associated with no upfront software expenditure?

Also, more development efforts can lead to greater lag times between requirements gathered and actual product delivery, adding to misunderstandings of solution delivery and lack of appreciation for IT development efforts. Unless good communication exists between IT and business units, more detailed development can also lead to more room for error and rework leading to longer development times and a feeling of BI's lack of worth, which traditionally involves business units feeling that they do not get value from BI due to long turnaround times. This leads to frustration and feelings of lack of value.

Long-term costs

Although OSBI provides free software access, the reality is that nothing is free. And within BI this means looking at two levels of costs — the initial BI investment and the longer term costs associated with BI. Basically, although less expensive in the short-term, long-term costs may actually be more expensive based on time and effort. Development efforts take time and effort to create effective solutions and to maintain them over time. Generally, IT staff are overworked and maintaining an OSBI initiative on a detailed level means that time and effort are required, leading to continued costs. And even though software costs may not be a consideration, hardware costs and time to implement are. And for many organizations, these costs over time may not be so different from traditional software offerings. This makes costs versus benefits a murky area because many organizations feel that there is a greater payoff by adopting free software, without the realization that real "free" does not exist. Consequently, this misunderstanding may enable solutions to be chosen by IT without adequate expectations being set for the business.

For commercial offerings, subscription costs add up and time to customize offsets costs with additional time required. Also, subscription fees change over time and generally have limitations. Once BI environments expand, businesses need more data storage to include more departments and users and, potentially more hardware. What this really means is that BI costs may really increase. In essence, if selecting community OS with the goal of expanding, it becomes very important to make sure that the commercial version can scale with the required growth.[4]

Unless organizations can attach ROI to these costs, these solutions can be hard to justify based on the potential unknowns associated with long-term use. After all, initial costs only represent one aspect of price in relation to BI, with IT developer time and expenditures over time representing additional considerations. This means that organizations have to look at costs in detail, as subscription fees may not represent fixed expenses over time. In Chapter 11, we'll look at return on investment (ROI), total cost of ownership (TCO), and look at costs associated with adoption more in-depth.

Business and IT collaboration and project sponsorship

Project sponsorship is slowly shifting towards business units, with business-driven BI applications becoming a central focal point. In many cases, or within mid-sized organizations, this means having projects led by CEOs or CFOs, which is a transition away from CIO-driven projects.[5] Companies now expect to drive initiatives from the business with less involvement from IT, due to continued trends such as self-service BI models, SaaS, and the like. Unfortunately, BI will remain a technology-driven application due to integration, customization, and overall project management requirements. Consequently, collaboration is also becoming more prominent, making it more likely that development and design will be more cohesive among departments. However, even with project sponsorships becoming more business-unit driven, IT project involvement will always be required.

This level of collaboration can be positive if and only if disparate business units work together for the betterment of the company. Unfortunately, companies that have holistic collaborative environments are few and far between when it comes to BI adoption and delivery. Within OSBI it can be even more so because IT departments are used to driving initiatives and developing solutions for business units. For organizations that are starting to drive IT initiatives through business

---

[4]Based on insight provided by William McKnight in our interview.

[5]Although I do not have any research numbers to back this statement up, based on my personal experiences, as well as several industry colleagues and interviews with vendors targeting small and mid-sized organizations, we all seem to be coming across the same thing when dealing with newer BI implementations from the SMB market.

sponsorship, issues might exist. For instance, politics within organizations still abound, and decision makers are still restricted by these power plays and relationships. This means that, depending on who pulls the strings, solutions might be limited or not be as beneficial to all who require them.

With all of this being said, the challenge exists in relation to identifying the project scope and the relationship that exists between IT and business units. This means that unless organizations set expectations in the beginning, there is a high potential for some level of product failure. In addition, businesses need to make sure that project sponsorship and scope match so that proper allocation of resources and expectations are met.

Scalability

Over time, organizations require the ability to expand their BI use. In some cases, this means increasing the number of end users. A good example is making sure that more people have access to reports or alerts based on changes in factory conditions or general sales performance or lack of performance. In other cases, expansion refers to data source additions, which can range from additional tables within a single database to completely new sources, such as geospatial or newer customer data management initiatives requiring integration from D&B.[6]

In many cases, traditional software vendors make sure to test their scalability to ensure they can support what their customers will require. Understanding how you might need to scale in the future may alter the type of software selected now. Basically, free software is great, but the OS model selected now might not be able to scale to support your organization's business and technical requirements in the future.

What all of this means for business justification

Despite the benefits of OSBI, its solutions might not be beneficial to all. Some of the challenges might be too far reaching to affect any benefits in a broader deployment. If companies cannot move beyond collaboration issues and work together to create a holistic environment, then an out-of-the-box or other type of offering might be best. Or if organizations do not want to pay for a commercial offering based on subscription fees but do not have internal IT developers on staff to help with the development efforts, they may want to consider alternative offerings. The reality remains that OSBI offerings might not be for everyone. And in order to develop a successful BI implementation, companies have to pick the right type of offering for their company.

Financial benefits and considerations when considering OSBI only look at one aspect of implementation. Broader benefits need to be weighed against challenges that affect businesses directly. Quick deployment times, flexibility, subscription fees, etc., need to be considered together to make sure that OS meets the needs of the company. Business needs and technology needs differ, therefore organizations require both to work together and to build a complete case to justify any OSBI investment.

---

[6]Dun and Bradstreet — http://www.dnb.com/

BI strategies for success – tying in OS adoption with BI success

The strategy behind BI adoption

Understanding the world of OSBI, some of the differences within the marketplace, and why vendors position themselves as they do are a first step towards identifying whether this type of BI deployment matches the requirements of your organization. If you are looking for an OSBI offering or trying to decide the type of deployment you should select, the next set of questions you and your colleagues should be asking are "what do I do with this information?" And "how do I decide what will work best for the organization?" After all, software selection is not as easy as closing your eyes and pointing to a vendor's logo on your computer screen. It requires being able to sell the value of BI to management and defining what isn't working in the current system, how BI can make it better, and what options might work best within your IT environment.

This chapter has the lofty goal of addressing these questions. After all, in order to identify whether OSBI is right for you, it is important to first consider how BI will support the organization's strategic goals. Once you make this decision, it becomes possible to identify whether OS fits within the company's business strategy. Obviously, some organizations bypass in-depth evaluations and select software based on previous use or recommendations from friends. Although this can also work, the greater the understanding of what exists internally, the more likely that the overall project will be successful. One of the problems with the BI marketplace today is that unless an organization is well versed in all of the solutions available, most solutions look alike and can provide similar things at face value. Yes, vendors have their key differentiations, but the reality is that most solutions can be customized to provide like features and functionality. Being able to optimize the solution, however, is one of the key differences when going the distance and taking the time to match vendor requirements with business goals and the existing IT infrastructure.

Let's take this one step further by looking at the role of developers and the process they need to go through to implement an end user facing BI solution. Generally, IT developers take a lot of time putting the pieces of the data puzzle together. This means they look at each table within each data source and identify if and how information is related and which fields are required. For instance, what product information exists and where it is stored, how it relates in one table to various other tables, what information is required, and what calculations are required to make sure that business users can get the insights they require to make the best decisions possible. Doing all of this effectively is no easy task. Some tables may house Product Number, while others use a separate Product ID descriptor, with others still providing a Name and Description. To create a singular view of data, all of this information needs to be consolidated and, in many cases, product numbers do not follow a specific structure. So, naming conventions might not be standardized and like names or descriptions might be used that mean different things to different employees. And even within data warehouse infrastructures that pull in all of the data without all of these data joins and additional preparation, these tasks are still required to develop strategic queries.

The bottom line is that to get the most out of your data from a business perspective, you need the following:

- An understanding of what you want to achieve and why BI is important as a key support to you and your organization's goals.
- Collaboration between business units and IT to help optimize information access.
- Insights into what you might require in the long run, whether from a business or data perspective.
- A broad understanding of your corporate culture, as different cultures will thrive using different types of BI applications.
- Visibility into your data assets and what you hope to glean from them.

All of these aspects apply to both OSBI and BI implementations. Understanding the value proposition of BI and the key benefits of OS (which will be discussed in the upcoming chapters) can help you decide whether it makes sense to take the plunge, or select a more traditional approach to BI adoption. Let's look at all of this in more detail by breaking down the strategic side of BI deployments — from a business perspective.

Adopting BI

One of the reasons I think it is so important to take a step away from OSBI and look at BI strategy and the general value of BI is because I speak with a lot of organizations about BI, whether conducting industry research, providing advisory services, or putting together case studies. One of the issues that constantly comes up is the fact that the industry is difficult to navigate. I am often asked, "Which product should I select?" Or, "I read an article about vendor X, should I implement their solution?" And in most situations, these questions require a lot more knowledge about the current IT infrastructure that exists, business needs, etc.

In addition, some of these same companies are new to BI. In these cases, they have been using Excel and it isn't working for them anymore — some even call it their "Excel Hell." According to these companies, being able to extract information, put it in a spreadsheet, and manipulate it to your heart's content ends up being the antithesis to developing a strong data infrastructure, or ensuring data validity, privacy, security, and accuracy. Consequently, where spreadsheets have been beneficial for the individual, the corporation is starting to suffer due to a lack of consistency across the organization.

This leads to a broader understanding of why many companies look at BI, which is basically to address the uncertainties that arise due to a lack of trust in the data that is available. However, there are also many other reasons. Let's explore some of the reasons behind BI's increasing importance within organizations and how its use is becoming essential to ensuring strategic decision making.

Goals of consolidating information across disparate data sources

The Excel example just discussed is a good segue into a discussion of the need for data consolidation. There is a common example used by BI practitioners and solution providers to illustrate why Excel on a larger scale does not work and why it is important to develop a secure and centralized access point to business information. Basically, it goes something like this. A planning meeting is called to help identify whether or not the said company is on track mid-year and to identify whether it will meet its overall sales goals. Each department sends a delegate with a prepared presentation to identify sales, accounts receivable, accounts payable, supply chain, partner networks, etc. And each representative has taken the time to prepare the key metrics related to his or her business function by exporting information into Excel, adding calculations based on departmental business rules, and manipulating it to suit individualized purposes.[1] When all of these decision makers come together and present their information, they find that their numbers don't match up. Basically, it becomes impossible to identify performance when the validity of the data is questionable. Questions arise, such as, which department is right? How can we trust our information? What calculations were applied? And where do we go from here? These are all valid questions that need to be addressed if organizations want to develop a consistent way of managing their data.

There is a constant debate over whether creating a "single view of the truth" is actually possible, which a general Internet search will show you based on the number of results. Although it falls outside the scope of this book, it is still important to know that even though information is consolidated and needs to be accurate and valid, that one version of the truth does not exist. Each department does have its own view of data and business entities. What does exist is the potential to create an accurate, centralized repository that is monitored for validity in a secure way. In this sense, consolidated data provides a better view of performance across the organization, which is not limited to a department or business function.

Better business visibility

All of this leads to better overall visibility. Once information can be trusted and accessed across the organization, it can be used to provide better visibility. Organizations used to silos can now gain a broader understanding of what is happening within their companies. On a high level this sounds simple, but when we look more deeply we see that this is actually a key reason that many organizations consider developing a data warehouse. Some companies actually start their BI projects with the goal of developing a strong data warehouse infrastructure, and the reason is to achieve exactly what we have been discussing — a centralized access point to information to provide better customer service, product allocation, and visibility into broader business operations.

Traditionally, many businesses develop operational systems separately, with information stored separately as well. Therefore, the only way to understand what is occurring beyond HR, finance, or supply chain is to create a central data store. Once companies want to understand how finance and accounting intersects with sales and distribution, or how customer satisfaction can be used to up-sell and expand sales, the ability to view information across the organization in a centralized repository becomes essential.

---

[1] In general, data manipulation is not as bad as it sounds. In many companies the concept of customer or membership date can differ. For instance, IT considers other departments' customers, whereas customer service looks at a customer as a person calling into the call center. Companies that deal with membership may have differing views on when a membership starts. In some cases, it might be when the application is submitted, in other cases it will be when payment is received, while in others it might be when a customer is invoiced. All of these situations mean that different people within businesses have different worldviews and apply separate calculations to their work, resulting in data that is considered "manipulated" to some extent.

Mitigating risk

Another reason organizations look at BI is to help mitigate risk. In the past, much risk management within BI remained within the realm of finance, insurance, and banking, but most organizations need to assess potential risk and help mitigate its effects on the organization. Within BI, this goes beyond information visibility and means using predictive modeling and other advanced statistical models to ensure that customers with accounts past due are not allowed to submit new orders unless it is known beforehand, or that insurance claims aren't being submitted fraudulently. The National Health Care Anti-Fraud Association (NHCAA) estimates that in 2010, 3% of all health care spending — or $68 billion — is lost to health care fraud in the United States.[2] This makes fraud detection in health care extremely important, especially when you consider that if you are paying for insurance in the United States, part of your insurance premiums are probably being paid to cover the instances of fraud that occur, making this relevant beyond health care insurance providers. Although risk might not be as apparent within all industries or organizations, many businesses still want to make sure they do not invest their resources in unprofitable products or projects. In these cases, the specific challenges of risk assessment may not be as great but still require a strategic development and use of BI and analytics.

Metrics/KPIs

The role of dashboards has taken center stage for many BI implementations. Ease of use and the ability to visualize data through charts and graphs expands the potential use of BI more broadly across the organization. More and more companies are starting their BI implementations from a vantage point of dashboard delivery[3] instead of from traditional reporting or OLAP[4] cubes, with the goal of taking advantage of self-service models.[5] Consequently, businesses are transitioning from historical analysis towards the monitoring of key performance indicators (KPIs) or metrics to help them monitor performance and to identify the cause and effect of various business processes and activities.

The use of metrics makes business analytics more business-process centric by making sure that business decisions and the way in which they are being applied within the organization are tied to the management of business performance. For instance, sales dashboards are very popular. The general goal of many of these dashboards is to identify how products are performing within various regions and to let sales managers manage their staff. The information collected and measured can

---

[2]For more information about this source and about the types of fraud committed within health care, please refer to the following white paper: Fraud Detection Using Data Analytics in the Healthcare Industry prepared by ACL Services Ltd.: http://www.acl.com/pdfs/dp_fraud_detection_healthcare.pdf

[3]On a personal level, I have been encountering more organizations that are looking at BI for the first time with the goal of dashboard deployment. In addition, many vendors are showcasing their dashboard functionality as a key component of their offerings, and many dashboard-oriented analytics solutions are becoming more popular.

[4]OLAP means online analytical processing and refers to multidimensional analysis — i.e., the ability to analyze trends over time and drill through various levels of data to gain more insight on targeted data sets.

[5]The concept of "self-service BI" will mean different things to different people, but essentially self-service means providing more freedom to end users and increasing ease of use and flexibility in design. For many, this means removing BI control from IT departments and enabling business users to develop their own front-end applications — i.e., dashboards and reports.

by tied into sales incentives or supply chain efficiencies. By using dashboards within mobile settings, line of business (LOB) managers and other employees can take these dashboards on the road with them, making BI transportable.[6]

Acquisitions

When people think of acquisitions, many times they think of large enterprises acquiring smaller ones. The BI market is no stranger to this. Solution providers such as SAP and IBM have acquired Business Objects and Cognos as well as many others over the years, shaking up the BI market. However, there are smaller businesses that also acquire other companies. A few years ago I was working with a sub-prime car loan company that offered loans to people with less than amazing credit. Although a smaller business, they were working on acquiring many other similar companies across the United States.

BI becomes important for acquisitions because information from multiple businesses needs to be handled as one large entity. Consequently, data needs to be consolidated and a system of record put in place to make sure that duplicates or other quality and business rule issues are taken care of.

Competitive edge — everybody else is doing it!

So, just because many companies[7] are prioritizing BI, does that mean that your organization should too? At this point I will admit that I am biased based on the fact that I am a proponent of BI and have seen its benefits. At the same time, I have also seen mismanaged projects or projects shelved, where organizations have wasted a lot of time and money. But obviously, if you have come this far, BI is a strong priority within your organization. And in essence, it is no longer enough to make decisions without having empirical proof. It is almost as if utilizing BI represents the entry point now but does not necessarily give you the competitive advantage you need. The competitive edge comes from how you apply BI, not from simply adopting a BI infrastructure and set of dashboards or reports.

Why these factors matter

All of these factors surrounding BI deployments lead to the types of features and functions that will be evaluated when selecting the right software. The types of applications and tools your organization adopts will be dependent on what you hope to gain out of the application. Not all companies will require the use of predictive modeling or the ability to provide stakeholders with risk assessments. But many will want to consider a wide variety of capabilities before selecting the solution they will adopt and the type of deployment.

---

[6]Mobile BI enables use that is broader than just dashboards, but mobile dashboards still represent the most visual and easiest way to interact with analytics access within mobile offerings.

[7]Based on a study by Gartner of 2300 CIOs: http://www.itwire.com/it-industry-news/market/52786-bi-analytics-top-priorities-for-cios

After all, whether selecting OS or not, organizations require the tools to develop and maintain a successful BI environment. And this means understanding why BI is important to today's business. Creating a list of key capabilities and how they relate to what your organization hopes to achieve can help narrow the playing field. What I mean by this is that some products are more mature than others and some provide features out of the box or use connectors to integrate other software within their applications that can be used to offset what doesn't exist natively to the solution. In addition, sometimes OS offerings are not as mature as other applications because they were not developed to meet the needs of paying customers.

The reality is that all of these factors relate directly to OS. Now that both commercial and community versions of OSBI exist, there is more flexibility in deployment and more businesses are evaluating multiple types of offerings side by side and looking at factors beyond the cost (or lack thereof) of software.

Why choose OS

What all of this discussion leads to is how to identify whether OS is the way to go. And the reality is that you might decide that OS isn't right for your organization. But this section will not cover cost. John Kearney, the Director of Administrative Systems at The Commonwealth Medical College (TCMC),[8] said that after being given charge of their BI project he was told, "look for OS" because of the lower costs associated with deployment. In Section 4: Justifying OSBI Projects, we'll look more at how costs factor in to the overall adoption of BI. But for now it is equally important to identify the other factors that make OSBI a viable option.

Already familiar with OS

In many cases, organizations that select OS already have a level of familiarity with its development. The TCMC, for instance, was looking for a data warehouse and reporting solution to take ad hoc queries from people and to be able to create a strategic view of information stored in multiple areas within the organization. Part of John's goal was to "give users a feel for what was available in the source systems" that would enable them to "run whatever reports they wanted to run." Aside from many homegrown applications, they also already had Linux Apache, mySQL, PHP, LAMP server,[9] etc., in-house and were looking to leverage mySQL to build their data marts. Therefore, when it came to OS familiarity, it was already in existence, meaning that skillsets existed and knowledge of where to go for resources was already known. TCMC became active in SourceForge[10] and used the resources to help with their development. Since they knew where to go and which resources to access, development was much simpler.

---

[8]http://www.thecommonwealthmedical.com/

[9]Here is a link to the website for more information on LAMP and mySQL independent of LAMP: http://www.lamphowto.com/ and http://www.mysql.com/

[10]Here is a link to SourceForge when searching for BI applications. It can be used for collaboration and even though John Kearney advises that it can be used for everyone, as it stands now it is mostly used by technical resources and not business decision makers. http://sourceforge.net/directory/business-enterprise/os:mac/freshness:recently-updated/?q=business+intelligence

Want to get off the ground running (as McKnight says)

In some cases, BI installations can take a while. Either the software install and putting it in the hands of those creating solutions or loading data takes weeks or it can take weeks or months to prepare data and develop initial outputs. For example, even a simple sales dashboard or admissions report may be simple in terms of getting the skeleton up and running, but weeks and sometimes months of effort are required to customize to make sure that the analytics represented reflect what is needed to gain valuable insights. One of the things that really resonated with me when speaking with William McKnight was the way in which he determines when he is more likely to use OS and that is when he "wants to get a solution off the ground running." When an organization wants a quick win, the ability to download an application and get it up and running quickly is essential. Even though more tweaks and bug fixes might be required over time, quick time to delivery goes a long way. And in some cases, organizations do not mind taking extra time to tweak a solution if it can be delivered quickly.

Budgetary constraints

It is virtually impossible to discuss OS without considering cost. As mentioned, the costs and lack of costs associated with OS deployments will be discussed in the next section when we evaluate return on investment. While we won't dwell on costs too much here, the reality is that many companies look at OSBI because they do not have unlimited budgets. They may have lofty goals and feel that what they want cannot be achieved by adopting traditional software and hardware due to costs and an infrastructure that might not be able to natively support what they want.

Want to experiment with BI before committing

Many organizations want to try a solution before they commit to dispensing with their budgetary resources. This is one of the reasons so many BI vendors now offer free trials. In many cases, IT developers may feel that they will develop a better understanding of the inner workings of a solution by installing it and using it on their own instead of developing a comparison of multiple offerings. For developers, looking at demos and going through the proof of concept (POC) phase may not achieve the flexibility they want. Downloading software and loading data, developing analytics, and the like can help IT staff understand the inner workings of the solution and see whether specific software is a fit before buying services, support, or even traditional offerings.

Why go traditional

Even though this is a book about OS, the reality is that there are many companies that should not select OS because it isn't the right fit. Even though many companies have similar infrastructures, work in the same industries, and have similar customers, their corporate culture, goals, and general needs may still be different. This means that some businesses may prosper using OS, while others might want to continue their use of proprietary software solutions. Within some of these environments, solutions that proliferate the organization also offer BI suites to accompany operational systems.[11]

The reasons why organizations look at OS are quite persuasive. Flexibility of development, quick deployment, and good experiences in the past are all reasons to expand OSBI adoption within the company. However, these reasons will not apply in all situations, and it should be noted that sometimes it may be better to select traditional offerings instead. So, let's look at some of the reasons why you might choose to forgo OS in favor of traditional BI.

Currently using proprietary software

In some cases, the expansion to BI might be as easy as adding a module available from your transactional software provider (i.e., the SAPs of the world) that also provides BI solutions. In other cases, BI might already exist within the organization and you have to decide whether to expand its use or select a new solution. Depending on outstanding licenses, costs of expansion, time to delivery, and many other considerations, it might make sense to expand general use. Within larger enterprises, it can be quite common for disparate departments to select their own BI solutions based on individualized use cases as opposed to adopting a BI platform to service the whole organization. SMBs sometimes approach BI use differently by standardizing on a single platform. In either case, there may be internal considerations that make it more appealing to expand use or work with a proprietary software vendor that has strong integration capabilities in relation to the transactional systems currently in-house.

No Java expertise in-house

Not all IT developers have OS experience or have worked within Java environments. From a business perspective this means that it is imperative to make sure that the right skillsets exist in-house or that there are external resources that can be leveraged for development and support. If no Java expertise exists, then businesses looking at OS need to identify whether they will hire new resources, use vendor professional services and long-term support, require their current developers to learn new skillsets, and what the implications of each of these actions are.

A few years ago I worked with an organization looking at developing a data warehouse for the first time. They went through an in-depth analysis, only to select Microsoft SQL Server in the end because the IT director was already well versed with Microsoft. Whether or not that was the right choice remains irrelevant. What is relevant is the fact that their choices were based solely on their current expertise and their lack of desire to think outside of the box. The fact is that many organizations are like this. Hence, if you don't have OS developers on hand, it makes sense that you might choose to select a set of software based on the level of comfort that currently exists.

---

[11]Oracle, IBM, and SAP are prime examples based on their acquisitions of leading BI providers. Many organizations with large SAP or Oracle deployments actually expand to use the BI solutions that exist. In some cases, this is because some proprietary solutions are more difficult to integrate due to some limitations of the connections that exist.

Uncomfortable with the concept of OS

Although OS is becoming more widely adopted, there will always be organizations that are not comfortable with the concept of its use. In addition, some organizations create their shortlists by selecting leaders in the industry, which tend to be proprietary offerings because of the breadth and depth of reach within the marketplace. Even though OS offerings are usually downloaded by tens of thousands of companies, most of those companies remain community users, making it impossible to know the true reach of use. Organizations that are risk averse might prefer to start out using solutions they are familiar with or that are based on traditional development methods.

In many cases, an organization is either a proponent of OS and is drawn to its use, or not. With the advent of commercial OS offerings, self-service models, and the like, more business decision makers are weighing in on the type of offering to deploy. I think that over time, more companies will become comfortable with the idea of OS, but will also understand that its value is not intuitive and depends on the outlook and goals of those looking to deploy it.

Looking to expand

Aside from the SMBs that I work with who are green field accounts and new to BI, many organizations already have some form of BI within the organization that extends beyond spreadsheet use. If a company is already satisfied with what they have in-house and want to expand use or types of analytics provided, or extend their solutions to reach more people, then it makes sense to not reinvent the wheel.

Takeaways

Each of these considerations could be looked at more in-depth. However, my goal is to make you think and identify the reasoning behind your choices to make sure that the BI adopted within your organization meets the needs of the broadest number of people possible. It is never easy to balance technical and business requirements, or to develop a solution that has broad analytics requirements with the goal of quick delivery times and low cost of entry. And although I see much value in OSBI adoption, I am also realistic and understand that OS will not be a fit for all organizations or address the needs of every BI-related business problem.

When selecting the type of offering, it is important to remember to look at:

1. Why you are adopting BI.
2. What you hope to achieve — both on a departmental level as well as organization-wide.
3. What exists in-house in relation to software, hardware, skillsets, and comfort factors.
4. Whether OS is right for the organization by looking at the potential benefits outside of initial software costs.
5. The long-term benefits of BI adoption and how the type of solution selected now will affect use in the future.

Although you may still not be convinced that OS is the way to go, the next chapter looks at the implications for users, expanding on what OSBI adoption means on a practical level.

Implications for users

It would stand to reason that once you have decided to select OS, your only additional decision rests on which solution provider is the best fit. The reality, however, is that organizations still have decisions to make related to selecting between community and commercial OSBI versions. When considering the strategic side of selecting BI software, what does this mean for end users and business decision makers? Organizations need to evaluate their potential decisions and look at the implications of those decisions. A good way to do this is to take a step back and figure out:

- Why do you need BI?[1] Is it to create a consolidated view of business performance, to mitigate risk, or to manage employee performance through management dashboards?
- What currently exists in-house? This includes looking at both the skillsets and technology that already exist.
- Why choose OS at all? Are additional support, training, documentation, etc., required?

IT developers have been using OS for years, with commercial OSBI offerings being fairly new within the marketplace. As vendors continue to move into the mainstream BI market, their positioning and solution offerings will continue to shift along with them. This change also leads to practical differences that involve the way business and IT departments interact with OS in general. The biggest implication for organizations and BI software selection is that commercial OS tends to relate more closely to traditional BI offerings, making it more likely for business decision makers to evaluate both types of solutions side by side. In the past, most OSBI initiatives were driven by IT involvement, whereas now many BI projects are driven by departmental needs, such as in the case of Nasza Klasa (NK),[2] Poland's largest social network.

NK is no stranger to OS, as they use MySQL and store customer data on over 200 servers. The problem that necessitated the need for a separate data warehouse was the fact that queries were not performing well when dispatched across these 200 servers. But the real issue was actually business related – with information being stored separately across these multiple servers, NK wasn't able to tell what types of activities members were performing online, such as how many people were playing games and how often. This shows that although technical in nature, the real driver is usually business-related, with the bottom line being the more insights on customers, the greater the ability to sell marketing dollars based on member behavior as opposed to general demographic information. What this shows is that no matter how technically oriented these projects are, the key focus should be on the business issues being faced and how to solve them.

---

[1]Hopefully, Chapter 8 has at least provided some of the starting points to address this issue and identify the key BI applications within your organization.

[2]http://nk.pl/ are currently using Ingres Vectorwise for their data warehouse and Pentaho for their front-end BI. At the time I interviewed them, they were only at the testing phase of Pentaho so our conversation focused on Vectorwise and data warehouse development.

Even though NK provides a good example of identifying the convergence of business and technical needs, the reality is that not every project starts out this way. Let's look at what differences exist within the evaluation arena and why these shifts are occurring.

A practical guide to selecting OS

Although not much different from traditional software evaluations, OSBI offerings do have some differences in relation to what businesses have to consider. These factors can be considered an initial guide to follow. Some of the factors to consider are:

- IT developer involvement: One of the first things to look at when evaluating the type of OS to implement is the needs of the business. Now business units that want to control the nature of development and rollout are driving more BI projects. Within traditional OSBI offerings, IT developers lead projects and are relied upon to update and edit offerings. This fact is nothing new. Commercial OSBI solutions still require IT involvement, but in many cases are geared towards business users. NK's use of data warehousing ties in the need for IT efficiencies related to query performance as well as the ability to tie in member behavior to potential profits. In terms of commercial offerings, many OSBI vendors have end users in mind when developing their commercial applications because of this trend of taking into account the needs of business users as an extension of technological efficiencies. With self-service models of BI access becoming a main focal point of many solution providers, business users have more access to manage their own BI experience. This includes the ability to edit and change the information being analyzed. Within these types of implementations IT involvement will differ. For IT departments that may not have the bandwidth to add another project to an overburdened staff, limited involvement may be an option with a commercial solution and professional services.
- Integration and use of OS source code: Irrespective of the involvement of internal IT staff, all companies should look at general integration and how the customization of source code fits within the BI infrastructure. Commercial OSBI offerings provide a finished product that can be implemented without editing or accessing source code. Although not a reason to choose one over the other, the level of involvement with the source code itself means that businesses might make their choices based on IT developer involvement and how solutions integrate with one another.
- Commercial OS and traditional BI implementations: Commercial OSBI offerings are becoming more like traditional solutions. Feature sets are similar as is ease of use and levels of interactivity. Consequently, OS vendors will have to justify OS offerings beyond price and OS value as these solutions become more intertwined with other types of BI offerings. Because organizations are increasingly expecting free access to BI and lower price points, OS will need to rebrand its value proposition. Even with this being said, as commercial OSBI becomes more comparable to other options, its popularity will actually increase, although differentiators outside of value-added services will decrease. Consequently, OSBI will have to continue to increase its value proposition to customers in order to keep its differentiated status.
- Expanding partnerships from OS offerings to mainstream software vendors: In addition, OS vendors tend to partner with one another due to similar frameworks and easier integration.

As more organizations adopt OS solutions within the full BI spectrum, broader integration strategies will be required. After all, OSBI adoption is expanding and leading to more diverse applications, and also to a wider array of integration combinations. Organizations are starting to use Talend with traditional front-end BI solutions or, alternatively, a front-end BI tool like Jaspersoft or Pentaho with a traditional data warehouse back-end. Organizations should identify the differences in deploying partnered vendors as opposed to other solution providers.

When initiating a BI project, organizations need to define their project scope and business and technical factors to help them identify the solution and how it will integrate within the current BI environment. But moving beyond the beginning considerations means looking at specific technical and business issues that will affect any organizations. So, two types of factors exist when selecting an OS solution — business and technical. But identifying these areas is not enough. Organizations need to look at the implications of each to bridge the gap between the general considerations and how they link to potential business value. The word "potential" is used because even though BI use provides increasing potential for organizations, the reality is that this potential may remain unrealized unless organizations make sure that OSBI is implemented strategically. And strategically means ensuring proper planning, requirements analysis, and tying this to technology.

Selecting commercial or community OSBI is no different from evaluating another type of BI solution. However, neither technological nor business factors can be overlooked to select the right solution and to implement it effectively. But in addition to all of these other areas of evaluation, collaboration within an organization becomes just as important as business and technical considerations.

Collaboration may be outside the scope of this chapter, but the level of cooperation between business and IT departments may actually influence the decision-making process. We've discussed the involvement required of IT developers and potential differences between community and commercial OS offerings. This adds another layer to both involvement and the software-selection process. Basically, before making any final decisions, businesses really should look at and define their expectations and level of involvement of each department to identify the requirements from each. Project initiation and sponsorship, stakeholder value, process changes and improvements, and the like are just some areas that expand beyond simple software choices but that directly affect BI initiatives and project success.

Now that you're ready to consider OSBI, the following factors need to be considered to get you there.

Business factors of adoption

Business factors are the considerations that go into a solution evaluation and that lead to success or failure of the overall project. The implications of not taking into account business needs, or driving project requirements through the business, are large and can lead to project stumbling blocks. Also, despite BI's heavy emphasis on database technology, integration, and other technical areas, a focus on technology only provides part of any BI picture. With community OS projects targeting IT developers, the business factors are sometimes overlooked. With commercial adoption, solutions are developed and deployed a little differently. These projects take into account the business requirements because vendors develop them as a way to provide BI to business users without having to rely solely on internal development efforts. Highlighting the different approaches to software delivery provides a good introduction into the importance of looking at BI from a business perspective — irrespective of delivery model or solution type.

So, why are business factors so important? As mentioned, community OSBI solutions target business users by providing out-of-the-box consumer offerings. Consequently, vendors take into account what business users may need and how they interact with technology. And although varying levels of comfort with technology exists, the push within the market is to create self-service models that enable broader visibility and greater decision making. This can only be achieved with business involvement and outlook.

Even though business factors can seem very broad, there are specific aspects that all businesses look at when considering either community or commercial OSBI. Some of these include:

- The purpose of the solution: Although not very different from other forms of offerings, the reality is that companies need to start at this point. Solution purpose moves beyond scope identification towards looking at the goal of the solution, including metrics, analytics, and reporting requirements. Although all of the data points that are required to actualize these features are a large part of any solution, organizations need to start with the business side first. Identifying the top 10 metrics helps provide the business rules required to make decisions, leading to broader corporate visibility.
- Matching solution purpose to vendor offerings: Once the business requirements are identified, the next step is to evaluate vendors to make sure that they actually provide the required feature sets. Luckily, within the OS world the number of players is limited, making this easier than within a traditional BI evaluation. But organizations still need to be careful and make sure they match their business needs to solution provider offerings.
- What vendor expertise is needed to support the business: Because commercial OSBI removes itself from community and IT developer involvement and tries to mimic other types of BI offerings (e.g., cloud-computing options, Web deployments, dashboards, data integration, etc.), organizations need to be sure that their business needs can be met. OSBI professional services differ by vendor and businesses need to match their expectations.
- What type of company are you?: Once these three factors are considered, decision makers are ready to identify the role of the vendor. This goes beyond professional services. For instance, just because OSBI might offer lower-cost alternatives does not mean that all companies will value the model. Considerations for OS may include comparing the differences between initial development and roll-out, etc.

Technical factors

We've looked a lot at the business considerations and factors involved in software selection and how it relate to commercial OSBI adoption. However, to create a full picture and be able to select the right model for the organization, technical factors also need to be considered. And to get the best possible view of what you need to apply within your business, technical factors need to be looked at in-depth. Unfortunately, for organizations that are not used to collaboration between IT and business units, this represents a challenge. Community OS generally looks at the needs of IT developers, with commercial options being more business-oriented. For IT departments this transition may also present some difficulties because there needs to be a letting go of control in relation to the decision-making process. Either way, technical factors cannot be overlooked.

These technical factors include the software, hardware, integration, and platform used that make up the development and deployment of a solution. For businesses this may mean looking at how much storage they require, or at the types of information they are analyzing and the number of disparate data sources. And although all of this seems relatively straightforward, the reality is that when shifting gears towards the more technical aspects of these activities, areas like integration, storage, and analytics capabilities evaluations become more difficult. Organizations have to go from looking at how often they want data to be updated to what types of servers are required, longer term hardware acquisitions, whether the new solution will integrate well within the current IT environment, and how all of the pieces fit together.

Looking at these factors more in-depth involves identifying the integration and hardware requirements. When considering BI specifically, organizations need to look at data warehousing and the options available. Even though businesses may want to apply OSBI, the choice of OS versus a traditional data warehouse or appliance can be considered a separate choice. Or organizations might go the opposite way and look at OS for their back-end solution and traditional BI for the rest. Any combination still requires the same (or at least very similar) type of considerations, which means that the same factors need to be looked at.

Here are some of the factors businesses need to take into account:

- Data warehousing: As discussed, different types of data warehouses exist. Within OSBI, most are relegated to traditional offerings that are based on OS software development and optimization to provide data-warehousing capabilities. Organizations should identify which one fits best — based on current platform, purpose, expenditures, perceived/identified TCO, and the like. Because so much detail is required to look at data warehousing in-depth, these factors will be discussed at length within the technical sections of this book.
- Data integration: Data integration represents another area that is complicated on its own. From a business perspective, organizations see the business problem as how to get disparate data into one place on a continual basis. From a technical perspective this is only the beginning. Data integration involves data extractions, transformations, validations, consolidations, and the list goes on. Add to this solution restrictions, data validation, data profiling, and the maintenance of quality standards, and data integration can represent the most time-consuming and time-intensive activities within an implementation.
- Hardware additions: All of the data considerations and new BI applications lead to additional costs and resources. In addition to software implementations and additional resources required, many organizations also require the addition of hardware (mainly in the guise of servers) to store and process new data. Some organizations are able to allocate current servers and existing hardware to BI initiatives. But even in these cases, hardware additions still require consideration.
- Overall platforms: What currently exists and why OSBI is being implemented and how everything will fit together is a huge technical factor. Although most solutions can be integrated within an organization's current IT infrastructure, not all integration processes are equal. Some solutions work better together, while others require much effort and are time consuming. The ROI of these solutions should be evaluated against other alternatives that might be easier to manage.

Overall, all of these factors lead to the evaluation of why data matters and the importance of data management to drive business information visibility. Irrespective of data warehouse choice or data integration requirements, everything relates to how information is managed within the organization. BI only represents the output of data entities, relationships, and insights. To effectively implement any BI offering, data factors are central considerations. But within the data integration space, limited OS options exist. The main OS data integration offering is Talend, with others having limited influence within the BI market.

Bringing this back to the discussion of commercial versus community OS means that technical factors may have an influence on what solution is selected in the long run. Even though both choices provide companies with the same environment, they require different efforts. Within technical environments, both types will require development efforts, but differences may exist within professional service offerings of vendors in relation to getting the solution up and running.

Considerations

Adding to all of these factors are the general considerations that are an expansion of the implications involved in adopting OS. Although similar discussions have been looked at in the previous chapter, the reasoning behind this discussion differs. The previous chapters focused on OS options and how to identify which option is best. These considerations actually take a step further and identify the implications of adopting commercial OS. Once a business decides to embark on commercial OS, many of the factors that have been considered in the evaluation process actually extend into how the solutions will be implemented. A good example is the discussion surrounding why IT developers flock to OS — basically, because of the flexibility and high level of developer interactivity. In addition, this community involvement acts as a source of support that may or may not overlap with professional services. Once companies have adopted commercial OSBI, the types of services provided move to the next level. And although IT involvement is still involved, businesses can limit that interaction through commercial OSBI application.

This example highlights that organizations cannot overlook detailed analysis of the pros, cons, and outlying factors related to their software evaluations. Their choices affect not only how the solution will look in the end, but also the amount of involvement and effort required to get the system up and running. The bottom line is that all of the time it takes to evaluate offerings and identify whether a company should select a community or commercial OSBI solution can be directly applied to ROI and TCO.

Overall, the implications of OSBI are mainly reflected within organizations in relation to value and cost. Within ROI identifications this might seem straightforward, but TCO is a little bit different. Return on investment normally applies to financial criteria only. TCO (which will be defined in detail, with a checklist to identify the level of TCO for any given solution within OS and how it differs from traditional BI options) takes into account the business factors outside of specific cost expenditures and how they affect performance. With this being said, organizations are starting to increase their view of ROI towards non-financial factors as well.

The categories discussed in the following sections highlight this fact by looking at cost-based implications.

Price and maintenance breakdown

The costs associated with commercial OSBI include more than just software and hardware provisions. The good thing about BI in general is the increasing flexibility in pricing and support. During our discussion of subscription models, it became obvious that not all pricing structures are the same. In the past, organizations were at the mercy of vendors, with high price points and maintenance fees paid yearly. The worst part for businesses in these situations remains the fact that these extra costs may have accounted for support but not for upgrades. In some cases, organizations needed to shell out additional expenses to remain competitive and take advantage of new features and functionality. And for many businesses, this is far from realistic.

Luckily, pricing has evolved to provide more benefits to customers. Whether this means a yearly or monthly subscription or a more traditional payment model, pricing has become much more flexible to meet the needs of the organization. For instance, most vendors price their offerings based on use. So solution providers will break up their offerings based on module or BI function (e.g., integration, dashboards, analytics, etc.). Because of this, BI's entry point is much more manageable. This is even more so for commercial OS.

With the development of lower-cost solutions, overall pricing tends to be less than traditional counterparts. This means that perception of value increases because organizations get more based on what they pay for in relation to competitive products. This translates to a better value proposition for businesses (hence higher ROI and lower TCO) and broader adoption once any uncertainties about OS adoption are overcome. The measurement of ROI and TCO has a direct implication on adoption. Even for businesses that might be less than enthusiastic about OS, or any non-traditional BI adoption, their views might change once they evaluate OSBI in relation to cost versus other options.

In addition, pricing factors also apply to maintenance. Traditional solutions charge about 20% for maintenance fees in addition to first year software costs. This includes areas such as technical support and fixes. With subscription fees, whether offered as a service or part of a more traditional model, maintenance is generally included within the fees. This increase in flexibility actually leads to a shift in the market and the expectations of customers. Many prefer the one payment option because it appears to provide more value due to the fact that an organization gets all services and access to software use without separating software costs.

These factors affect solution choice. Organizations develop in-depth evaluations based on features, functions, professional services, support − the list may be endless depending on the business pain being addressed. But final decisions are made based on the technical requirements and budget constraints. An organization plans its OSBI adoption partially around the money it can spend. Project scope may be changed based on cost limitations. SaaS provides a good example of a BI solution that provides subscription offerings that are priced based on amount of data storage and type of analytics. Aside from pricing not being the same for each customer, the same limitations exist for OSBI solutions.

Each vendor defines its own commercial model of OSBI, making it difficult for businesses to compare solutions based on the same criteria. But companies should still be able to compare costs based on the features they are getting and matching that list to their must haves, with cost expenditures. Add to this growth and longer term costs and the implications surrounding software costs, maintenance, and decision making becomes even more complicated. The overall adoption of commercial OSBI, however, is still expanding based on its merits.

Long-term costs

This flows into the long-term costs associated with commercial OSBI. If we take a step back, some companies look towards OSBI vendors for continued support over time but still develop independent solutions in-house (i.e., community solutions). These are still long-term costs but the implications for businesses involved in this type of development differ from commercial offerings. Commercial OS has a similar model to traditional software models based on newer subscription models. Most OSBI offerings follow subscription models, meaning that customers pay for what they use.

However, when looking at long-term costs, OS may differ from other solutions with a subscription model. In many cases (the market is slowly shifting, meaning that more mainstream BI vendors are moving towards subscription models as well), hosted solutions or SaaS are the drivers of this software model. In these instances, organizations may pay for professional services to get the solution up and running, but once everything is up and running, no internal involvement is required. This is not always the case, as sometimes organizations choose to develop or maintain applications on their own. This means that overall costs include the time involved in maintaining the solution. The difference with commercial OSBI solutions is that this development and maintenance is a given. In addition to the time and effort involved from internal IT staff, additional hardware may be required, meaning that even though the subscription fees are outside the norm, other cost considerations reflect the traditional models of BI.

When changing gears and looking at free OSBI offerings, the longer term costs may differ. It is very important to identify whether these are better than commercial software options – especially when looking at community OS. Sometimes organizations think that free software equals no costs. But the time it takes to develop internal applications from source code may actually increase implementation times and overall costs associated with software development. Depending on how much it would cost an organization in time to develop and implement a solution, roll it out, support it, and expand over time, long-term costs might actually be equivalent or higher than commercial solutions.

As discussed, in some cases commercial options are less expensive due to their developed solutions. Although IT resources are required for data integration and some level of implementation, the overall solution is a ready-made and easier-to-install alternative. Consequently, depending on overall scope and the business and technical factors identified over the past two chapters, organizations should perform an in-depth analysis to see which option works best.

On a broader level, this leads to the question of whether OS solutions are really less expensive (or free) in the long run. The common adage that "OS is free as in a puppy and not in beer" is a good one. Efforts of IT resources – whether community or commercial – reflect complex tasks within a BI implementation. Companies place different value on what it means to have access to free software with a large development effort versus an initial cost of software expenditure with less involvement over time.

IT development

The debate related to the level of IT development and general involvement expands beyond costs towards time to value and implementation times. This chapter has already looked at the difference between community and commercial OSBI offerings. Obviously, the perceived benefits are different depending on the goal of the BI project. In some cases, individualized projects may require a lot of customization anyway, meaning that companies will lean towards free software with broader development efforts. On the other hand, more traditional applications, such as sales and marketing dashboards, retail analysis, or supply chain management, are sure bets with out-of-the-box offerings.

Business and technical requirements

The past two chapters have broken down the factors on both business and technical levels, after providing an overview of both commercial and community options. In addition to the types of OSBI models and the factors that contribute to their selection, companies are tasked with identifying which model if any will suit the organization's business challenges. The one thing companies should remember when delving into the implications of implementing OS is the importance of both business and technical considerations in order to get a full picture of what is required to implement a solution successfully.

Checklist for software selection and implementation

The business and technical implications of OSBI give companies a roadmap that can be highlighted by the following checklist. Basically, after drilling similar concepts within a series of chapters, having a takeaway hopefully makes it worthwhile. The following checklist puts all of the pieces together to give decision makers the ability to break down the steps required to make the right OSBI choices for the organization. Hopefully, these choices also lead to successful BI implementations and broader company adoption.

- Project roadmap: Has your organization developed a strong scope and mission for the project? It is not enough to identify that visibility is lacking or that decision makers only have access to a limited amount of information. For BI to be effective organizations need to identify what they hope to accomplish. In many cases projects involve the ability to define sales goals and have the analytics to identify potential opportunities and challenges as they occur or to understand the cause and effect between customer behavior, sales, marketing, supply chain, and partner relationships. Without a way to consolidate information across the organization, manage it, and derive valuable insights, companies are only working at half their abilities.
- Making sure the timing is right: Even though businesses want to jump on board with BI or enhance their current environment, the reality is that timing is just as important as anything else. And sometimes that timing is not right. IT- and business-related initiatives, or future project dependencies, should be taken into consideration before commencing any OSBI project. For instance, if a company is migrating to a new system or acquiring a new company, it might be better to wait until completion before taking on a new project.
- Allocating proper stakeholders to the initiative: Once your company decides to move forward, one of the first steps is including the right people. A mix of business, technical, and management level provides a good start. These resources need to have insights into the business

processes, information assets, and analytics to help create a committee that has a broad view of the business.

- Features and function alignment to project scope: As discussed earlier, feature alignment with solution choice provides a good basis for businesses to use as a starting point to design a relevant solution. Sometimes members of the organization will want specific features, like up-to-date views of data, when realistically, to remain competitive, a daily view is enough. In these cases, you may need to formally define what the scope is and how it relates to business processes to identify software features and requirements.

- Understanding data sources and integration: The level of detail required to successfully implement a BI solution remains substantial. Where data resides, how it interrelates, and timeliness are the business aspects of data. For that, technical details are required. In most cases, this is where collaboration becomes essential because more than one business unit will be required to understand how information interrelates. On the IT side, data issues represent one area where collaboration cannot be overlooked. Even commercial OS offerings will require some level of interaction with IT to understand the current environment and BI integration issues.

- End goal and delivery: The end goal closely relates to the project scope and goal, but this checklist item refers specifically to how BI will be delivered. What aspects are required and how should they be accessed? Will end users access reports, dashboards, detailed analytics, etc.?

- Audience: Delivery and audience go hand in hand. Once your team identifies all of the rest, and how BI will be accessed by end users, looking at the skillsets of those users becomes a natural extension. Comfort with technology and level of expertise actually affects adoption and BI interaction. Therefore, if your audience is only used to interacting with predefined reports, changing how they access information without their input might backfire.

- Future requirements and anticipated use: Although it is not always easy to identify how BI will be used in the future, businesses should still look at anticipated data storage growth, new applications or departmental use, and potential growth.

Justifying OSBI projects

Selling an OSBI project to the business

The fact is that the value of BI is not always self-evident. Organizations have struggled for years to sell the value of BI beyond data consolidation and faster query delivery. Depending on the type of analytics applications and who in the company is sponsoring the project, BI's value proposition might be more or less difficult to prove. I have spoken with many companies that have reiterated this point while being very adamant that although they are satisfied with their use of BI, they may have put more thought into how to sell the value of BI and how to measure the benefits received through its use. Therefore, irrespective of the type of BI deployment, the ability to sell the value of BI and its adoption across the organization can, in some instances, make or break its general success.

So far we've looked at the value of OSBI offerings in detail through developing an understanding of how these offerings differ from traditional BI solutions and the benefits and considerations involved in evaluating what OS can bring to your organization. We've explored time to value, commercial offerings that combine end user oriented solutions with community input, and the considerations associated with business-driven OSBI projects. All of these provide a beginning point to actually selling OS to businesses. But at the same time, business unit perceptions of OS and confidence in its deployment as the main BI infrastructure within the organization is slowly gaining momentum, but they still have a long way to go. Although some companies like the value proposition of OS (as discussed throughout the previous chapters), others feel that there are greater risks associated with its implementation.

The reality that some organizations are unsure of BI is really based on the fact that OS provides a different way of looking at the world of software development and BI delivery. Questions surrounding security, viability, scalability, costs, value, and so on can create stumbling blocks to adoption. In reality, there are reasons to not implement OSBI and to go a different route, some of which we've looked at while others might be more individual to the business. After all, depending on who does the selling, the purpose of the solution, and general sponsorship, how to address business units and sell the value to the business in a way that businesses can understand may be a challenge. Organizations may not be aware of the different benefits varying stakeholders will achieve through OSBI. What makes this even more complicated is two-fold. The first being that different stakeholders within the same department might have disparate viewpoints, and the second being that various stakeholders and project sponsors might have goals that are not aligned with one another.

As a caveat and something that requires mentioning, whether using OS or not, BI projects involve risk. Granted, all IT-related projects and software implementations do, but it's important to be cognizant of this fact to try to avoid it. Not all BI projects are a success or turn out the way expected. Sometimes projects are shelved, integration stumbling blocks occur leading to longer data preparation and implementation times, or business requirements change and project scopes need to account for new features and functions. Another challenge remains adoption. If no training is provided, adoption remains slow or unlikely, creating another form of failure. But if an organization gets sidetracked by these potential BI initiative risks, it will become impossible to expand or to create a successful BI infrastructure.

A closer look at ways of selling OSBI

There are many aspects involved in selling OS to organizations. These can include companies just learning about the market, businesses adopting commercial OS after community use, business units looking at adopting OSBI solutions independently of IT department management, or organizations looking to replace traditional BI models with OS offerings. The reasons companies choose OS have expanded well beyond IT developers accessing source code and customizing offerings for their company's benefit. Between expanding offerings and better education, companies now consider OS offerings as a viable option and alternative to traditional BI models. And for many of those that don't, their awareness is slowly growing to include a general understanding of the types of offerings in the market.

However, there are still some businesses that do not know OSBI options are a consideration when evaluating BI offerings or that are unsure about the viability of OS due to its newer entry into the traditional BI marketplace. Alternatively, there exist stakeholders within companies that are champions of metrics management and BI adoption but who are not the actual project sponsors. These people need to adopt a sales outlook to sell the value of OSBI to individual business units or the overall organization. Unfortunately, this role is not easy due to potential resistance that adds an overall challenge of selling the benefits and value of implementing OSBI instead of another model.

Additionally, a lot of education is still required to bridge the gaps between general education, software selection, and the creation of a strong business case for OSBI. Hopefully, this chapter will help OS enthusiasts do just that by providing a business case for the virtues of OSBI adoption and use — both throughout the company or for one business application. To do so, this chapter has been divided into digestible chunks that can be read based on the specific business challenge being faced within your organization.

The sections within this chapter provide a breakdown of the types of choices companies make, the stakeholders involved, and aspects to consider when selling to business. Each section is self-contained. This means that a certain level of repetition will occur. The purpose of this is to let you pick the sections that meet your needs and skip the rest. Obviously, you can go through the chapter in detail, but if you are involved in an OSBI project and need additional ideas on who to involve or how to get broader buy-in, each section will point you to the right path based on the type of deployment your organization selects.

Community OSBI adoption

Community OS still represents the most widely applied type of OSBI (or OS in general) due to its long-term popularity within the broader IT development community.[1] In some cases, IT developers have looked to OS offerings to build up a whole platform for both operational and analytical solutions. In other cases, these offerings are used as a starting point and evaluation period for potential commercial offerings later on. As OSBI moves towards more of a commercial solution base, community versions will still exist, but vendor focus may not seem abundantly supportive of this model. Even so, many organizations that have built their BI platform within an OSBI framework will continue to expand their use, while other businesses that are open to OS models will adopt OSBI as a way to increase BI use within their organization.

Who benefits on the business side from using OSBI?

In previous chapters we've discussed why organizations and specifically IT developers choose community OSBI and some of its benefits. Here is a more in-depth look at some of the scenarios involving community adoption of OSBI offerings.

If development efforts within community OS projects are collaborative between business units and IT, then reporting and analytics can be created based on specific needs defined by the end users. Although commercial offerings generally provide 80% of the features required out of the box (the same as any traditional BI offering), companies still require customization to get things up and running effectively. In essence, OS offerings are similar, but on a larger continuum community versions that provide general source code give organizations the shell and then enable expanded use through development and customization.

In some cases, business units have been accessing OS reporting or analytics for years without even knowing it and want to expand their BI use or address a specific need within the company. For instance, if sales and marketing have been finding success based on the reports provided for them by IT, it makes sense that other departments may want to have access to a similar set of reports. In the case of OS, expanding use across the organization may be more timely and cost effective than evaluating a new set of solutions independently. With an infrastructure and skillset already in place coupled with past successes, the use of OSBI in these cases almost sells itself to the business, providing reports can be delivered in a timely fashion.

In other cases, such as those that are similar to TCMC and their search for OSBI, there might be a mandate to procure OS. In these instances, companies might be more attracted to the promise of community OS to test the solutions and see which one makes the most sense. Since the decision to implement OS comes from the top, in these cases, an understanding of what the implications of OS are to account for potential longer development times in order to tweak the solution to the

---

[1]Generally, many organizations will download BI servers or reporting solutions but not become paying customers. http://sourceforge.net/projects/pentaho/files/Business%20Intelligence%20Server/stats/timeline provides the number of downloads of Pentaho's BI server over a week-long period. Just under 1,800 downloads are recorded, whereas the commercial customer base is listed at 1,200, which is based on an analyst briefing provided.

proper business specifications can help provide the knowledge required to make sure that OSBI is being selected for the right reasons, and not just because of its free software component.

What is involved in getting buy-in and in developing these offerings?

Getting buy-in always remains similar irrespective of the type of IT requirements. Within BI specifically, project sponsors need to identify the stakeholders involved, business unit champions, and additional potential project sponsors within other departments. In some cases these might be the same people, while in other cases multiples of each might exist. Based on the goals of each individual, selling OS might be unique based on each business case. For instance, some employees want to accomplish higher sales while others want to become more effective in their jobs and have better access to data so they do not have to work large amounts of overtime and can spend more time with their families. Whatever the driver, each should be handled individually, as non-technical users most likely will not care about open standards or the ability to customize and control development efforts. They might care about the interactivity and time to deployment, however. So all in all, buy-in requires the ability to match product benefits with the goals of the stakeholders involved.

The IT side of the organization also requires consideration. It is important to realize that community projects are driven primarily by IT developers. Making sure they are onboard and have the proper skillsets or can acquire them quickly becomes important to future development and potential product expansions over time. Therefore, top-down community adoptions need to be coupled with IT support to ensure that there will actually be a certain level of dedication to the project.

Why should the business side of an organization consider community OS as an option?

In some cases, it already exists and end users just don't know it. As mentioned above, in many organizations instances of OS are being used by departments in the form of reports or even full applications without end-user knowledge. Therefore, when looking at additional BI applications, the infrastructure is already in place and additional development might not be as hectic as developing something from scratch. This means that companies can develop new applications with quicker time to value without having to spend the time developing a new BI infrastructure or allocating additional resources for additional hardware and/or software. Basically, business users can have more autonomy in the development process without having to rely on IT departments for new integration activities or to create a new BI platform.

Other times, IT developers choose to create solutions in-house and prefer to control the design and general data access. In these cases, departmental costs are low because software development remains within the realm of the IT cost center. Add to this free software and free perceived development/customization, and departmental use can be broad without breaking the bank. However, as BI becomes more self-service over time, more businesses may want to participate in the decision-making aspects of OSBI adoption on a broader level. Therefore, it makes sense to include them in the beginning phases to ensure support from the start of the project.

When is community OS BI appropriate?

Organizations select community OSBI for many reasons, but the easiest aspect to sell to decision makers includes the ability to develop solutions in-house with current skillsets and resources available. This level of availability needs to expand towards support and on-going maintenance, with the realization that hardware and software requirements may change or expand over time. This also relates to the next selling point in terms of companies that have limited budgets for commercial software. Even though cheaper solutions exist, they are generally limited to a specific number of users, servers, data connections, etc., creating a limited picture of what BI can provide.

In some cases, and if the above criteria apply,[2] then one of the other benefits is the level of collaboration between the business unit and IT development efforts in relation to the design of the solution and the gathering of business requirements. Obviously this does not always occur, but for organizations that do have high levels of collaboration between the two, OS options are a great way to develop lower-cost solutions across the organization.

Commercial after community
Who evaluates commercial OSBI?

The answer to this question is twofold:

- Companies looking to broaden their internal BI use and that require better support and broader deployment through commercial OS — in essence, by expanding their current community use, they have access to formalized support, upgrades, and solutions that are part of a broader vendor roadmap.
- Organizations wanting to take advantage of what they've developed in-house, as well as product support, additional features and functions provided out of the box, and the community interaction as a whole — these organizations want better services and quicker time to development with the goal of getting more value out of their solutions.

What benefits does switching from a free model to commercial OS provide to the business unit(s) involved?

Some companies are still under the impression that community OSBI is free. Therefore, the switch to a commercial model translates into a new set of costs. But for some organizations the cost of software may be offset by not needing internal development efforts to the extent of community offerings. For instance, instead of having to spend additional months of developer time on customizing an offering, costs may be spent on the software, saving months of time to implement. The cost of the developer, therefore, is almost offset by the cost of the software. In some cases, this may actually balance itself out in the long run. Commercial OSBI also leads to quicker

---

[2]In reference to collaboration and open communication between business decision makers and IT developers. The reality, however, is that in many cases this might not be the reality. In my experiences working with smaller companies, collaboration is more likely, but the issue with me making these assumptions based on broader OSBI adoption is that most businesses adopting BI are on the larger side, even if they are not considered enterprise organizations.

development times based on broader solution availability. What this means is that business units are no longer reliant on developers to create their BI applications from scratch, as commercial offerings closely mimic other traditional BI offerings with many features being provided out of the box.

With commercial offerings, end-user support remains external to the organization, and in cases where more of a self-service model exists, there becomes an increase in end-user autonomy and customization potential. In these cases, end users can bypass IT departments to get the answers they want more quickly. In addition, costs are lower (in general, but not in every case) than with other traditional models because no proprietary aspect exists, lessening the development costs and having updated offerings developed using community input.

Why do organizations want to transition from one model to the other?

As commercial offerings become more viable and BI more important within the organization, businesses want to be able to take advantage of technology, support, and quick deployment times. For instance, better time to value may occur when using commercial offerings over having to develop solutions only from OS source code. In addition, companies can integrate new technologies and take advantage of new technology partnerships as they become available. Because BI maturity necessitates formalized structure and OSBI is generally less expensive in relation to traditional software to deploy, companies can be more dynamic with their deployments. The hope is that because many of these solutions are newer market entrants, they require less effort to get up and running and do not require the robust platform development in comparison with the solutions required many years ago.

When should organizations progress towards commercial OS?

There comes a time when expansion seems inevitable. As BI adoption expands and as the types of uses diversify, IT departments may not be able to support each function optimally. Consequently, the adoption of an out-of-the-box solution built on the same framework as the current BI infrastructure provides a nice extension to what already exists and enables companies to reuse what they've already developed.

In addition, there's no point in breaking something that doesn't need to be fixed — meaning that if IT is satisfied with the way the current infrastructure works, and if consumers are happy with their BI interactions, then expanding on the same general platform can help create a more robust BI platform without any rework required. This makes commercial use a natural extension.

Commercial for the first time
Who chooses commercial OS over traditional BI models?

For the past several years, OS vendors have been enhancing their commercial offerings and messaging to compete head-to-head with traditional BI offerings. Now these solutions are more mature and have use cases that can back them up beyond commercial customers that use community versions with support models attached. In essence, many of the BI offerings available are starting to create differentiated products based on whether you are using community or commercial versions. Consequently, these newer offerings are giving organizations more BI choice, irrespective of requirements or general needs.

Comparable BI offerings exist that don't cost as much due to OS development-related activities and that do not require proprietary development. Vendors such as SAP, IBM, and Oracle provide broader feature sets than many other vendors but also require more robust infrastructures to deploy due to limited integration capabilities. This means that organizations encounter more challenges getting these infrastructures up and running. OSBI offers a different value proposition because of the open framework. In addition to lower costs, organizations can integrate offerings more easily based on these open standards and also have access to a wider array of tools and services that natively integrate with their solutions. However, this is not to say that implementations are without hiccups. In some cases, OS can be just as difficult as these other proprietary vendors depending on the IT and BI infrastructures that exists within the company.

Even with this being said, the cost savings might offset this other perceived downside of OSBI adoption. This means that businesses looking at saving costs — at least in the short term through subscription-based delivery models — can enjoy what OSBI has to offer. Overall, this may include SMBs that want to take advantage of broader BI but that don't have the resources to maintain a large-scale deployment, or larger organizations that have other OS solutions within their company. Unfortunately, the general benefits identified do not always only apply to OS. In many cases, companies need to figure out whether this type of model fits within their overall BI infrastructure and goals.

What are the benefits of OSBI for businesses not familiar with the model?

In general, each organization will look at benefits differently, but there are also some overarching advantages that organizations may attach to looking at commercial OSBI offerings. Some of these include IT familiarity with OS models.[3] Although not a benefit in itself, it may help when projects are developed in terms of collaborative buy-in and overall development time frames.

But obviously a look at the business side is different. Organizations look for solutions that are tried and true, tested and successful within many business scenarios. They don't always consider or care about how to get there as long as there is a short time to value. With subscription models and multiple deployments, OS offerings are ahead of the curve in the sense that organizations now expect a level of "free" when evaluating solutions, with OSBI paving the way. In essence, organizations know what they are paying for and can have the IT side of the house test it out beforehand.

How are the benefits of this model sold to the business?

Although cost differentiations within the market are lessening, OSBI models have the largest levels of developers working to expand their products on a continual basis due to large amounts of community involvement. This means that support issues can be addressed more quickly. This in turn leads to quicker development times and better time to value. Add to this lower costs and BI's value

---

[3]This is definitely a generalization, but developers are familiar with various operating systems, programming languages, and the like, with some of these being based on OS frameworks.

proposition increases. The reality, though, remains that all of this is only as effective and true as the organization and its effectiveness at making sure that internal processes are aligned with business needs and the BI frameworks. Without this, all of the potential benefits will most likely not be realized.

New to BI
Who is new to BI?

Based on market reports and industry analyses, it would seem that all companies have some sort of formalized BI. But this is not the case. Some businesses use old versions of Excel or other spreadsheets as a way to analyze information without any processes or security features in place, while others (especially within the SMB market) want to achieve higher levels of business visibility and metrics management but don't know where to start. In addition, new BI users who want solutions that are quick to develop gain value from and look to newer entrants that do not require large IT infrastructures to get started.

What are the options for companies starting out with BI for the first time?

For these organizations the marketplace is open to many different options, and although the potential for any type of deployment exists, since this book focuses on OS options, we will stick with OS-related options only. Both commercial and community versions of OSBI are feasible for small and mid-sized companies as well as any organization starting out, but depending on internal IT resource limitations or skillsets and the number of projects already tasked to IT and the maintenance of other initiatives internally, developing a solution only using source code may be beyond general company resources. In these situations, looking at commercial options might be more feasible. Organizations want to know that vendors being selected are viable, will provide long-term support, and value long-term relationships between vendors and BI consumers.

In these cases, commercial OS may provide a good starting point, as organizations can generally have access to a free trial and then pay a subscription fee for use. In addition, OS vendors have based their commercial versions on community success and place a lot of emphasis on community interaction and feedback. Therefore, even if not on par with traditional vendors in perceived viability, these vendors still have success stories that can be used to identify whether this type of deployment is a fit.

Why consider OS over traditional BI when new?

Taking this one step further, when companies look at BI they are normally hoping to solve business inefficiencies and a lack of information visibility. How they do this remains a cross between requirements gathering, enhancing their technical infrastructure, defining long-term goals, and increasing overall general knowledge. In addition to short-term and long-term costs and solution maintenance, many businesses select software based on their industry knowledge. The depth and breadth of knowledge within non-profit, government, general SMBs, and the like are quite broad among OSBI vendors. These types of organizations have general familiarity with the OSBI framework and are more likely to apply it within the organization. For other organizations, however, it may be hit and miss, as some companies select software based on industry reports or what other colleagues or friends are doing in lieu of large-scale software evaluations.

BI expansion
Who benefits from BI expansion through OS?

Organizations continuously expand and improve upon their BI use. As time goes on, these companies require more BI to move to the next level. With new developments in technology, this means that if organizations do not take advantage of new BI offerings, they will be left behind. Looking at traditional BI, for example, until recently data warehouses provided a way to consolidate data and provide a historical view of information. Now, data warehousing enables near real-time data updates and the ability to process large and complex data sets that take BI to the next level. Therefore, to adequately take advantage of technology and BI use, technology advancement and new BI applications are required.

When it comes to the actual benefit of BI expansion, any stakeholders involved in BI initiatives on the end-user side will benefit. Advancements in technology generally translate to broader ease of use within BI offerings, which help enable broader use of these tools. On the development side, IT developers can optimize processes and technology efficiency. This, in turn, can make solutions easier to maintain. Many offerings now enable development using graphical user interfaces that are easier to interact with and that include drag-and-drop environments.

What benefit does expansion provide?

Companies usually get to the point where they need to improve what they are currently doing. This means looking at new offerings and expansions. In some cases, organizations have already allocated a large amount of budget for developing a BI infrastructure and may not want to invest heavily in new software. In these cases, the ability to take advantage of free software is perfect. Organizations can expand their BI use without having to invest additional funds in software acquisition.

Why do organizations choose to expand with OS?

As discussed, the paragraph above probably highlights the reason behind the use of OS for BI expansion, and this is price. Although the concept of free is subjective because no such thing as free BI really exists, the perception of the benefits of free software means that many companies flock to OSBI despite the additional development requirements. Some of these businesses might feel that internal involvement will be required no matter what selection they choose. Therefore, limiting the amount of professional services and transferring that effort to internal development seems to be a good payoff for many.

Rip and replace

The last type of OSBI use looks at the concept of organizations looking to replace their outdated BI infrastructure and start fresh. The companies that choose to do this are generally unsatisfied with the limitations of proprietary offerings and robust BI architectures. Overall, ripping and replacing a BI platform is becoming more common. Organizations have been tied to out-of-date data platforms that provide limited value in terms of analytics performance or the ability take advantage of new technologies. Because new offerings enable broader BI visibility and flexibility, many organizations are looking at OSBI as their new BI platforms. However, even with this being said, there are also many organizations that choose other traditional BI offerings when looking to rip and replace their current BI infrastructure.

Who decides to replace their BI offerings with something new?

As businesses become more dynamic and want to grow their companies to the next level, they need to consider how they gain visibility into their organizations. This includes looking at:

- Internal efficiencies — What works and where potential gaps exist. Identifying inefficiencies in process, design, and use can help IT identify what is required to transform a BI environment that obviously wasn't working into one that will provide business users with benefit.
- Gaps in analytics — The identification of what end users want to analyze and access versus what they can see. Depending upon the structure of a data warehouse or a series of data marts, the information being accessed might be limited. In addition, structuring analytics and providing specific views of data means that organizations are unable to analyze information dynamically.
- Information delivery — The hows, whens, and whos of information access. What type of latency exists? Is data stale by the time it arrives, and what information access is required and when in order to make informed decisions? Answering these questions can help identify what type of data updates are required to deliver the appropriate information to relevant decision makers in a timely manner.
- Integration of multi-structured data sources — Mature BI infrastructures may be limited in their ability to capture multiple types of data. Aside from relational databases as data sources, organizations are starting to look at geospatial and social media-related data. Add to this customer sentiment, emails, the integration of content management with BI-related information, and the like, and organizations require a BI environment able to support multiple data types.
- BI platform — Ripping and replacing means that the current BI platform does not work. Identifying the positive aspects and what is not working will help IT with the new platform by identifying inefficiencies and stumbling blocks that are not to be repeated.

Because BI and the technology supporting it continuously advance, companies are starting to realize that old-style BI does not and will not help organizations achieve the next level of what BI is supposed to be. Organizations want to leverage new technology without having to spend the time tweaking what they already have in-house — basically they want to remove the stumbling blocks to near real-time complex information analysis and access. Newer BI offerings are more robust and generally provide lower TCO and quicker time to value than their outdated counterparts. For companies looking at lessening the overall costs of maintaining their BI platforms, OSBI and the move away from proprietary software can provide a valuable switch in strategy for BI delivery.

What do companies need to know about replacing solutions with OSBI offerings?

The previous chapters have looked at the general benefits and types of OSBI available to organizations. Therefore, it doesn't make sense to go into repetitive details about the offerings themselves. However, organizations strongly considering a rip and replace BI strategy do need to relearn technology. Some of the roadblocks such as complex analytics using large amounts of data updated in near real-time that were not available in the past are now considered factors that are integral to and part of a BI infrastructure. What this really means for businesses is that technology isn't the only challenge to a new BI implementation. Lack of current knowledge might create a scenario whereby companies do not know what is or isn't possible. And because OSBI differs slightly in BI outlook, the ability to look at BI from a new vantage point and learn what open platforms offer becomes as important as general industry and functionality knowledge. Because of the many changes that have been made over the past several years in relation to the evolution of solution offerings, companies need to spend the time to evaluate what products are available and to look at the customizations required by OSBI.

Why does OSBI provide value that mature traditional BI platforms might not?

Organizations no longer want to take years to optimize and fully develop their data warehousing platforms that are limited in scope and analytics provision. In some respects, OSBI solutions can be said to be more dynamic and customizable based on specific requirements in relation to older traditional offerings. Consequently, the ability to develop offerings that integrate more easily, provide general data integration without heavy investments, and provide community support are areas that are viewed as valuable based on many companies' histories of paying a lot and not getting much in return. In addition, IT developers have the ability to optimize database platforms to provide DW functionality and analytics based on the specific requirements within their companies without having to struggle with support or maintenance limitations.

What should a company's expectations be regarding a rip-and-replace model?

Unfortunately, the ripping and replacing BI option represents the most challenging of OSBI. A whole new project and all of the issues associated with it need to be considered. And even though beneficial in the end, organizations should identify whether the effort will be worth the risks. Add to this the need for new training for end users to learn a new set of tools and potentially for developers to learn new skills, and a lot of effort is required to make the new initiative a successful one. Overall, organizations should make sure that the new set of solutions are actually easier to use, otherwise adoption may not occur. In essence, project sponsors need to treat a rip-and-replace initiative as a net new BI project and take into account all of the considerations associated with one.

Embedded applications

Even though not directly related to the discussion of OSBI validation and adoption, the fact remains that many OSBI applications are embedded within other software offerings. For instance, software vendors want to deliver a certain amount of analytics or reporting within their solutions but do not want to acquire technology or invest in developing their own offerings as an extension of their products. ERP and CRM are good examples of operational solutions that manage to track what is happening in the present but that do not provide insights into time series analysis or help with strategic planning. Obviously, simply embedding reporting within these solutions does not solve the problem fully without a data warehouse or data management architecture.

Businesses require an infrastructure to manage data over time and to identify trends and provide statistical analysis, which means the marrying of operations and analytics within a BI framework. But embedded applications do provide access to BI without having to develop a different platform that remains separate from operations. Because operational reporting is becoming more popular, companies are better able to be more proactive with their reporting and operational insights.

What all of this leads to, however, is the fact that many people are using OS solutions without even knowing it. Because of the fact that OSBI is more widely deployed than expected, it becomes important for project sponsors to identify what solutions currently exist within the organization. After all, if a specific department already uses an embedded form of OS, the transition towards a broader OSBI deployment might not be as difficult as starting BI from scratch. In these situations, end users will already have a level of familiarity, lessening the amount of training required and hopefully increasing the adoption rate.

Sorting out the different models and what it means to business units

After providing outlines of the types of decisions businesses find themselves facing, we need to take a step further and identify the commonalities and what all of these decisions mean for the business. After all, many BI solutions exist that are low cost and that focus on providing BI more quickly and less expensively than traditional or large-scale vendors. In these cases, the true differentiators of OSBI may not be clear for companies. Why should organizations look at OS especially when free software does not mean quick implementation times or ease of use? And how do commercial offerings differ?

As discussed throughout this book so far, considering OSBI means changing your overall mindset. Although differentiations are becoming less and less, the outlook of OS still differs from the traditional software market. OS provides a broader outlook. The premise of these solutions is based on community and collaboration, and even though vendors are starting to monetize these offerings, the access to documentation, online support, and colleague insight cannot be matched using other methods. In many cases, traditional BI vendors are now launching their own communities and developer portals to try to mimic the success of OSBI communities, but these are still behind the curve in comparison with OS community involvement.

Each organization and individual business unit will fall into one of the categories above if OSBI is a viable option for expansion and BI growth. Business units should understand that each of the choices above will have similar outcomes even though they may require different methodologies. And although OSBI is slowly becoming a mainstream BI option, non-technical users should strive to learn the differences involved in developing an OS perspective to BI adoption and use.

Why sell to the business

The concept of self-service is making headway into the general BI marketplace. The goal of self-service is the following, based on Claudia Imhoff's[4] and Colin White's[5] definition within a recent industry report[6]:

- To make BI tools easy to use
- To make BI results easy to consume and to enhance
- To make data warehousing solutions easy to manage and quick to deploy
- To make data easy to access — from its source

What all of these aspects have in common is easy access to data and its interaction. Unfortunately, what this really means is that vendors still have a long way to go to provide business and casual users with an intuitive way to interact with information. On the other hand, this push towards self-service BI use means that business users become a more intricate part of any BI deployment. No longer is BI deployed to super users enough to justify the value of its deployment. Now companies want to get information and business insights into the hands of end users to empower them to do their jobs better and to make more informed decisions. In terms of the overall relation to business, this means that vendors are starting to target their offerings to business users by increasing interactivity, design, and the ability to address business questions. Consequently, this ends up leading to business decision makers have more input and driving BI projects. The implications of this are large, as traditional BI offerings are built from the back end first — in essence, as a transition from technology to business as opposed to the other way around, which is the goal of self-service BI models.

Within OSBI specifically, the same can be true. Community OS targets the IT developer and IT collaboration. With the advent of commercial OSBI, the target audience is shifting towards the business user. Whether done effectively or not remains besides the point. The reality of BI is as follows: Without the ability to answer business questions and to probe into the cause and effect of daily operations, its implementation and justification will be hard pressed as organizations strive to identify the benefits of broad BI deployments that do not provide interactivity to many business users throughout the organization.

---

[4]http://www.intelsols.com/aboutus.cfm/Who%20We%20Are
[5]http://www.bi-research.com/aboutus.html
[6]The Data Warehousing Institute (TDWI) — *Self-Service BI*, July 2011 Report — TDWI.org

Selling framework

All of this comes down to the fact that despite the differences in approach to OSBI, the goals are the same — to provide enhanced information insight to business users across the organization. Whether OSBI is or is not the answer to a historical lack of large-scale BI success does not negate the fact that organizations are starting to look at alternative ways of accessing analytics due to limitations in traditional BI models. With newer and more dynamic BI platforms and a focus on self-service information access, organizations are no longer satisfied with traditional BI deployments and maintenance efforts. Consequently, this leads to more business involvement.

Whether across the organization or within individual business units based on function, the sales framework remains the same as discussed above. Project sponsors require an understanding of what end-user roles are in order to make sure that the benefits of OS can be applied to what they hope to accomplish through OSBI adoption. And the value proposition of OSBI needs to be stated based on the individual role within departments and how BI will be interacted with.

The new importance of including the end user within the parameters of sales and the value proposition of implementing a new type of BI or expanding its use will only continue to increase as businesses rely more heavily on access to multiple information sources to drive business decision making. Add to this the increase in embedded analytics and the role of BI will become supportive in nature to daily business operations. The increase in business involvement in OSBI projects as well as broader BI implementations means that IT departments will no longer be able to work independently of their end users. Looking at this from the perspective of vendors' shift towards commercial OSBI models means that self service access to BI will continue to increase, with the focus being on commercializing BI access in a similar way to other BI vendors. However, at the same time, OSBI vendors will have the added bonus of community involvement and an open framework to drive continued adoption.

Why IT has to work with business units and why business units need to collaborate with one another

To develop successful initiatives organizations need to understand the complementary role of both ends of the spectrum — technical on one end and business on the other. Interviews collecting general requirements are no longer enough to drive BI access points. IT should understand how each business unit operates to develop an infrastructure that provides access to relevant information while still maintaining security protocols and privacy measures. Additionally, business units should work to see beyond delivery delays as working together may help BI end users get solutions that they can more easily work with.

As an extension, this includes the realization that different business units will have varying outlooks on BI deployments and use. Therefore, in addition to IT collaborating with business units, business units also need to work together. For instance, for retailers, supply chain needs to have an understanding of sales and marketing and vice versa to identify where and when to supply items and the success of strategies. In addition, marketing departments need to be able to analyze customer sentiment and how previous campaigns have affected overall sales by product, region, etc.

As organizations strive to consolidate information and pull relevant facts together based on ad hoc query analysis, disparate departments are going to have to learn how to balance information sharing with maintaining customer privacy. However, without higher levels of interaction, organizations will be unable to develop BI initiatives that provide a broad level of performance management and visibility into operations across multiple departments.

The bottom line for OSBI adoption in organizations

What most organizations want more than anything is to lower costs while increasing revenues. The adoption of any BI system that enables broader visibility and quicker access to information will help organizations achieve this goal. With OSBI offerings the benefits extend a little bit further as, depending on the method used, software costs are waived and developers can work with developers outside of the organization to optimize their BI environments.

Evaluating ROI and TCO

Organizations require a good understanding of the costs and benefits associated with BI adoption and where OS fits within the perspective of return on investment (ROI), total cost of ownership (TCO), and how it compares with other types of BI offerings. In addition, companies need to justify these numbers to project sponsors and management. How organizations do this on an individual basis may differ due to the fact that companies evaluate what is valuable within software evaluations and how applications fit in a way that ties into their company value, not based on an industry-wide standard.

Some organizations are more focused on cost savings in comparison with fixed and variable expenses, whereas others want to know about the business value and time savings using BI provides. Either way, companies ask similar questions to get the answers they need. These include: Do real cost savings exist overall? How does this relate to time to value and developer hours required? What about maintenance and licensing fees? How does OSBI stack up against other BI vendors in relation to long-term viability and the ability to take advantage of newer technologies as they become available within the marketplace? And what makes the evaluation of ROI and TCO more complicated is that all of these questions just scratch the surface of the factors companies consider when selecting their BI vendor of choice.

Additionally, because most organizations do require ROI and TCO calculations to justify IT projects in general, and BI projects specifically, many calculations and frameworks exist that help guide companies through the process of defining whether a solution will provide value or not. But in order to apply the right one, it becomes important for businesses to understand the nuances of each area for evaluation. Therefore, this chapter provides an outline of how businesses evaluate the costs and benefits of OSBI, how this relates to general ROI and TCO calculations, and what organizations should consider on the whole. This includes providing a breakdown of the different business and technical considerations that are part of TCO and ROI calculations. Also, the next chapter will tie in checklists and ROI and TCO calculators so that your company can adapt your unique requirements to industry-standard calculations and select the right criteria and calculations to make your OSBI assessment valid for your unique business needs.

Developing valid definitions of ROI and TCO

Luckily, when it comes to ROI and TCO a lot of information and calculations already exist that can be applied within organizations. Even so, companies do not always place value on the same factors, meaning that calculations should be tweaked to account for these differences. Based on company structure and the goal of the BI initiative, factors organizations consider differ to the point that one industry-defined calculation will not suit the needs of all businesses. But, the benefit of these calculators is that they do provide a basis for the customization that can be used to reflect the direct business requirements of these companies. So, let's look at what constitutes ROI and TCO for OSBI projects.

According to Interim Technical Management Inc., the traditional definition of ROI for enterprise software is the ratio of costs to savings for an investment, and it's usually expressed over a period of time.[1] And although a great general definition, the reality remains that few organizations can adequately identify what these monetary benefits are in relation to their BI use. In some cases, full-scale BI solutions with data warehousing have enabled organizations to cut costs and increase profits in a way that can be thoroughly measured, but in other cases these projects only provide intangible benefits, making concrete ROI hard to identify.

Based on this fact, calculating TCO is a bit easier. According to businessdictionary.com,[2] TCO is the estimate of all direct and indirect costs associated with an asset or acquisition over its entire life cycle. Luckily, in this case, organizations have a better chance of identifying the TCO of a BI project. It is fairly easy to identify how much an implementation will cost over time as well as considering the time costs of efforts associated with BI implementations.

But, what do these definitions mean for businesses?

Return on investment

Basically, ROI represents the financial payoff for a project. In essence, costs and benefits are weighed to determine whether the solution will provide potential value and financial reward. How organizations effectively do this within BI, no matter what the type, still remains elusive. According to Mark Madsen, founder of Third Nature, "vendors try to compete on numerous features as points of differentiation, which confuses comparison. It's best when evaluating BI software to stick to the features you plan to use and not try to factor in added value of unique features and their relative cost." Madsen also feels that "new projects are a better deployment model for open source because the high cost of acquisition is a significant barrier to starting a BI project. Traditional vendors' products have been too costly for most department budgets or small to medium-sized companies."[3]

What all of this means for ROI evaluation is that companies need to identify their must haves and be able to allocate a cost to each of those factors to make an apples-to-apples comparison across BI offerings — whether only considering OSBI or a mix of OS and traditional solution offerings. With this being said, the question remains of what factors to include and which to dismiss to get an accurate assessment of the overall value of OSBI. Therefore, the questions asked in reference to ROI represent the first step in the development of a BI framework. However, the way to adequately evaluate and get a full perspective of the potential ROI of any given solution is not only to look at the ROI of an OSBI project, but also to develop a framework that compares various vendors in the same way and based on the same merits. This is not always easy, as many vendors are not forthcoming with pricing until they receive the in-depth requirements of the project, making it impossible to accurately assess vendors at the beginning of the process.

---

[1]http://www.answers.com/topic/return-on-investment#ixzz1WWLg9rI8

[2]http://www.businessdictionary.com/definition/total-cost-of-ownership-TCO.html and http://www.interimtechexec.com/blog/roi-for-enterprise-software/.

[3]Lowering the Cost of Business Intelligence With Open Source: A Comparison of Open Source and Traditional Vendor Costs — Mark Madsen, Third Nature, Prepared for Pentaho, 2010.

ROI requires organizations to identify the key areas of importance, place a price tag on those activities, and identify which solution will best meet the needs of the business while providing the best-use case in terms of cost and value. In addition, these numbers have to be offset by the benefits incurred. For instance, if an automotive manufacturer currently has 11% market share based on its three top-selling vehicles but eventually hopes to capture 15% market share, the use of analytics and the ability to gain a full view of the marketplace can provide the insights that may lead to a direct performance increase. Aside from looking at overall car sales and buying habits, the organization can look at buying habits, average lifecycle of a vehicle, and how to up-sell customers based on their needs as well as their preferences, industry trends related to green initiatives, price, demographics, quality issues, customer sentiment, and the list goes on. What this means is that all of the outcomes of analytics directly relate to ROI calculations and the benefits acquired through OSBI adoption.

But figuring out how organizations make the leap between identifying these aspects and how they translate into financial outcomes is the challenge. As we look at the individual factors below, we will identify how this can be accomplished.

Total cost of ownership

TCO, on the other hand, almost goes one step further. TCO takes costs into consideration and identifies the value of the implementation on the whole. However, costs alone do not guarantee project success and do not take into account the additional aspects that make a successful BI initiative. They only provide a partial picture of all of the considerations that go into evaluating the TCO. Measuring value is also something that remains subjective in nature. Obviously the ability to provide business insights and increase revenues while lowering costs provides direct value. But within other organizations, increasing collaboration and process efficiencies also provide a value that is less concrete in reference to mathematical calculations. Nevertheless, TCO may provide a more adequate view of OSBI offerings due to its broader evaluation of what the TCO really means for business.

Both ROI and TCO enable organizations to identify, based on their solution choice and implementation requirements, the amount of time it takes to make up their costs. TCO also lets companies look beyond that towards some of the implications of those costs. A good example is what the solution translates into when considering ongoing maintenance. For instance, one solution may cost less in terms of overall software and hardware but may require more long-term and regular maintenance activities, meaning that TCO will be higher even though the initial fixed costs are lower. Community OS actually represents a good way to expand upon TCO. Extra development efforts can lead to longer development times. This may or may not offset software costs, but in some cases the TCO can be considered longer because it can take more time to get the solution up and running in a way that is valuable to the organization. Going back to what William McKnight said about using OS to secure a quick win generally refers to getting OSBI up and running, but its optimization is another story.

Therefore, the evaluation of TCO requires looking beyond ROI towards the value entailed in deploying and maintaining a BI platform/framework, which may include the time it takes to get a solution up and running. As discussed earlier, the definition of value differs based on the organization's outlook. When looking at TCO, this value has to have the ability to attach a dollar amount to it. For instance, access to community source code or lack of proprietary software only provides monetary value if there is a direct relationship to ease of integration that leads to lower costs or quicker implementation times. The reality is that ideological reasons for selecting OS do have their merit but are not tied directly to TCO calculations. To do so requires attaching a dollar amount to the time it takes to develop solutions that takes into account how many resources are working on the project and how much continued effort will be required over time.

ROI and TCO similarities and differences

As seen, ROI and TCO are similar in many ways. Both provide general cost-benefit analyses to give businesses an estimate of how beneficial the expenditure will be — in essence, both calculations aim to justify a BI expenditure. What companies need is to identify how much solutions will cost and what the benefits associated with those costs are. In essence, we can break this down as follows.

ROI provides an assessment of software, hardware, and development costs within a predefined amount of time. Executives need this information to make informed decisions on software selection and to identify the costs and benefits of a given solution. All in all, the benefit of ROI is that it provides insights into the long-term financial gains of deploying BI. This includes looking at other related cost savings over time, such as costs incurred before BI that are no longer relevant. Whether replacing solutions or ending support contracts that are no longer in use, there are usually costs that might not be directly related to new software purchases but that may affect ROI. Therefore, assessments require broader analyses that take these aspects into account.

TCO, on the other hand, identifies the cost to the organization of maintaining a BI initiative. Questions such as how much do development efforts cost in addition to time savings of spreadsheet and analysis development represent the types of queries needed to identify TCO and take into account when developing appropriate models.

Why ROI and TCO are important to software selection

What all this shows is that both ROI and TCO are fairly similar and important to software selection — whether evaluating community and commercial OSBI offerings or comparing them to other offerings. After all, the process of software selection requires a lot of effort and information, with ROI and TCO calculators providing the framework for adequate value assessment. Looking at the features and functions and related costs only provides a partial look at the benefits of deploying a BI solution. By conducting an ROI and TCO comparison, justifying budget allocation for a BI project is much easier. Why is this?

Through ROI and TCO evaluations, organizations are able to:

- Develop more accurate spending estimates that will translate into project budgets. Because vendors develop different pricing structures in relation to their sales strategy it is accurate to say that creating cost comparisons requires some flexibility and creativity. The benefits, however, are partially the fact that organizations can gain a broader understanding of how much they will actually spend and what factors may affect their future costs. Many BI projects fail — irrespective of the type of solution implemented — and one of the reasons remains costs. Organizations budget a certain amount and don't realize that other costs haven't been considered, or don't build in contingency plans based on their cost assessments.

- Make vendors accountable for their pricing estimates and what they provide for that price/amount required to get started. Since vendors are not always forthcoming or develop different levels of end-user access (i.e., community OS with training and documentation versus commercial editions with varying levels of interaction, including enterprise, departmental, and individual levels), it becomes important for a software evaluation to include some sort of vendor commitment or promise as well as an outline of what the costs include. Alternatively, organizations should make sure that the costs associated with the TCO evaluation actually meet their business requirements. This means looking beyond features and functions towards support, upgrades, etc.
- Educate the organization about expectations that include current needs, future expansion, the initial requirements, etc. Basically, buy-in and adoption become an essential component of any BI success story. After all, successful IT projects that are not adopted by targeted end users are actually failures. TCO and ROI evaluations can be used as tools to work toward OSBI adoption. What this really means is that education is knowledge. Developing a framework and setting BI goals through these evaluations can also be expanded towards selling the value of OSBI to the broader organization by identifying the ROI and how BI adoption can affect productivity and even the bottom line.
- Make it easier to sell the potential benefits of a BI solution. As mentioned, ROI and TCO evaluations should act as springboards for new opportunity. If done right, BI can become an exploration tool to give business users the ability to gain valuable insights and information visibility more broadly across the organization. Also, many OSBI projects start at the IT layer of business. To get business units onboard with the potential of these offerings, it sometimes takes the bottom line and the benefits associated with cost savings. If these calculations provide this, then it becomes easier to generate support for a full BI implementation.
- Potentially sell the advantages of OS deployment over traditional BI offerings. Most BI solutions require IT developers to implement a solution. Free software takes a large chunk out of BI implementations and in some cases there is not a big difference in development efforts or time required to deliver end-users reports and analytics. By comparing different solution types side-by-side, organizations can see this directly.

The figure below identifies the average cost of OSBI usage versus traditional BI offerings based on Madsen's evaluation of the TCO of OSBI versus traditional offerings.[4] The deployment size is based on looking at deployments of 25 users, 100 users, and 500 users, respectively. However, these numbers are based on large-scale traditional vendors. As we'll see later on, newer offerings are minimizing these differences and potential barriers to entry, but OSBI still has the benefit of no-cost software.

---

[4]Lowering the Cost of Business Intelligence With Open Source: A Comparison of Open Source and Traditional Vendor Costs — Mark Madsen, Third Nature, Prepared for Pentaho, page 4.

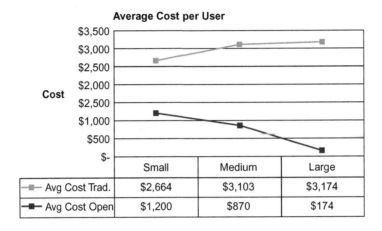

	Small	Medium	Large
— Avg Cost Trad.	$2,664	$3,103	$3,174
— Avg Cost Open	$1,200	$870	$174

FIGURE 11-1

Average Cost Per User, Comparing Traditional and Open Source Across Scenarios.

Developing an evaluation framework for your OSBI project

Now that we've looked at the basics and the importance surrounding ROI and TCO calculations and provided a glimpse at high-level pricing differences, we can identify the factors to consider when evaluating ROI. Even though we've identified that many calculations exist, and even if your organization selects one that is formalized, it is still important to understand the individual factors that contribute to overall ROI and TCO. After all, because different companies have different needs and BI goals, there may be factors that need to be added or changed to customize aspects of the calculation. Unless the details are understood in great detail, the ability to make those adjustments will remain limited.

The first step to developing an independent framework enabling proper evaluation of the desired toolsets involves looking at the factors that require consideration. The following sections identify the general requirements organizations should consider when developing an ROI calculation. Whether developing one independently or using one that is already defined, understanding the business requirements behind the calculations are essential to being able to match requirements with what vendors have to offer. And for OSBI offerings, this takes things one step further by understanding the value proposition of community versus commercial variations and being able to compare this to any traditional offering being considered as part of the evaluation. Additionally, by understanding each factor independently, decision makers can develop a greater sense of clarity into the decisions they make. Whether this is due to weighted requirements or important initiatives that align themselves to BI implementations, the extra time commitment required to understand these calculations in detail is minimal in relation to the benefits incurred.

Software costs

As mentioned multiple times, looking at software costs is important. Questions such as:

- How much does the initial software cost?
- Will there be additional software costs for future upgrades?

- What are the payoffs of free software?
- How will these short-term cost benefits (i.e., free software) affect the organization in the long term?

And the list goes on. The evaluation of software costs alone provides insight into the structure of the solution provider. For instance, even though software costs might be minimal, many solution providers are starting to offer subscription fees, meaning that companies pay for implementation activities and add the yearly subscription. How this compares to no initial software costs and internal or professional services for development is an area that may be important to evaluate. In addition, models and pricing will differ significantly for the same vendor when looking at community and commercial versions, meaning that ROI calculations may include two evaluations for one vendor.

Answering these questions, however, helps provide companies with the initial bulk of the tangible items within an ROI and/or TCO evaluation. There may be additional criteria to consider or variations on algorithms to determine costs, but these will only apply to a very small percentage of companies. Overall, general software costs seem to be the most straightforward. Organizations need to identify the cost of entry and look at whether the price of software will only be a one-time expenditure or potentially require more investment (a good example is software upgrades, with some vendors including updates within the initial price while other vendors charge for each release).

As mentioned, some vendors charge initial fees and may also charge for future upgrades. In addition, some solution providers charge on a per module basis, making initial costs manageable but expansions expensive. The general implications are that initial TCO calculations may need to have time-based scenarios to identify the total cost of BI ownership for not upgrading versus upgrading. And even beyond this, these calculations may need to account for multiple business scenarios. For instance, what happens if expansion occurs more quickly than anticipated? Will monetary resources exist to make the necessary expansions? How will this be handled and by which cost center?

Within the OS world specifically this is doubly important, as organizations that define their ROI criteria based on community OS may be shocked at how much those numbers change when transitioning over to commercial OSBI offerings. Whether due to software costs alone or subscriptions, an awareness needs to be developed to understand the range of potential software costs within the spectrum of OSBI.

Professional services or outside consulting

Many organizations have preferences related to internal development versus using outside expertise for development efforts or requirements gathering. Either option has its payoffs and downsides in terms of costs and rewards. Both, however, should be considered within an overall assessment of ROI and TCO to make sure that organizations understand what potential higher consulting costs mean in relation to time to develop. Or alternatively, how bundled vendor services may lower overall costs or enable a quicker learning curve among internal IT development staff. This option can lead to less time learning the new environment, leading to quicker development times for future use. This fact alone can lead to a lower TCO over time.

Overall, considering whether to use external consulting or professional services may add to total implementation costs, but may provide quicker implementation times based on expertise used to design and deploy solutions. Internal developers will always require a learning curve and a new skillset to manage the solution over time. But getting a solution up and running without additional training or by collaborating on development efforts may increase the value over time. And for perceived ROI, this could mean the world to adoption across the organization. Because many BI complaints come from the time required to actually get access to applications, the quicker solutions can be up and running may offset some of the additional costs associated with actual deployment.

Development efforts and time to deployment

This leads to the next consideration — what development efforts are required and associating a cost structure with this. In some cases this requires creating an estimate of how long it will take to develop the solution multiplied by people hours and number of resources. It is also important to keep in mind potential additional time or other projects that might interfere with rollout. A good example is data integration. For many BI projects, both for OS or traditional, data integration activities and the ability to integrate information sources makes up the bulk of the work and ends up being more complicated than expected. Organizations that don't take this into account in the beginning may encounter a rude awakening when issues arise surrounding the integration and centralization of disparate data sources.

In addition to all of this, the time to develop solutions will differ for community and commercial OSBI versions. Although community offerings may not require software costs initially, long-term development efforts will most likely require a substantial amount of money. Remember that when looking at TCO and ROI, identifying the financial payoff is important. These costs should not be taken lightly or considered the same as within traditional BI solutions.

New hardware requirements

Even though many OSBI projects will not require additional (or initial) software costs, the reality is that many BI projects do require new hardware allocations. In some cases, companies will be developing a data warehouse, whether an appliance or adding new servers, and require a budget to account for this new hardware. Even for businesses not considering a data warehouse, due to additional space requirements and processing times for Service Legal Agreements (SLAs), new hardware may be required. Also, some companies will not require new hardware immediately but will as growth occurs and should factor this into potential long-term costs.

One of the benefits of OSBI offerings is the lack of proprietary restrictions that may exist with some traditional BI solutions. In terms of costs, this broadens the spectrum of what remains available to organizations. In essence, the ability to install any hardware can lower hardware costs and make it easier to achieve integration activities, leading to quicker implementation times.

More efficient processes — time savings

Unfortunately, this is where things get sticky. Building up more efficient processes through the use of BI may be obvious, but associating a financial value or TCO equivalent is not. Organizations need to have a good understanding of what isn't working and what the value of added efficiencies equals. The most obvious is the time saved through BI, but other factors can also be considered. More complicated analyses might include the profits achieved through the deployment of OSBI or how much quicker decisions can be made because of BI.

The time savings of process efficiencies can lead to a lower overall TCO based on a long-term assessment. This means that even if not considered as part of ROI, it can be included within an assessment of TCO. If solutions take less time to deploy and can provide insights more quickly, then the TCO lessens over time. And even though identifying what the actual value is, organizations should still make sure that added process efficiencies account for the overall value add of implementing a BI offering.

Maintenance costs

Traditional vendors generally charge 20% maintenance yearly, which also includes support. However, newer models might differ due to the increasing popularity of subscription models. Organizations need to be aware of nuances without making final choices before understanding how vendors compare with one another based on these factors.

Commercial OS offerings tend to charge subscription fees, enabling organizations to identify the cost structure beforehand. In some of these cases, they may be higher or lower than the 20% maintenance fees of traditional offerings. In other cases, internal maintenance required still takes time away from other projects and may require more than one resource to maintain the offering depending on the scope of the BI project, leading to higher maintenance costs over time.

Even for OSBI solutions that do not have additional maintenance fees associated with vendor pricing, companies still need to identify the costs associated with internal maintenance and identify what that means in terms of general maintenance fees. This might mean attaching a dollar value to maintenance over time. Otherwise, it might require similar requirements as development efforts by developing a cost per resource and estimate the time in hours per week or month required to maintain the offering.

Licensing fees

As an extension of maintenance fees, many vendors charge licensing fees based on CPU, number of consumers, number of developers, etc. Depending on the broad scope of deployment, these fees can be large initially or grow astronomically over the course of usage based on use. Understanding licenses is very important, as pricing is not so straightforward. Subscriptions may seem straightforward, but when companies compare OSBI with traditional BI difficulties appear. For instance, traditional BI vendors each have their own way of identifying licensing costs.

On another note, organizations need to identify, or at least anticipate, growth in this area as the amount of ROI may change year after year. Even with subscriptions, some contracts lock customers in for a number of years, whereas others provide subscriptions or general licensing options based on specific factors. Therefore, if usage changes, so do fees. When evaluating alternatives and the that value of each, these changes need to be considered within scenarios to address the possibility that expansion of data or end users may change within the first few years or even sooner.

ROI comparisons of multiple vendors also require this knowledge. In the case of OSBI offerings, many licensing fees are bundled within general subscription models to lower the overall price points of these options. However, this doesn't mean that OSBI adoption is immune to various price points for different levels of use. There may be a payoff in the short term, but long-term costs may not be as low. As mentioned, if based on user, the ability to expand BI access may be severely limited.

Putting everything together

All of these factors together create the basis for both ROI and TCO calculations. The next chapter will look at specific calculations and applications, but let's look at how these various aspects are put together to develop an overall cost benefit analysis of BI use.

- Software costs and hardware costs — account for the first level of pricing. Basically, these initial costs can be considered fixed based on hardware depreciation or defined costs determined by the vendor and agreed upon by the customer. Hopefully, these costs represent initial costs that do not become exorbitant over time due to their static nature. In some cases, these costs will be $0 based on free software, making this portion less expensive than traditional or commercial BI options, but might not affect other aspects of either calculation.
- Professional services/consulting and development efforts — are supporting services that enable organizations to get up and running more quickly. In some cases, this affects the overall implementation times and solution roll-outs. What this means for ROI and TCO depends on the financial benefits of a quicker implementation. In addition, training, new skillsets, etc., can be more easily attained by taking advantage of external expertise (or alternatively, by taking advantage of the community). Some solution providers offer packaged services, while others charge between $185 and $250 an hour.[5]
- Maintenance and licensing fees — represent recurring costs to the business that will be applied as long as the OSBI solution is in use. Depending on the structure of vendor services and longer term usage, companies may have to face the fact that these costs will increase over time, and in some cases astronomically, depending on overall use.
- Business process re-engineering — getting things done faster — unfortunately, this represents the most subjective part of any ROI and TCO calculation, but is also one of the most important soft factors of BI adoption. Here, organizations require the ability to evaluate general inefficiencies and identify how BI can help make business processes more effective. In many cases, organizations can leave this out of equations unless there are specific equations that apply or that can be identified.

---

[5]These prices are based on my general interactions with vendors and don't represent a study of hundreds of offerings. I have placed them here to give you an idea of what to expect. In other cases, services are packaged, with hourly rates being offered above and beyond agreed to services.

What is time to value?

All of these items lead to time to value. The general TCO of a project/solution is based on the costs associated with use and deployment. For instance, some organizations only look at the software and hardware costs, whereas others include the ability to perform tasks more quickly. Moving beyond costs means evaluating the actual time it takes to gain value from a solution. This requires not just looking at how long an implementation takes but how long it takes to acquire a general learning curve, complete training, and actually get some benefit out of the solution. Although seemingly simple, the reality is that even if a BI project takes 3 months to implement, the actual benefits achieved may only become visible in 5 or 6 months. This means that a lag time between deployment and value exists, lowering potential ROI and increasing overall TCO.

Even though similar to increasing process efficiencies in terms of being more subjective, organizations should be able to include value within their evaluations. The type of value will depend on what the company hopes to achieve through BI use. Obviously, applying cost to end-user autonomy or information access is much different than the value associated with successful marketing campaigns, but both represent the types of value that can be achieved through OSBI use.

Overall, different offerings have varying times to value and depending on the ease of use they also have different points of access that can increase ease of use or general access. The easiest way to address what value means is to associate the time savings of employees. But at the same time other types of value exist and can be individual to the organization, providing they can be justified within the framework of ROI and/or TCO.

A look at long-term ROI and TCO

As a last thought on TCO, it's always important to not just consider the initial cost of ownership. Obviously value is achieved by implementing a solution more quickly, but ease of use, integration, support, and the like are also relevant factors that help improve the overall usability and benefits associated with the solution. Consequently, general calculations do not apply to all organization, and companies require an open mind and broad understanding of what is important to the business in relation to BI in order to develop an adequate view of ROI and TCO.

Obviously, ROI provides a good first step to evaluating TCO. After all, companies need to first identify the associated costs before broadening the outlook to include how BI affects the organization from a value standpoint. Even with this being said, both are important and should not be looked at as either one or the other. Using both as complementary elements to software selection and BI value helps companies understand all of the costs associated with any BI implementation.

For OSBI specifically, the ability to break down the differences between community and commercial offerings allows people to look beyond the trappings of free software and gain an understanding of what that means within the scope of an overall BI implementation. Also, costs for both models can be compared in addition to the time to value and implications of moving from one model to the other.

Developing a cost-benefit analysis for OSBI: A practical look at ROI and TCO calculations

Organizations need a clear understanding of the factors that affect their solution choice. As mentioned previously, each company's validation of potential ROI and TCO will differ slightly based on:

- The size and structure of IT
- Previous BI use and knowledge
- Planned resources
- Overall purpose of the solution

But at the same time, all of the factors discussed in Chapter 11 will also be a part of any TCO and ROI evaluation, even if to varying levels. Consequently, understanding the components behind each aspect of a calculation also leads to better knowledge of what goes into a successful implementation, and maybe even more importantly, a broader understanding into the factors required to assess project value can help attain the required buy-in when decision makers are not familiar with OS and how it differentiates from traditional BI options.

The first step involves making sense of the last chapter. What all of the considerations discussed in the last chapter have in common is that when combined, they lead to an accurate ROI validation. Combining these factors provides organizations with the framework they need to justify OSBI to their organizations, or at least the ability to identify the costs and benefits associated with OS solutions. And these justifications also apply to identifying the TCO of a BI initiative.

One of the ways to transition from the factors to consider towards an actual evaluation is to identify what other organizations are looking at and how they are using their ROI calculators to justify their BI investments. Because consultancies and research firms have broader expertise due to their reach, using what already exists can keep organizations from reinventing the wheel. Therefore, this chapter will use some of these ROI models as a way of providing practical examples of how to apply ROI within your company, and hopefully expand on these calculations enough to enable you to take this to the next level and apply variations of these calculations to your particular project.

General TCO/ROI models — a look at what exists in the market

Since so many ROI and TCO calculators already exist that target BI initiatives specifically, it makes sense to use them as a guide by either tweaking them to suit your needs or to use them as is. Within the next several pages, we will look at how three consultancy/analyst firms evaluate ROI for BI. All of these models are applied to the BI industry broadly, but they still apply to OSBI and provide a great starting point to evaluate the validity of any BI initiative. Organizations can apply one of these models as is or make changes, with the important fact being to remember that ROI provides the basis for a BI project and should be evaluated before embarking on a BI project.

The first was developed by TDWI[1] (The Data Warehouse Institute), in collaboration with Hall Consulting & Research LLC[2]. Called the TDWI Business Intelligence ROI Calculator,[3] its goal is to help organizations with their BI evaluation. Figure 12-1 identifies the aspects involved in ROI.

This calculator looks beyond the factors discussed in the previous chapter to include:

- Overall revenue and company size: helps identify budgets and overall use.
- Current BI maturity: looks at scope of project, which can lead to the identification of size and scope of project.
- Assessment of use: looks at adoption and current use to anticipate growth.
- Key performance indicators: places emphasis on non-financial factors that benefit the organization and attempts to place a dollar amount on them to tie in the indirect project costs.
- Net profit of revenue: identifies potential revenue enabled by the new project.

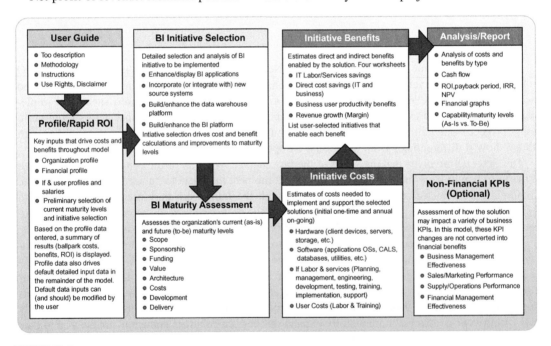

FIGURE 12-1

TDWI Business Intelligence ROI Calculator Model Components/Flowchart.

[1]http://tdwi.org/

[2]http://hallcr.com/

[3]http://hallcr.com/BI.aspx – developed by Hall Consulting & Research LLC (hallcr.com) and TDWI (The Data Warehouse Institute) www.tdwi.org.

Hall Consulting & Research LLC provides organizations with a breakdown of factors in separate tabs to provide individualized assessments of each aspect, which leads to a full cost-benefit analysis to identify ROI. The example provided lists sample data but gives an overall picture of what businesses should expect.[4]

One of the key things to note about all of this is that this is not a traditional ROI calculator. This shows that the first step of any type of value-focused evaluation is to look at factors that expand beyond numbers, whether this means looking at your BI maturity and how it has affected the current need for a new solution or if you are starting from scratch. In the first case, BI maturity and expansion may account for new servers or may mean a shift from traditional BI offerings towards an OS framework. And if this is the case, it means identifying whether any of the older BI applications are usable and, if not, the amount of effort required to rebuild solutions from scratch. The second case requires the same considerations, but new implementations do not have the road-blocks that are associated with reviewing contracts, or being limited by current BI infrastructures.

Figure 12-2 moves beyond all of the more abstract aspects and looks at the initial costs with a 3-year look at ongoing costs associated with the solution, identifying the initial investment and what costs will be over a number of years. The importance of a longer term assessment can mean avoiding larger costs in the long run, as some solutions cost less initially but may have higher maintenance and support over time, lessening their overall ROI. Also, the reality is that many organizations are unaware of what costs are. The push towards community OS shows this. The promise of free software is pushing adoption without initial evaluations of whether or not these missing costs will have to be paid somewhere else or become an implication for future use. For instance, does a free initial solution have the ability to scale to meet the needs of the company in 3 or 5 years? The skills and time required to build "free" applications should certainly offset potential redevelopment due to a lack of ability to scale in the future.

Hall Consulting & Research LLC goes one step further by providing a cost breakdown per user:

The benefit of taking it to this level is that organizations can identify how costs break down based on specific vendor offerings. Most vendors base part of their pricing structures on the number of users that will be using the product. Overall pricing may appear similar, but upon closer comparison pricing could be widely different based on end-user adoption. Another potential benefit of breaking costs down by individual user or department is the ability to allocate costs to specific departments. For organizations where BI budgets are the responsibility of the business unit, this may enable broader implementation due to the ability to allocate costs to the appropriate departments.

Nucleus Research has also developed a Business Intelligence ROI Tool (Figure 12-4) that provides a survey to help guide users through the ROI evaluation process. Factors considered include Net Present Value (NPV), a breakdown of hardware and software costs, as well as an attempt to quantify the benefits achieved through BI adoption and use.

Figure 12-4 is one of many, but it provides a good continuation of the above identified ROI outline because it takes the totals from the costs and benefits of an initial evaluation one step further by tying in the overall value to the organization. Some of this might not apply for private companies, but this shows that a key aspect of an ROI evaluation includes the overall effect on the organization. In addition, it guides the user through the process by making general assumptions and

---

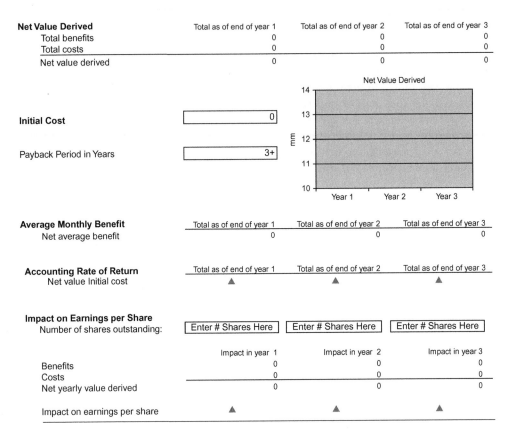

FIGURE 12-2

TDWI Business Intelligence ROI Calculator Total Cost Summary (Including Labor).

applying overall calculations. For companies looking for a quick way to evaluate the benefits of BI, selecting a premade evaluation tool can be beneficial.

The problem with this, however, is that for organizations new to BI or new to OS, identifying how its use will benefit the business at a dollars and cents level might be limited to speculation. Companies that are within the BI maturity curve and looking to expand to the next level will be better poised to identify what those benefits are. For others, the ability to identify how OS will benefit them may be a mystery. In these cases, the first areas to look at are development and customization. Therefore, Figure 12-3 provides a breakdown of the costs associated with implementation and how this is broken down by an individual user, in essence, providing a way to identify the value BI brings to each user and what those expenditures translate into.

For instance, questions such as:

- How do development and customization within OS lead to more usable products?
- Do these offerings provide better value to the business users?

Implementation Costs (Per BI User)

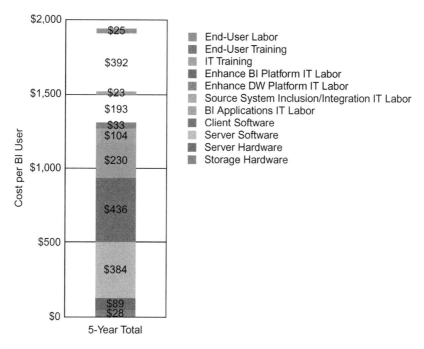

FIGURE 12-3

TDWI Business Intelligence ROI Calculator Total Implementation (Cost per User).

- How do internal development efforts offset software costs, and do they offset enough to justify community OSBI offerings?
- And finally, what is the difference between commercial offerings?

Obviously, these represent the first set of questions, leading to others, but they provide a basis for the value of the solution and what businesses should consider. Therefore, the quick financial analysis provided by Nucleus Research also provides a way of breaking down costs to help newbies to BI get past the hurdles of having to apply a series of assumptions to an initial ROI calculation.

Nucleus Research tries to make it easy for companies to integrate initial and longer term costs with the benefit BI provides the organization. This is definitely the ideal to strive for but not one that all organizations can achieve initially. For companies new to OSBI, this might be even more difficult based on a lack of familiarity with the model and, if not the model specifically, lack of experience with OSBI deployment, maintenance, and use.

Therefore, it is always important to remember that many of these ROI calculators for BI have been created with traditional BI in mind. Just because there may not be a specific cost associated with server software (based on the line item above) does not mean that it won't be a factor over time. Also, in the case of subscription-based offerings, maintenance fees will be larger than for traditional offerings but may offset larger initial costs.

Cost/Benefit Category	Costs ($ per PC)				Costs ($000)		
	One-time	Annual On-Going % of Initial	Annual On-Going	5-Year Total	One-Time	Annual On-Going	5-Year Total
Hardware							
Storage Hardware	$ 20	8%	$ 2	$ 28	$ 81	$ 6	$ 113
Server Hardware	$ 63	8%	$ 5	$ 89	$ 253	$ 20	$ 355
Total	$ 83	16%	$ 7	$ 117	$ 334	$ 26	$ 468
Software							
Server Software	$ 192	20%	$ 38	$ 384	$ 768	$ 154	$ 1,536
Client Software	$ 218	20%	$ 44	$ 436	$ 872	$ 174	$ 1,744
Total	$ 410	40%	$ 82	$ 820	$ 1,640	$ 328	$ 3,280
IT Labor/Services							
BI Applications IT Labor	$ 131	16%	$ 20	$ 230	$ 526	$ 79	$ 919
Source System Inclusion/Integration IT Labor	$ 74	8%	$ 6	$ 104	$ 296	$ 24	$ 416
Enhance DW Platform IT Labor	$ 22	10%	$ 2	$ 33	$ 88	$ 9	$ 131
Enhance BI Platform IT Labor	$ 121	12%	$ 14	$ 193	$ 483	$ 58	$ 773
Total	$ 348	46%	$ 42	$ 560	$ 1,493	$ 170	$ 2,239
Training & User Labor							
IT Training	$ 15	10%	$ 2	$ 23	$ 61	$ 6	$ 91
End-User Training	$ 314	6%	$ 16	$ 392	$ 1,256	$ 63	$ 1,569
End-User Labor	$ 25	0%	$ 0	$ 25	$ 99	$ 0	$ 99
Total	$ 354	16%	$ 17	$ 440	$ 1,416	$ 69	$ 1,759
Total Costs	$ 1,195		$ 148	$ 1,937	$ 4,883	$ 593	$ 7,746

FIGURE 12-4

Nucleus Research Net Value Derived Table[5].

The third ROI model was prepared as part of a vendor presentation by Jonathan Wu[6] based on his work with BASE Consulting Group.[7] How this one differs is that organizations move through a set of calculations to determine the overall ROI. The first looks at what ROI is — basically, the NPV of the benefit associated with the project divided by the initial investment.

In many ways, this calculation is more complicated than the previous two. The main reason is that identifying the project benefit is not always easy. Many organizations will be attracted to this model if statisticians or lovers of math are involved in the evaluation. But unless a company can actually identify the benefit, using this calculation might be a challenge. Whenever I interview a company for a case study, I make sure to ask about the benefits received through BI adoption. In some cases, I have been told, "we identified process inefficiencies and have been able to save 11% of our overall production costs." While in other situations, I have been told, "we love our BI, but can't quantify the benefits." For the latter organizations, identifying the NPV of the project benefit might be difficult even though both Nucleus research in Figure 12-5 and Base Consulting as shown in Figure 12-6 consider it a key component of any ROI for BI calculation. After all, ROI and TCO is lacking in their ability to measure qualitative improvements. So basically, even though this calculation is based on quantitative factors, there are cases where it is not possible to ascertain qualitative BI benefits, but where you might want to.

---

[5]http://nucleusresearch.com/Nucleus%20Research_ROI_Case_Study.pdf
[6]http://www.navinture.com/company/leadership/
[7]Content Copyright © 2002 BASE Consulting Group — All Rights Reserved Template Copyright © 2002 Business Objects — All Rights Reserved

Basic Assumptions

Fully loaded cost of an "average" employee | 0 |

Cost Information

Total cost of server software | 0 |
Consulting costs | 0 |
Hardware costs | 0 |
Maintenance cost per year | 0 |
Number of IS personnel needed | 0 |

Benefit Information

Improved information organization and access | 0 |
Improved decision making | 0 |
Improved customer and partner management | 0 |
Other benefits | 0 |

Financial Calculations

Total savings over three years   0
Net present value (NPV)   0
Average monthly benefit   0

Annual Savings

FIGURE 12-5

Nucleus Research Quick Financial Analysis.

However, if businesses fall into the first category of company — the ones that are able to quantify their BI value — the next phase is to look at the internal rate of return.

Both Hall Consulting and Nucleus Research provide similar calculations by looking at the costs associated with BI that are applied year after year. With the rate of acceleration of technology development, it can be assumed that every 2 to 3 years BI use will have evolved (as shown in Figure 12-5). In many cases, this also means that the hardware requirements, number of end users, and types of applications that permeate the market will change. What this means for each business will differ. I strongly believe and advocate in taking these considerations into account during an initial implementation to anticipate growth but know that it is not always realistic. Therefore, many organizations associate 20% of initial software/first-year expenditures as maintenance costs year after year. But this doesn't take into account additional licenses, data volumes, or hardware required.[8]

Using both of these calculations brings you to the cost-benefit analysis, which is the basis for many ROI formulas. In essence, the goal becomes identifying how long it takes to recuperate your BI investment. This expands beyond identifying how many months it takes to develop an OSBI solution to how long it takes to make money from its use. This, in turn, brings us to the final ROI formula.

What these three models provide is the ability for people with different skillsets to develop their own ROI calculations. For instance, some business users prefer a straight spreadsheet application over a set of calculations, whereas others prefer developing a set of calculations that provide the

---

[8]I mention these three aspects, but they might not apply to all deployments. For instance, many SaaS solutions do charge based on data volumes being stored. With OSBI providers moving towards the cloud, companies need to be aware of factors that may differ from traditional implementations.

NPV formula

$$NPV = \frac{CF1}{(1+r)^1} + \frac{CF2}{(1+r)^2} + \frac{CF3}{(1+r)^3} + ... + \frac{CFn}{(1+r)^n}$$

Legend

CF	The net cash flow for each year that the NPV is to be applied
r	The borrowing rate or investment yield rate for the organization
n	The total number of years for which the calculation is to be applied

FIGURE 12-6

Jonathan Wu/BASE Consulting Group NPV Formula.

IRR formula

$$\text{Initial Investment} = \frac{CF1}{(1+r)^1} + \frac{CF2}{(1+r)^2} + \frac{CF3}{(1+r)^3} + ... + \frac{CFn}{(1+r)^n}$$

Solve for the "r" to calculate the IRR

Legend

CF	The net cash flow for each year that the IRR is to be applied
r	The Internal Rate of Return
n	The total number of years for which the calculation is to be applied

FIGURE 12-7

Jonathan Wu/BASE Consulting Group IRR Formula.

straight financial payoffs of a BI initiative. Either way, there are valuable ways to take advantage of what exists in the marketplace to avoid reinventing the wheel.

Applying these models to ROI for OSBI

Now that we've looked at some ROI calculations, let's apply these models to real-life scenarios. All of the pricing represented in these examples is fictional. Each solution provider will have its own pricing based on your requirements. Some vendors are upfront and list their pricing on their websites, whereas others are pretty cryptic, based on what you need. Even vendors touting subscriptions will have different levels of use based on amount of data, users, developers, servers, etc. Consequently, these numbers will provide a deeper look at whether these solutions are realistic and how they compare with other offerings. And as always, we'll look at the differences between community and commercial solutions. One tip, based on personal experience, is not to give too much information about budgets away to vendors that are not upfront with their pricing. I have personally worked on projects where vendors have provided estimates at the top end of the budget provided but were really willing to sell solutions for a discounted rate between 20% and 40%. Although this is not always the case, it is something to be aware of.

Payback Period formula

$$\text{Payback Period} = \frac{\text{Initial Investment}}{(\text{NPV of project benefit/N years})}$$

FIGURE 12-8

Jonathan Wu/BASE Consulting Group Payback Period.

ROI formula

$$\text{ROI} = \frac{\text{NPV of project benefit}}{\text{Initial Investment}} \times 100$$

FIGURE 12-9

Jonathan Wu/BASE Consulting Group ROI Formula.

Overall, the three models looked at above provide a good basis of what companies need to look at within any ROI assessment irrespective of whether it is an OSBI project or not. Some of the important factors to keep in mind are:

- Corporate information that includes yearly revenue and general financial data — basically, how much you are willing to spend and how much of it represents your overall budget.
- BI maturity and anticipated expansion of use based on project scope. As mentioned, this is not always easy but will help when identifying the rate of return on your OSBI project.
- Software and hardware costs — this applies to both community and commercial OS options. In some cases, and as we've discussed before, organizations transition from community to commercial. If this is the plan, then a year 1 software cost of $0 still might have a year 2 or year 3 software cost of $30,000.
- Overall support, maintenance, and the depreciation of hardware over time, which may lead to new hardware needs. Make sure to identify the scalability, both in terms of data warehousing and hardware optimization.
- Commercial versus community OSBI selection, which can lead to differences in development efforts and the evaluation of how these differences affect time and cost.
- Number of users and planned use, which may affect costs over time. Vendors may base their subscription fees on the number of users, making expansions challenging for organizations selecting OSBI based on the assumption of low-cost deployments and maintenance over time.
- Long-term payoffs and the number of years it will take to see the financial benefit of the implementation. As shown above, different businesses will look at the benefits of use and evaluate which aspects provide the largest pay off.

Evaluating TCO for OSBI

Now that we've looked at ROI, we can provide a general look at TCO. In general, looking at TCO is very similar to ROI, but organizations can dig more deeply into specific benefits of features and functionality that affect the costs of maintaining the solution as well as compare solutions against each other. For instance, a couple of years ago I was asked to develop a TCO model for a traditional BI vendor based on features and functions provided out of the box. Organizations were rated based on whether or not they provided the capabilities below as part of their stack without the need for customization. Part of the reason this was considered a component of evaluating the TCO is based on an assumption that the features provided out of the box relate directly to the ability to get a solution up and running more quickly, thereby getting it into the hands of end users more quickly. When looking at OSBI, there can be arguments for and against this point. On the one hand, and as William McKnight mentioned, for a quick win, he likes to use OS solutions. On the other hand, he also realizes that more iterations will be required. For the TCO capabilities below, the whole point is to get a solution up and running quickly and also provide business users with value.

Taking this one step further, vendors within this particular TCO study were rated on implementation times, support provided, cost of solution, etc. The assumptions made included the fact that vendors with more features automatically built in to their applications provided the basis for less customization, leading to quicker implementations.

Figure 12-10 identifies the types of features identified within the study. Organizations can do something similar and create a point system based on the factors they are interested in. These may include support, development efforts, additional hardware required, time to implement, etc. In addition, depending on the importance of each, the criteria can be weighted to provide levels of importance based on IT and business requirements, in essence, developing different assessments based on the needs of the end users targeted.

Also, in the previous chapter we looked briefly at Mark Madsen's TCO evaluation of OS against other offerings. Figure 12-11 (on page 140) shows a vendor comparison based on licensing and support with the last one representing OS. This comparison represents community OSBI versions, but commercial versions can be compared in a similar vein. Obviously, I have removed the vendors to eliminate potential bias.

ROI and TCO calculations

What all of this shows is that there are multiple ways of evaluating ROI and TCO. And although TCO can be more flexible and customized, overall calculations do follow a pattern. ROI generally looks at the costs and benefits associated with BI, all the while taking into account corporate information and attempting to place value on the implementation of BI, even if it falls outside the realm of quantifiable benefits. TCO, on the other hand, enables organizations to take their analyses further once they have justified BI spending. TCO gives companies the ability to compare the alternatives available and evaluate their potential use of OS against traditional BI alternatives and, more importantly, different alternatives within the realm of OS.

In general, despite all of the calculations required, if you are tasked with justifying the ROI or TCO of an OSBI project, the use of a simpler calculation will enable you to reach various audiences. Therefore, looking at the costs associated with deployment including the following:

- Software costs
- Number of IT resources × time allocated to project

Features and Functionality	Features and Functionality	Features and Functionality
Content creation that includes reusable data view elements (such as data tables, graphs, and animated charts)	Performs calculations based on date and time for trend analysis	Real-time access to multiple data sources per report or visualization (examples include XML Web Services, RSS/ATOM, and traditional data servers)
Drill down capability within crosstabs and charts	GIS reporting (support for ESRI, Google Maps, or MapInfo)	
	Creates personalized views for analysis (using cubes/relational data)	Write back capability into operational data
Report wizards to guide users through analytical and reporting tasks	End user reporting out of relational data via Web browser	Zero footprint and multi-platform client
Exports to common formats, including Microsoft Office, PDF, and Google Docs	End user analysis out of OLAP data cubes via Web browser	Supports user and group role-based security
Enable interactive drill down into multiple detail levels	End user dashboard building through a Web browser	Integration of 3rd party BI, application components, custom HTML, and JavaScript
Report prompts to give multiple selection criteria, ease of implementation (scripting and coding)	End user report and alert scheduling	User interface customization via standards (such as CSS)
	Creation of analytic workflow with built-in alerts and notifications	Platform availability for integrating with existing infrastructure – multi-platform support (.NET, Java)
Multiple nested report prompts support (scripting and coding)	Row-level conditional class to Identify problem areas in real-time	
Changing graphical views in real-time	Uses dashboards to deliver personalized information across the enterprise	

FIGURE 12-10

Assessing TCO of BI[9].

- New hardware
- Expansion of servers/new software allocations
- Licensing (if relevant)
- Maintenance over time – both support and internal IT resources

And the benefits are as follows:

- Time savings – time allocation/number of resources required to gather and analyze information
- Hardware/network efficiencies
- Additional revenues/profits
- Realized opportunities such as sales
- Etc.

How these benefits and costs are reflected at any point in time or after a longer period of time, such as 1, 2, or 3 years, will change. Many organizations are able to identify the benefits of initial OSBI implementations. Mark Madsen's calculations in Figure 12-11 provide a good example of this. But the implications over time might be different. Expansions to commercial offerings, new modules, broader integration requirements, etc. will all affect the ROI and TCO over time and may change depending on how BI is applied within the organization.

---

[9]http://www.logixml.com/content/10_AssessingTCO_WiseAnalytics_2010.pdf?ResourceCenter

Size	Total License Cost	Total Support Cost	Total Cost
Small	58,184	43,618	101,802
Medium	182,356	136,707	319,063
Large	543,584	407,608	951,192
Small	10,100	21,666	31,766
Medium	174,500	115,170	289,670
Large	845,800	558,228	1,404,028
Small	36,000	23,760	59,760
Medium	131,750	86,955	218,705
Large	1,595,670	1,053,142	2,648,812
Small	17,600	29,040	73,040
Medium	254,800	168,168	422,968
Large	1,124,200	741,972	1,866,172
Small	0	30,000	30,000
Medium	0	87,000	87,000
Large	0	87,000	87,000

FIGURE 12-11

Lowering the Cost of BI General Assessment of TCO.

Looking at commercial versus community offerings

Overall, these calculations won't change if an organization is looking at one OS model versus the other. However, organizations should look at the value of commercial and community versions in comparison to one another and what the implications are for their organization. In many cases, at first glance, companies look at community OSBI offerings as free. Even though software is free in terms of available source code, organizations need to look closely at what other benefits they get in terms of costs, time to develop, and services. As this chapter has shown, the value of free software does not negate the other solution expenditures or payback times. On the other hand, commercial OSBI offerings are becoming much more comparable to traditional BI offerings and, as time goes on, it seems like many of these offerings will continue to mimic the traditional.[10] Either way, the evaluation of OSBI solutions in the context of ROI and TCO are becoming much more similar to traditional offerings as solutions start to move towards more robust commercial models.

[10]This comment is based solely on my opinion and on my continued discussions with OSBI vendors. When I started covering the BI space, many of these vendors were working on becoming known within the traditional BI space but were clearly proponents of OS. Now when I speak to many of them and am provided with analyst briefings, the focus is on their capabilities and commercial offerings.

Understanding the technology behind business value

A look at technical considerations

Historically, BI deployments have been very data centric and IT-focused. Data warehousing, data integration, and multi-dimensional analysis were the cornerstones of BI use and development. Most of the time this meant that those involved were technically-inclined resources. As the market shifts towards self-service and SaaS models, more and more business people are getting involved in managing their BI platforms. Within OSBI, there are two ways of looking at things. First, community development is still highly dependent on the technical resources that download the software and get it up and running. Second, commercial deployments are starting to follow the shift in the market with a greater focus on business involvement. Basically, both types of resources and their outlooks require consideration and, up until this point, much of the focus of this book has been on the business side.

What this really means is that even though BI is developed for business users and the so-called "super users," its development is almost still completely IT-centric. Even within self-service models, much of the initial set-up requires IT departments or external consultants to get the solutions up and running. What this means for organizations is that looking at the business components associated with deploying OSBI is not enough to make informed decisions. Yes, organizations require business buy-in if IT is not sponsoring the project, but much of the effort involved stems from IT development staff. Therefore, the ability to understand technology and how OSBI fits within a current IT infrastructure may be one of the key areas for developing a solution that meets both technical and business unit requirements.

The technical role goes beyond developing an end-user tool for analytics and/or reporting. Whether community or commercial, companies require an in-depth look at their current IT architecture, what platforms they use, what skillsets currently exist in-house, what technology projects they have in the works, and the list goes on. The toughest part about all of this is to also make sure that these IT-based activities' outcomes provide the relevant tools for business users and meet the SLAs required for business activities. If this isn't enough, organizations should factor in the costs for each of these activities to identify the overall costs associated with the initiative — in essence, creating a link between ROI identification and technical considerations.

Because OSBI projects can be quite time intensive due to in-depth development efforts, it is quite important to make sure that technical considerations are looked at to meet company expectations. Consequently, to help you do just that we will look at the technical challenges that exist when organizations choose an OS approach to BI development. My main goal is to provide an explanation of these potential risks from a business perspective so that business decision makers understand what the implications of these initiatives are at the technical level. Most of the implications will be discussed from the vantage point of decision makers. Obviously, a certain level of technical understanding is assumed, but not to the point of having to be a developer. For the more technical audience, looking at these considerations in a different light might help with the process of collaboration required between business units and IT on a growing level. In addition, we'll be expanding on these considerations in Chapter 17 when we discuss the technical benefits and challenges of OSBI deployments.

How do technical considerations help with the evaluation process?

Many organizations want to jump right into new BI projects without understanding the implications of their choices. For instance, the type of BI infrastructure your organization selects will affect query performance, integration activities, and the timeliness of data delivery. If businesses lack the information they need at the beginning, there is a chance they will develop ineffective solutions, wasting time and money. OS adoption is no different. Even though community OS offerings are considered free based on the lack of upfront software costs, the same risks exist based on the amount of time required to develop internal solutions using community version source code from available offerings. To make sure companies understand these implications, it is important to understand the issues related to the technical infrastructure of any BI solution.

In all reality, within OSBI projects this may be even more so. Many developers like OS because of its flexibility but do not always check with business units to have the defined requirements in advance of development. In some cases, the software is selected based on broad merits and then expanded to include more departments without really understanding the needs of more than a subset of business units within the organization. The problem with this is that different departments will require different approaches to analytics. In addition to defining the role of data entities independently, the importance of timely information access or complex analytics for one department may not be the same for another. Making a choice without adequately understanding what these needs are leads to risk. Even though there isn't a single solution that will meet the requirements of everyone within the organization, fine-tuning a solution to meet the needs of most will eliminate the need for rework later on.[1]

Applying this directly to technical considerations means identifying all of the factors that affect the business from a technical standpoint. For example, manufacturers require the ability to manage

---

[1]http://mimiandeunice.com/

parts – how many exist in what place at any given time, defective parts, just-in-time delivery, supply chain and parts management, as well as placements in warehouses before use. For e-commerce and retailers, similar requirements exist. Not only do products need to be tracked, but sales trends and customer preferences need to be identified to make sure that consumers have positive experiences to induce them to become and/or remain customers.

Aside from all of the implications, taking the time to look at the impact of technology on the business provides a great starting point to develop a short list of possible vendors. In many cases, businesses are now evaluating OS options with traditional counterparts and understanding the technical considerations can make final decisions easier.

Evaluating the current IT infrastructure

So what is the best way to figure out what technical considerations apply to your organization and BI-related project? Although different companies may approach the evaluation phase differently, the overarching theme lies in the analysis of the current BI platform and general IT infrastructure.

In many situations, even if your department isn't using BI, someone in your organization is. Advanced users may download their own free version of software to perform independent analytics. This type of BI lacks the ability to create a broad view of information and performance within the organization. Collaboration and information sharing are also severely limited. Outside of this type of individual usage, companies generally have one or many BI solutions implemented within the organization, and these may be on a single platform or on more than one. In addition, OSBI tools may have been developed. The reason many business units or disparate roles within IT departments might not know what exists is because of the fact that most companies work in silos and conduct initiatives independently of others. By evaluating what currently exists in-house, project sponsors gain a sense of what has been done before and the level of success or failure of each. More importantly, project sponsors may be able to lessen overall costs based on reusing solutions already in-house.

Looking at the following questions will give you a good starting point and general overview of the technical areas that should be discussed and evaluated in-depth:

- What servers and databases make up the IT framework? This helps identify implementation requirements. Some solutions only work within a subset of proprietary hardware offerings, meaning that to look outside the box requires additional hardware provisions. In other cases, the organization is tied into contracts for several years, meaning that there might be areas to take advantage of or to be aware of. In today's world, many different systems can be used together, but the ease of integration may be what differs.
- Do any data warehouses or data marts exist? If an infrastructure already exists, it may be possible to add additional data to what has already been developed, or even take advantage of the data that is already being housed within the warehouse. If the system is a partnership solution,[2] then integration with OS or pulling data that has already been prepared to create individualized reports and analytics may be possible. If not, then only considering a front-end

---

[2]Many vendors partner with one another to ease integration requirements.

OSBI solution will not be enough to get the most value out of a BI tool. In these cases, understanding what exists under the hood is the only way to discover what the requirements are to build a broader data warehouse. In general, if using a common data warehouse market offering, most BI solutions will be able to support the data.

- What operating system is used? For instance, is it Linux, Windows, etc.? This may end up determining or limiting the solution choice. This can also extend to programming languages and the ability for offerings to work together. Even though most solutions can be made to work together, the time and effort involved differ. Since integration activities take up the bulk of the development and implementation process, it is always best to try to keep things as simple as possible. Also, organizations with an infrastructure that includes OS architecture already may be better poised for OSBI adoption because of the skillsets that already exist in-house.
- Does extra space exist to accommodate a new project or additional data storage? Operating systems, data warehouses, and BI tools may all sync up but may lack additional space or performance capabilities, which means that even for OSBI projects that were initially free, installing new servers or a data warehouse appliance might create a new set of costs, turning a so-called "free" project into one that requires a large budget.
- What expertise and skillsets are available? Although most companies implementing OS choose to do so because they have the required skillsets in-house, with increasing business unit sponsorship, the choice to adopt OSBI may be done without the identification of who already possesses the required skillsets to use OS. At this point, the question becomes whether to invest in training for current resources or to hire — either way costing the organization more time and money. Or another option is to look at consulting or professional services.
- Does the organization currently value collaborative efforts between IT and various business units as well as between disparate business units? Although outside the scope of technical considerations per se, the reality is that collaborative environments are better able to define project goals and develop solutions that best meet the needs of the business. Because OSBI can be so development intensive, the only way to create effective BI without multiple iterations is to be in constant communication with the business users to identify what they require.

Technical differences between community and commercial

Much of what has been discussed applies to both community and commercial OS options. After all, the development effort and support provided remains outside the scope of whether or not the platform will actually be functional and how to get it to where it needs to be. With this being said, differences do exist between both types of OSBI offerings. For businesses making changes to source code, they fall outside of support, meaning that an organization is on its own if something goes wrong. Yes, community support can be an option, but it will probably not include the extra support from the vendor, creating potential implications over time. If customizations are made that deviate too much from the original source code, then it might be difficult to find other organizations to help with any support issues.

Commercial versions, on the other hand, mimic traditional BI offerings in relation to technical requirements. Many are very similar to their traditional counterparts and require the same considerations when evaluating software and once implemented. Aside from more upgrades and releases due to the constant focus on development, commercial OSBI vendors want to compete with traditional BI vendors to expand their market share and to increase their profits.

Aside from these minor differences, which aren't always so minor depending on the situation, considerations remain similar. Organizations cannot overlook the need for an in-depth look at IT infrastructure irrespective of whether community or commercial solutions are chosen. So, either way, the considerations remain the same but should be evaluated based on the type of solution. Also, some companies start off with community versions to see if the commercial version would suit them. Others know that they will never go that route. Although this might not matter in the short term, the long run might be different. During your evaluation, keep this in mind so that you don't have to start from scratch when looking at the next iteration.

The next sections look at individualized considerations based on where you are within the OSBI adoption life cycle. You can skip ahead to the section that applies to your organization. Although some of what we'll look at has been discussed in the past, the points expounded upon below take the business considerations discussed and integrate these into what technical requirements should be looked at.

New to OSBI

If you are new to OS, all of this might seem quite overwhelming. The good part is that all of these considerations should be evaluated no matter what type of BI solution is being implemented. So, for future implementations or BI iterations, decision makers will already have an idea of what exists in-house — providing this information has been communicated to others across the organization. In addition to defining what exists, this exercise also helps identify the business owners of data, where resources exist within the organization, and who the go-to people are for different business activities, which in turn ties the technical to the business areas.

For first-time projects it is important to look at:

* Project scope — The "what," "who," and "when" type questions are important first steps to making sure that alignment exists between business and technical concerns. Even though businesses tend to want to do everything at once, starting small helps optimize business processes by making sure they are reflected in metrics management and what is being measured within the company. However, smaller projects may lead to oversights in understanding the true technical requirements, as managing one business area with seven data sources is very different than understanding the technical requirements for 15 data sources that take into account the entire business structure.
* Business rules behind the data — The term Big Data is very popular these days and basically refers to large data warehousing projects: large in data volumes, big in velocity, and most importantly in the complexity of design. Applying this to new OSBI initiatives and technology means identifying how information is connected. For instance, online gaming requires complex algorithms identifying player habits, preferences, and the like. For betting this even goes further to identify the odds.
* Storage — How much information needs to be stored, including historical data and the ability to merge data sources? The importance of storage is based on the ability to anticipate data volume growth while still understanding how compression affects the amount of storage required.

- Data latency – Different information requires different types of interaction. Banking and certain retail establishments require up-to-date access to information. The stock market and managing portfolios means that prices and transactions need to be up to date within seconds. The amount of latency required will influence the type of data warehouse selected, as some do not support real-time data feeds or subsecond query response times. For other types of businesses, this might not be an initial requirement but should still be understood for potential future use and BI expansion.
- Current hardware – If the organization currently has hardware that can be allocated to the BI project, overall expenditures might remain low based on a no-cost software solution for community OS adoption. However, many companies set aside separate budgets for hardware expenditures. In some cases, businesses might still want separate hardware for their BI projects and will want to take into account future storage and data latency requirements to identify which hardware will work best. In addition, there is the proprietary versus open approach in the sense that some data warehouse vendors only function using specific hardware. This may have implications for existing hardware use.
- Internal resources – In addition to the data and where it's stored, the fact remains that to get the solution up and running and to make it function effectively, there need to be people behind the effort. Who currently exists in-house and any gaps in skillsets may affect the project and what can be done. Whether choosing to hire new resources, train current employees, or use professional services, the amount of cost and effort will differ and the time to see value and get everything up and running will also change. In addition, skillsets might determine the type of hardware and software chosen. For instance, if a developer has worked on Jaspersoft projects in the past, using Jaspersoft might be intuitive and organizations might choose its use irrespective of the organization's business requirements.

These areas are just the tip of the iceberg in terms of considerations but do provide insights into what new adopters need to be aware of and the factors that affect the technical aspects of an OSBI project. For companies that are new to BI, and especially to the concept of OS, it's important to identify "why OS?" and to discover which type best suits your organization. Simply selecting a community model because of the no-cost software entry point may actually turn out to cause more hassle in the long run if you have not planned out the project properly.

OSBI expansion

On the other hand, many organizations are already familiar with OSBI and are looking to expand what currently exists in-house. In these cases, the above points are good for review to make sure that nothing has changed, as general considerations for expanding BI environments are different. These factors will include:

- New hardware – Moving from the type of hardware to asking essential questions that include, do we need new servers? Do our old ones work for us or do we need more space, processing power, data virtualization, an appliance, etc.?
- New data sources – What are the new data sources required? Or are we using additional fields within the current data feeds? Looking at the data sources may bring up issues such as data latency and different information being needed at different times, the amount of history, how

information relates to each other, the value of data and how it is currently being presented to the business, and the list goes on. Because data is the source of BI, the analysis of its worth and use cannot be overlooked.

- Integration – The data sources required and the integration of information are interrelated. Bringing in data sources and preparing data for data integration activities can take most of the work during any BI project, whether OS or traditional. BI expansions may mean that integration requirements change. Looking at how these changes affect other processes in the organization is important to ensure an easy transition and/or expansion.
- Business rules – To effectively integrate various data sources into a combined data structure, it's important to identify what business rules apply. Does the project expansion change the way information relates? Now that more information is being considered, it is quite possible that new business rules apply. For instance, are there new customer considerations now that buying patterns and demographic trends are being captured? What about customer loyalty programs?
- Resources – The identification of skillsets and internal resources are the same as for new deployments. However, there is a general assumption that companies that have already deployed OSBI and are managing current projects have the resources required to maintain these solutions. When expanding, however, it is always a good idea to reevaluate whether you need more people involved and who those people should be.

Integration with non-OS sources

The reality is that few IT infrastructures are fully OS. OSBI solutions need to be able to integrate with broader proprietary IT environments. How organizations do that may differ. Some of this integration might be specific to other BI applications or database solutions. Either way, IT resources need to understand any of the nuances that exist within specific software and/or hardware solutions. Generally, OS touts itself on open standards and being able to work with a broader range of offerings. This may or may not be the case depending on the type of offerings that need to play together.

Overall, organizations need to look at what exists and what activities are required to get their BI offerings up and running. In many cases the non-OS sources that already exist within these businesses are proprietary offerings. Certain proprietary solutions require APIs to enable integration between disparate offerings. Even with these, integration can be complicated. Consequently, before expanding any application or toolset it's important to look at how integrating various offerings will affect the current BI environment as well as end users' access.

Implications of trends

Trends within the BI software market actually affect the technical considerations. Database technology is constantly evolving, making it easier to process large amounts of complex data sets in near real-time. Acquisitions are being made that change vendor focus and product roadmaps. Pricing for storage and expectations for in-memory and analytics access is changing, with price points lowering to accommodate more for less. Add to this the social aspects of increasing self-service and ease of use at all levels, and BI is becoming more accessible. What this means for OS is that as OS solutions start to move towards commercial models, the features and functions they need in order to compete with traditional offerings are more robust.

For organizations looking at OS offerings because of the free software availability, other vendors can also be considered. The past few years have seen an increase in free trials or limited free versions, with the only difference between free software and OS being the availability of source code. The implication of all of this is twofold:

- OSBI vendors need to differentiate themselves beyond free. The ability to deploy software free without any initial costs is no longer unique. Now many vendors offer varying levels of free BI to expand the reach of their solutions, with hopes of increasing their customer base. OS vendors do the same, with hopes that a certain number of customers will adopt their commercial BI offerings.
- Increasing competition among free software offerings means that price is no longer a competitive factor. In the past, organizations wanting to implement BI for less would look to OS as a main contender. Now these organizations have broader offerings to choose from. What this means for businesses is that vendors have to try harder to differentiate their offerings and sell the value of OS.

Looking at data integration

We've provided a glimpse into first-time and expansion considerations to identify what factors are important for a bare bones evaluation of OSBI and how to integrate it into your current IT environment. When it comes to integration itself, however, the importance of understanding the various steps cannot be underestimated. Even if you are not conducting these tasks on your own, you should understand the process so that the effort it takes is not underestimated and can be scheduled for appropriately within the whole project timeline.

For instance, aside from identifying the data sources required, an organization needs to identify the fields required within those data sources, the business rules that apply to help transform that data into valid information, and joins/interrelations between tables. In addition to conceptual design, data ownership and business applications of the data should be identified. In essence, all of the business-related tasks that relate to the information being identified. Even though this preparation does not include touching the data sources or copying any information from actual source systems, its preparation beforehand can ease a lot of difficulty in the future.

In terms of development efforts and data integration tasks, each vendor will have its own requirements. Some BI offerings do not require transformations or even identifying primary keys, etc., while others need these things to be done upfront and therefore require more preparation in advance. These differences will vary and require different efforts leading to disparate time frames. Overall, though, the important thing to remember is that following these tasks and making sure that data integration activities match business requirements are essential aspects of a successful BI initiative.

Generally, OS offerings have built-in ETL functions or formalized partnerships with data integration vendors so that you can get general integration functions using the community versions required. However, for organizations with complex integration requirements, paid versions, or developing your own processes becomes essential as free tools, although many are easy to use, they only provide the most common data integration activities as opposed to supporting complex joins and processes out of the box. And although many businesses looking at OS do so for the price, data integration is not the area to skimp on in resource or budget allocation.

Disparate data sources

Identifying the data sources required might seem simple, but information exists in different formats that do not always integrate easily with one another. In addition, end users sometimes identify spreadsheets as sources that are actually secondary data access points and do not represent the most accurate information sources. Other business users may only know the interface or program they access the information from, but this doesn't mean that this is the actual source data.

Making sure the right data sources are identified and the integration requirements that go along with them helps speed the implementation process along. What businesses need to be aware of, however, is that some vendors have limits on the number of data sources that can be used for free or the amount of storage. Looking into this in advance of selecting a solution is the best way to go to avoid surprises. For instance, some free software offerings only allow information from one data source, which limits the types and number of analytics that can be performed.

In addition to identifying where the data comes from, it is important to identify the types of data. Sales and operations are common applications that BI draws on when creating analytics, with supply chain and risk management additional areas that are very popular starting points. But as BI environments become flexible and interactive, disparate types of data are also being added. Social network analysis is becoming much more important in terms of enabling organizations to identify their customers' behavior and interactions as well as what the public is saying about products, competitors, and the like.

The following sections look at the general types of information that can be pulled into a data warehouse and/or used for the purpose of analytics.

Internal structured data

Structured data represents the most common type of information stored in a database — rows and columns with numerical information such as sales by region, parts, or customer information; sales and marketing analytics, and generally any of the common information that is analyzed within an organization — basically the transactions that take place.

Much of this information is the first that is captured within a data warehouse or BI infrastructure. This is no different from OSBI offerings. Organizations look first to structured content to analyze trends, customer behavior, partner and supplier management, and design marketing campaigns. Even though this information can be complicated, the ability to go beyond the obvious is where other information comes from.

Internal unstructured/semistructured data

Information contained in emails, documents, call center notes, etc., represent good examples of unstructured content that is increasingly being captured as part of BI initiatives. Organizations are trying to identify why customers stay or leave and what their levels of satisfaction are. Because of the increasing competitive nature of the marketplace these days, businesses can no longer ignore multiple types of data sets.

Industries such as legal, healthcare, and finance need to identify trends or potential risk factors within documents and contracts. The ability to identify fraudulent mortgage applications or submitted health care insurance claim forms helps save companies billions each year. This is the value of unstructured data analysis and the ability to look beyond numbers to identify correlations and interrelations between disparate information.

External structured data

External and internal structured data is the same in format. However, integration requirements and data preparation might be different. Organizations need to look at the considerations discussed above in relation to integration and available adapters. Salesforce.com represents a good example of vendors developing adapters because of the large number of organizations using their solutions. When looking at BI, organizations can no longer only use internal data for their analytics. The combination of internal and external data sources helps provide better visibility overall.

External unstructured/semistructured data

As with internal and external structured data, the same exists with unstructured or semistructured sources, geospatial information where companies integrate Google Maps with internal sales and demographics to identify sales by region, trends based on geography, etc. This level of integration between many different types of information provides a broader view of overall performance because of the enhanced access to a variety of information sources. But in order to really take advantage of this level of integration, companies need to let business owners (of data) define the relationships and help develop the analysis required based on their industry knowledge. IT developers using community versions will have the opportunity to customize these relationships. The risk, however, is that if the source code is changed, it will probably not be supported and there is no guarantee of community support.

Social network data

A discussion about unstructured data cannot exclude social media. This goes beyond Twitter and Facebook towards actually looking at how customer social networks interact. This is obviously not possible with all industries, but in vertical markets such as telecommunications, where it becomes possible to manage interactions between customers, it becomes possible to see who are the important members of your customer base. This expands beyond how much a person pays each month towards who are the influencers within the customer base.

Storing this data and defining trends and the considerations associated with this type of information is quite challenging. As these types of information sources become more common, vendors will become more accommodating. The issues are not always about bringing the data into a BI infrastructure — the question becomes what to do with it. Although some dashboards do exist that stream this type of data, developing complex analytics based on social networking data is still in its infancy. Organizations need to be aware of how data integration, storage, and query processing will react based on their hardware and software choices.

Database technologies and what the differences mean in terms of end-user delivery

In many cases, OSBI will either include an OS data warehouse or database that can be optimized for data warehouse use. Whether OS or traditional, different types of data warehousing exist and can affect the way information is streamed and how quickly and complexly queries are processed. These differences need to be looked at in-depth to determine which features are important for the type of analytics:

- Row versus columnar — Refers to the way in which data is processed. For analytics, columnar-based databases process queries by looking at the columns first and then going through the rows to pick out the right information. For analytics, this type of structure is more efficient and provides better query response times.
- In-memory or data virtualization — For companies looking at a more dynamic approach to analytics, the ability to create queries and identify analytics on the fly provides a more vibrant approach to BI. Unlike more traditional offerings that require detailed specifications in advance, in-memory analytics allow you to create one-time views of performance.
- Query performance — Which brings up the ability to perform queries quickly, service-level agreements, and the ability to sift through large data sets to uncover valuable information in a timely fashion require consideration. Different solutions have various strengths and some are better poised to process information more quickly than others.
- Data streaming and near real-time data demands — Although not all organizations require information on a real-time basis, the fact is that businesses are starting to look at information intra-daily, even if only a subset. More data warehouses are providing this capability, but not all do. If you are interested, you need to look at the specific capabilities of each solution to make sure it meets your specific requirements.
- Storage and optimization — How much information you store, whether historical or simply large data volumes, will vary with each solution. Cost per terabyte is one consideration to be looked at in addition to the items above.

Takeaways

The good thing about technical requirements is that organizations can create a checklist by taking the items discussed within this chapter and making sure that all of the considerations are taken into account. Although both vendors and IT staff tend to discuss the technical factors in technical terms — i.e., storage space, query response times, and other performance measurements — the reality is that business decision makers can also work through the technical checklist. This is because these factors are a bridge to the company's business requirements. Overall, it's important to remember that although projects should start with a business need or pain being faced, many technical factors still require consideration before deciding on a solution that best meets your organization's needs.

Understanding integration and data preparation

Traditionally, organizations have developed BI solutions that were all encompassing. What this means is that many companies implemented BI offerings that included a robust data warehouse, a development environment that required strong technical skills, canned reports, analytical engines, etc. Developing this took a long time and required great effort. And this effort was required, not only for implementations but also in reference to overall maintenance. Although OS is not inherently different in terms of the overall BI environment that traditionally exists within organizations using it, what is different is the fact that most OSBI projects require a knowledge of traditional offerings and infrastructure, whereas knowledge in the opposite direction does not always exist. Organizations require this knowledge because it is rare to find an IT infrastructure that does not include some level of proprietary solution.

Organizations incorporating OSBI within their IT environments, therefore, require an understanding of many different types of solutions and how they fit together — whether through formalized partnerships, integration activities, or within the current infrastructure. Different solution mixes will have potential differences in terms of the way they integrate as well as the implications for management, technology, etc. After all, different software categories may have disparate integration requirements or business rules that create a more difficult environment when considering how everything should work together.

What all of this really means is that most organizations looking at OSBI offerings will also have some type of traditional BI applications in-house as well as other traditional software. Any data sources that require integration within a BI application will require consideration in terms of how it integrates with OSBI. Luckily, the broad range of use and large numbers of downloads mean that within the scope of OS use is quite broad, making integration capabilities a focus of solution providers.

Therefore, even for organizations within a fully OS environment for their analytics, there are still required knowledge sets about different solutions and how they integrate with other applications. Although APIs exist, the reality remains that integration activities are not intuitive when it comes down to actualizing your business goals. This is generally why vendors build in buffer zones when discussing their implementation times. For instance, when asking a vendor about how long it takes to implement a solution, they may ask a series of questions about the desired outputs and number of inputs. Even armed with this knowledge, they will still provide a buffer — for instance, between 3 and 6 months, to ensure that any issues that arise are taken into account within these estimates. Aside from the number of data sources and general complexities of business rule integration, consolidating multiple types of data and developing a framework to gain valuable insights out of information requires in-depth knowledge irrespective of platform.

This chapter looks at the components of BI in relation to what OS offerings are available. In addition, this chapter explores the reasons behind combining OSBI with traditional complementary offerings and/or other solution offerings that work to create a full BI platform. This includes the types of offerings that organizations may consider, the implications for business, and examples of the types of projects organizations are currently undertaking.

Looking at the components of BI

Although talks about BI components generally provide a cursory glance of introductory views of BI, this discussion does not reflect an introduction to BI but actually provides some insights in relation to the various possibilities of OSBI and how this fit in with other components of BI. For instance, some organizations like to develop their own reporting applications, so they select OSBI-reporting solutions to create reports based on legacy or other information sources. In some cases, this provides faster development times because developers create solutions for business users independent of budgeting constraints or broader software implementations. The implications may include more flexibility — both for development staff and for the types of solutions developed.

Also, companies no longer look at one solution to fit their needs. In many cases, they take a piece-meal approach by combining multiple solutions to create the best possible solution. Now that OSBI is becoming more like traditional offerings in terms of robust functionality and commercial offerings, they are starting to be compared alongside traditional vendors more often.

What this means for companies is that it becomes important to understand the implications of these options, how they compare with others, and what the implications are for integration with complementary solutions. For instance, many organizations are just now realizing the benefits of data quality and building in the proper processes that enable long-term information quality at the source. Unfortunately, many of the solutions available are out of the price range of many SMBs, making it more difficult for them to achieve on a company-wide level. This makes OS a valid alternative for businesses looking to get a full range of solutions to meet multiple business needs without the added software costs (depending on the type of OS used, of course).

Taking this one step further, Talend provides a good example of a general data quality tool that can provide organizations with the stepping stones needed to get to the next level. Within their data integration platform they offer master data management (MDM) and data quality (DQ) that can be used effectively at the free level to get organizations on the road to better data management — all of the essentials required to make BI more effective. Organizations can use the free products and expand to the commercial version as needed. In some cases businesses do, but in other cases companies choose to continue with the community version without expanding to a commercial option.

In other cases, some organizations may feel that a traditional data warehouse is out of their reach. Consequently, developers may choose to develop solutions internally. For example, by taking an OS database solution and optimizing it for data warehousing use. Or alternatively, taking a free version of a solution like Ingres (which does not provide the source code with its free downloads) and customizing it to integrate with a front-end BI framework.

All of these examples lead to the fact that BI contains many components and multiple ways of creating a BI infrastructure that will depend upon individual organizational needs. Although no one answer exists for all businesses, understanding the options and how it all work together can provide the basis for a strong OSBI infrastructure and overall analytics. The next section delves into the reasons behind considering complementary offerings within an OSBI framework.

Why organizations should consider complementary offerings

At this point, you might be asking questions related to the whys surrounding the validity of looking at other types of offerings when OS provides a full breadth of BI solutions. But the reality for most organizations falls into one of the following scenarios:

- The organization already has a BI infrastructure in place that has become the standard for analytics but is not meeting the growing or changing needs of the business, so IT looks towards OS offerings to minimize additional software costs while expanding BI reach throughout the company.
- OSBI exists but the organization wants to look at other software providers to address a newer business pain — for instance, enhanced data quality or data migration activities.
- Organizations have a mixture of solutions and are replacing their traditional offerings with OS.
- Companies are transitioning from a community offering towards commercial adoption.

No matter which situation, the reality for most companies is that there will be some sort of integration of OSBI with non-OS solutions, BI or otherwise. In addition, aside from the effort involved in internal development projects, most organizations do not have the unlimited resources or will to recreate the wheel when other opportunities for quicker time to value exist. Therefore, OS projects tend to be strategic in nature, making BI a valuable area for developers to focus on should they choose OS as an option.

Also, there are implications involved in only looking at traditional or OSBI. As mentioned, OSBI requires internal developers with specific skillsets, potentially new hardware, and adequate time to develop and maintain developed applications. On top of the obvious, the following implications should be evaluated to identify whether they affect your organization and current BI environment and if so, how.

Limited capabilities

Even though many OSBI offerings provide most of the features and functionality required for a robust BI infrastructure, each organization has unique requirements and business needs that may fall outside of the scope of specific product roadmaps and current offerings. Some organizations might prefer to wait for a one-stop shop solution to their every need. Vendors such as SAP and Oracle are good examples of software vendors that offer various types of business solutions to meet organizational operational and analytical needs. The problem is that these solutions require high budgets, complicated integration, and long implementation times.

Basically, for many businesses this option is far from realistic and not at all ideal. The reality is that single solutions generally do not meet the needs of an organization. They do, however, meet many of the business requirements and provide the option for companies to customize or "tweak" the solution to individual specifications. But what happens if this is not the case, or if an organization is looking to integrate MDM or data profiling within their OSBI environment (or alternatively, wants to use OS products as a complement to their traditional BI infrastructure)? In these situations, the integration of OS with traditional BI or complementary offerings to get all of the features required for an integrated solution is obvious because of the limited capabilities that exist within any one given offering.

Long-term development and internal maintenance

Two of the common arguments both for and against OSBI are the development times needed to build solutions and the maintenance required to maintain and support OSBI offerings. The "for" argument looks something like this: Organizations can bypass the 80/20 rule and develop targeted applications. After all, even with out-of-the-box solutions, developers still require customizations to hone in on the features and functions they need to create a set of analytics, dashboards, reports, and the like. And by creating something from scratch OS developers develop greater expertise, enabling broader skillsets that translate to a greater ability to maintain the solution over time without having to rely on external support.

The "against" argument involves the fact that developing a BI solution within a community OS environment from scratch can take extra time, even with community participation. Depending on the availability of training, skillsets, other internal projects, and overall time, the payoff to creating BI applications independently may not be within the realm of community development. Even with commercial offerings, the key differentiators between models (i.e., OS versus traditional offerings) are not as broad as they once were.

What all of this means for organizations looking at complementary solutions is that depending on the types of BI components required, it might make more sense to mix and match. In the past many businesses chose to standardize on one centralized platform. This is no longer the case. Now organizations select dashboard or analytics applications based on their merit. This means that the possibility of integrating OS with traditional BI solutions is much greater.

Integration

The reality is that most OSBI solutions will require integration with non-OS offerings or the ability to integrate data from many disparate data sources. Consequently, a fully OS environment that only includes data from other OS sources is far from realistic. Even though focused on OSBI offerings, in some cases the OS portion may fall outside the realm of BI specifically and include the back-end or integration portion. Although the same principles hold true in this case as well, IT departments have to be aware of special circumstances that may exist.

One of the benefits of integration within an OSBI environment is that in many cases community users publicize the connectors they create to share with the community, making integration with specific tools easier — or less complicated. Developers can also create their own connectors or pay for external services to do this if one doesn't exist.

Many solution providers have specific implementation processes that provide estimates of implementation times. Community OSBI projects should still have general guidelines that can be followed to identify realistic timelines, however, buffer zones are very important whether adopting commercial or community versions.

Expansion

Traditionally, organizations start with a community version of OS to see whether the offerings fit what they hope to achieve. In some cases, these organizations expand to commercial offerings to extend features, functions, support, and the like. Either way, BI infrastructures and business requirements will continue to grow over time. In some cases, growth occurs due to new and increasing amounts of data, while in others expansion is based on additional users or departments with new requirements.

Once maturity reaches a certain point, however, businesses need to address whether a community OS solution will really meet their requirements, is scalable, and if so, how to maintain a growing infrastructure. In many cases, resources do not exist that can continually expand and adapt to consistent changes in a fast enough way to provide adequate value to organizations. In these situations, something more formal may be required, meaning that expansions may or may not include additional OS or may be a hybrid. Whether or not this is the case, companies should evaluate both. Due to community versions not requiring software costs, initial investments still have value, even for projects that combine both OS and traditional offerings.

Evaluating the current BI environment

What all of this leads to is the reality that organizations need to evaluate how the current BI environment works and whether what currently exists remains effective. For instance, a number of best-of-breed solutions exist for companies evaluating adding dashboards to their internal reporting needs. Many organizations are moving away from one platform and a standardized approach and integrating diverse offerings to make sure they get the best of everything. This does not mean that one solution outperforms another, but that based on changing price structures and lowering barriers to entry, organizations can develop a piecemeal approach. Within the realm of OSBI, this may mean that OS only represents one portion of BI or that disparate offerings pull data from the same sources or may need to interact in specific ways. For instance, no matter what exists on the backend, business users need a seamless business experience.

Once organizations define what they have in-house, they can identify which aspects require OSBI considerations and which don't. For example, implementing OSBI can complement solutions but will require different considerations when looking at the differences between new deployments versus BI expansions. In addition to the use of more than one BI offering, BI requires data integration, in many cases data warehousing, and the availability of other complementary offerings. Whether all OS or a combination of OS and traditional, there are many ways to implement a full BI framework. The following section looks at some of the complementary OS offerings that can be integrated within an OSBI environment. We've already provided some examples, but this looks at general technologies that fall within the spectrum of BI.

A brief look at Hadoop

One of the big game changers for traditional BI applications is Hadoop. With the ability to query large amounts of data and distribute data as needed without the infrastructure required to support a broad data warehouse environment, some businesses are choosing to integrate Hadoop within their organizations due to its accessibility. Especially due to the fact that it is an OS project, companies with a pull towards OS that extends beyond BI specifically will look towards Hadoop over Mapreduce.

Because the amount of information and data stored is growing at astronomical rates, organizations need to find valid and cost-effective ways to manage data. Until more recently, data warehousing had many roadblocks as well as benefits. For some companies, the hope that Hadoop will replace the limitations of dealing with complex data means that more organizations will look at Hadoop to implement within their organizations.

As data becomes more complex, diverse approaches will be required to manage the data and create valuable insights. With OS helping pave the way to broader information management, more organizations will evaluate the benefits associated with OS offerings and the ability to create a full range of internal solutions while lessening costs associated with maintaining a similar environment within traditional environments.

Integrating OSBI with traditional offerings

Overall, looking at how to integrate aspects of OSBI with traditional offerings can be complicated. With the number of partnerships and general options available, organizations really have to identify what they want to adopt internally. This means evaluating the features and functions of multiple OS offerings and how they integrate with the current BI environment or vice versa. One-stop shopping no longer exists for organizations that hope to optimize every level of analytics and operations within companies.

With OS broadening in popularity, its continual focus on increasing commercial availability means that organizations should be aware of the differences between a vendor's community and commercial offerings in addition to new partnerships and expansions in feature sets and overall offerings. The good part about OS is that development cycles are quite quick and relatively constant. On the flip side, businesses need to be aware of these changes to take into account what will work best for them — both in the short term and in the future as the BI environment grows.

The reality of the market

The reality of the market is that few, if any, organizations will use OS or traditional offerings exclusively, with Hadoop's increase in adoption being a good example of how organizations not familiar with OS will still apply OS within some aspect of their organization. Many companies, however, will use a mixture of both, especially since OSBI is becoming a much more viable offering for companies. This value exists for two reasons:

- SMBs are looking for their BI entry point — making the need for lower cost, easier-to-implement solutions a broader industry requirement.
- Organizations are demanding greater flexibility based on the ability to expand offerings and move from one model to another.

Out of the many solutions within the BI playing field, OS actually tries to meet that need more broadly than most. Aside from newer niche players, OS is providing greater BI access points, meaning that more organizations will start to integrate OS offerings within their traditional BI environments.

Working within an OS environment 15

Whether through source code flexibility, support, or general integration, many developers prefer to work within an OS environment. However, issues also arise depending on comfort levels, etc. Therefore, it makes sense to take some time to discuss what it means to work within an OS environment. In many ways, this chapter is targeted towards developers. However, it should also be said that my specialty does not lie in technical banter or within the world of development. So my goal is to provide an introduction to working within an OS environment so business users can gain a broader understanding and also bridge any gaps that may exist between development teams and the business users driving these projects.

Hence, we now turn our focus to developers. Normally much of the material discussing OS and what it entails targets IT developers and looks at specific platforms or product offerings and how to optimize these solutions through step-by-step guides. In essence, these guidebooks provide additional support to developers but do not always discuss what it means to work within an OSBI environment. But none of this helps provide more cohesion or project management ability. Obviously, it stands to reason that what business users need to know about working within an OS environment versus what is required of developers is quite different. My goal is to present the information in a straightforward way so that business users can also attain some benefit, without needing to understand technical jargon.

Additionally, not all developers are knowledgeable about OS and may also be thrust into its use due to organization initiatives focusing on OSBI or because of software evaluations that end up with an OS offering as a best fit. Therefore, this chapter targets developers and those looking to understand the OSBI development environment, what the steps are, and the challenges that exist.

Introduction to developers

Now that we've provided a small introduction for general readers, it's important to set the stage to identify what this chapter is and what it is not. If you are a developer, then you are probably used to technical documentation and guidelines needed to ensure quicker development cycles than if you were developing an application independently. If you are looking for a detailed description of steps to take, you might be a little disappointed in this chapter because there is very little of that. This chapter does shift the focus from business to technical requirements but does not provide the steps required to get there. Although generally similar, the goal of this chapter is to educate readers about the general requirements for OSBI, so it is not a step-by-step guide to developing specific applications. Therefore, this chapter looks at the steps required to work within an OSBI environment, with more detailed discussions in the following chapters.

A word about Java

As mentioned in the introduction, some organizations are familiar with OS environments while others aren't. In general, OS requires knowledge of Java programming. For many developers comfortable with proprietary options, this means learning new skills, which in turn can lead to longer times to develop solutions due to the time it takes to either transfer skills or learn new ones. Consequently, organizations need to identify whether the payoffs are worth it in relation to the costs and benefits of an OSBI implementation versus a traditional one.

To give you an idea of whether this is the right way to go for your organization, this section provides an overview of Java for those readers who are newer to OS and the differences between development languages.[1] Hopefully, this will be enough of an overview to give resources the knowledge needed to make informed decisions while providing a better understanding of the development process.

Java is a programming language like C++, which uses a compiler to transform the programming done into a usable language that can be read by a computer. Figure 15-1 shows how Java is transformed into a usable programming interface. Although a different bytecode interpreter is required for each type of computer, the benefit of Java is that once this bytecode exists, it can be run on any computer.

Because of the series of steps required to interface with the Java program itself, the first iterations were considered slow because its use was through virtual environments. Even though this is still the case, just-in-time compilers provide translation into machine language, which makes it easier to develop solutions more quickly. Either way, any programming language selected will

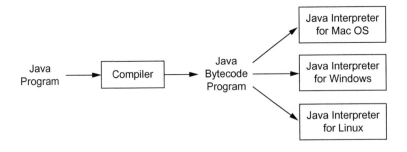

FIGURE 15-1

A Look at How Java Gets Converted to a Format Understood by Operating Systems[2].

---

[1]The introduction to Java relies heavily upon http://math.hws.edu/javanotes/index.html, *Introduction to Programming Using Java*, Sixth Edition, June, 2011, by David J. Eck. Much of this section is taken from this guide to provide a general explanation.
[2]http://math.hws.edu/javanotes/c1/s3.html

have benefits and challenges. Some are easier to justify than others. Within an OS environment, the fact that it is an open programming environment makes it easier to use and to transfer.

For OSBI, the openness of a solution is the key component. Proprietary programming or limited integration capabilities would be an impossible route to take, therefore Java is required to get solutions up and running and maintain the openness of the solution. Once developers choose this route, the flexibility to develop and customize personalized solutions increases, but the responsibility of the IT development staff also increases, making the onus of maintaining solutions up to the developers themselves (unless they select commercial offerings).

Development within a community OS environment

So what does this mean in relation to community OS development? Community solutions require the ability to develop a solution from beginning to end. Obviously, OSBI source code provides the bones of the solution but not the interface or specific features required to fit to your needs. Overall, these solutions are built to provide a skeleton of BI offerings with the ability to create a strong offering that can be delivered to business users. At this point, you have probably already made your decision in relation to selecting OS. The reality, though, is that there are still considerations and things that you need to know when embarking on community OSBI initiatives. And this is especially the case when adopting OSBI for the first time.

Here are some of the development considerations and what developers should know when selecting community development:

- Most OSBI community offerings are not final products. Although access to source code provides more flexibility, in most cases the source code provides the ability to install a blank slate of working BI offerings. Depending on the solution, different modules will need to be developed separately or require a large amount of effort to create final solutions. Although most developers are aware of this fact, business users may not be. The ability to sell this understanding to business sponsors is an important factor to remember when considering developer involvement. These factors are important when looking at the development efforts and the amount of customization required. The implications of this potential customization are large when looking at the time and effort involved.
- Considerations are the same irrespective of solution choice. Developers need to understand that selecting OS does not mitigate the need to evaluate offerings based on their merit and to develop an understanding of which solutions best meet company requirements. In many cases, one OSBI offering might be better than another, but in other cases the right choice may be a traditional software solution. Although business sponsors and decision makers might push companies towards OS even though it might not be the right choice and many developers prefer having control over product development, there still needs to be collaboration between business and IT involvement to determine the right solution. This decision from a technical perspective and resource availability should be left to the lead developers involved.
- Integration requirements. Data integration requires a lot of detailed requirements identification. Profiling, ETL processes, quality − the list is endless. Developers need to identify whether their solution choice can integrate source data natively, requires a little customization, or the

development of new APIs to ensure long-term management. In addition, the general assumption is that data integration processes take about 80% of development time. The more prepared developers are with knowledge of the solution requirements the better they will be able to manage their time more effectively. Essentially, the goal of OSBI development should be to create effective and efficient BI applications for business users and try not to figure out how to get data into the BI solution stack.

• Developing a full stack versus niche solutions. OS offerings provide the ability to apply reporting or dashboards or develop a full BI solution. This is a consideration for developers in terms of looking at what areas of BI they want to apply within their organizations. Is this an expansion, new adoption, rip and replace? All of these potential implementation types will lead to different ways of adopting BI. What this means for developers is that the level of involvement will be different based on involvement required. This might include amount of time, complexity, and data required.

• What about expansion? Over time, BI use expands based on business requirements and general expansion of use. Consequently, developers need to manage this expansion and identify the requirements. Some factors to consider for expansion include time, data additions, new algorithm development, and maintenance over time. Basically, expansions involve the same evaluation and requirements gathering strategy as a general software implementation.

• Transitioning from community to commercial, or from traditional to OS. Developers looking at expanding to the next level may consider commercial offerings. In many cases, this will involve getting access to features out of the box and better support. For those looking at OS for the first time, more flexibility may be the key. Either way, developers need to understand what the implications are. In the first case, data infrastructures and data integration requirements may be the same, whereas future development and expansion efforts may be less encompassing. In the second case, OS requires more development in addition to a total re-haul of the organization's BI infrastructure.

Development within a commercial OS environment

In many ways, commercial OS solutions are similar to traditional BI offerings. Because commercial versions provide ready-made and tailor-made solutions, the amount of development effort required is much more limited than with community OSBI offerings. The advantages of this type of solution are generally seen as lower price points in relation to many larger traditional offerings. In relation to development, the amount of time to develop offerings will be similar to those of traditional BI projects. This means that the time savings for commercial OSBI might offset the financial benefits of community versions.

In terms of differences, the ability to access source code enables future customization that extends beyond what traditional offerings can provide. Even free trials and solution offerings are limited beyond what OS can provide. However, commercial offerings are not free. What this really implies is that commercial OS and free software are not comparable, at least not in the way of development capabilities. Consequently, the development process of commercial environments will resemble traditional BI offerings.

Comparing traditional software offerings and developer roles

The reality is that irrespective of the solution choice, developer involvement is still required. The breadth of involvement will differ, however, and potentially to a great extent. Traditional software offerings require developer involvement as a way to ensure that the technical considerations are being accounted for. Within OS initiatives, this ends up being a more involved role encompassing actual design, customization, development, and the like. Some of the differences are highlighted below and can help organizations move beyond financial considerations when looking at whether to select OS over a traditional BI offering. These include:

- Pre-built solutions versus the need to develop. With organizations looking at cost and time to value as key decision factors, the fact remains that in today's marketplace traditional offerings that enable BI out of the box are better poised to get solutions up and running more quickly. Therefore, if organizations are looking for quick times to implement, then traditional offerings might provide more value; after all, businesses cannot expect to get everything out of one solution and may need to evaluate the trade-offs of the extra time it takes to develop applications using OS. This involves looking at the time it takes to design and create offerings and estimate whether this extra time offsets the costs completely or enough to justify this time-cost balance. In addition, organizations need to evaluate the time to customize traditional solutions and balance that with OS developer involvement.
- Managing solution development and delivery. For organizations managing solutions from the business side, traditional offerings enable business decision makers to use professional services to manage the process. IT staff will still be required to provide insights into data collection and algorithm design, but their resources will not be needed on a broader basis. Traditional offerings, therefore, enable BI to be implemented without the reliance on IT to manage and maintain these offerings from the onset of project initiation.
- Time to develop. As discussed, time to develop is a factor that is sometimes overlooked because of the offset of lower software costs and acquisitions. But the time to develop offerings will differ from a few months to many months, making the scope of the project just as important as general financial considerations. And depending on these factors, development roles may be similar irrespective of the type of solution chosen, especially when commercial OS offerings are selected. Community projects may involve more time but may result in similar efforts when comparing potential integration and customization issues that arise.
- Project sponsorships (in general, the differences between business and IT sponsorships). In many cases, traditional BI implementations are shifting towards being managed by business units. In these cases, developer involvement can be kept to a minimum. OS projects, and specifically community ones, differ. Generally, these projects are more likely to be sponsored by IT departments and involve much more developer involvement. Organizations need to make sure that the right developers are managing the initiative in terms of having project management skills in addition to development efforts.

Awareness of future commercial OSBI focus

Even though OS is a market within itself, the reality is that different vendors place emphasis on different aspects of OS. The traditional definition of OS in relation to BI remains providing free source code to developers. In addition to this, community collaboration, version control, quick timing for bug fixes, etc., are the aspects that many people are most aware of. But vendors also have individual roadmaps and strategic goals that align with their goals of increasing revenues and expanding market share. Although individual to each vendor, these may include:

- Expansion of commercial offerings. Many OSBI vendors have slowly shifted towards more traditional BI models. This is most obvious in the push towards commercial offerings. This creates greater symmetry between OS and traditional BI models. In general, OS has influenced the broader BI marketplace as well. Not only is OS starting to mimic traditional BI offerings, the same occurs the other way as well. For instance, we can see this in the fact that many BI vendors now offer free trials or limited access to their software based on certain restrictions, but for free. OS is slowly shifting in the other direction. Over time, these solutions will start to resemble traditional offerings more and more. The implications of this are broad because the integrity of OS can be lost when shifted towards a monetary-focused venture.

- Less community development support. As transitioning toward commercial OS takes resources away from community development, these solutions are likely to become less community-centric over time. Obviously, OS will always include a level of community involvement, but depending on the available resources, this focus will be limited due to research and development budgets, etc. In terms of support, OS already has a two-tiered approach with more detailed support for paying customers. As this transition towards commercial continues, these gaps between paid and unpaid may continue to grow. Although unique to the solution deployed, organizations need to understand these differences and how it will apply to their specific project. To identify the future focus and support interactions, it becomes important to discuss any concerns directly with vendors. Obviously, this does not mean that support will not be available anymore, just limited to specific community involvement.

- Separation of community and commercial product roadmaps. As commercial OS offerings start to take hold within the marketplace, more of an effort will be placed on developing these solutions to target the needs of paying customers. In some cases, this might lead to divergent product sets, or in other cases, solutions might be developed with different goals or time frames in mind. Most customers, whether community or commercial, will either not initially be affected or will not notice. However, implications arise when looking at longer term deployments. As developers, you need to ask whether the goal is to continue with community development and internal customizations or whether the company will eventually transition towards commercial OS. If this is the case, it becomes important to identify what potential differences will exist in the future in order to make these transitions simpler in terms of integration and migration requirements. As long as both types of solutions are similar this might not be an issue. Once community and commercial BI offerings are handled individually, transitions towards one model or the other might include additional hardware and/or software requirements.

- Transitioning free users towards becoming paid customers. One of the main purposes of commercial OS is to monetize offerings and increase profit margins. This means that community customers are viewed as potential paying customers even though the rates of transformation are small. Aside from a development focus on commercial versions from the vendors themselves, this focus creates an environment whereby there is a continual effort at up-selling customers and providing added value by subscribing to services. This has implications in the way of customer relationships and focus on development by potentially creating a disparate set of offerings making a two-tiered approach to OSBI.

- The convergence of free. The BI market is at a crossroads. As mentioned, traditional vendors are starting to offer free solutions, with OS software offerings transitioning towards commercial offerings based on traditional BI models. What all of this leads to is more free applications, broader BI adoption, and fewer differentiations between OS and traditional BI solutions. For vendors moving into the realm of commercial OS, this blurs the lines between community OS, free trial versions, and traditional BI. For software vendors expanding their offerings towards commercial OS, it may become more confusing for organizations to identify which free offerings are most beneficial and what transitioning to commercial OSBI will mean for their company now and in the future.

Free software access without source code

Most OS offerings are similar, but some differ in small ways — and one in particular, providing OS without access to source code. Therefore, some vendors pass themselves off as OS but do not provide source code to their customers. They do, however, offer free solutions and community access. The issues surrounding this include the ability for organizations evaluating software solutions to understand the differences and the implications of selecting an OS offering without direct source code access. Looking at data warehousing as an example (i.e., Ingres), this means organizations can optimize their data warehousing environments but need to stay within the confines of the OS vendor. Whether this differs from traditional data warehousing environments remains to be seen. Aside from cost differentiators, organizations should identify the differences related to features and performance. After all, aside from initial costs, it might not be enough, depending on the overall benefits and challenges.

With so many trial versions and free offerings on the market that offer free limited access to solutions free of charge, developers need to understand the differences and their implications. Obviously, there are the general solution choices that organizations need to make that might push a company to select OS versus a traditional data warehouse solution. The differences should be discussed at length because in some cases OS integration may be a better option.

Support available to developers

By looking at community and commercial opportunities, it can be seen that there are different support levels available to developers, depending on the type of interaction with the OS environment. Based on the flexibility that exists, developers can define the levels of support they require or want over time. In some cases, this might include more than one of the following, while in others developers my use little support beyond the documentation available online. However, based on general flexibility, organizations can negotiate with the vendor to create their own support package. This obviously will be on an as-needed basis or based on the project, but the potential does exist on a broader level.

The following lists covers general support options and how they can benefit developers:

- Commercial BI. Support options within commercial OSBI offerings can be as different and diverse as the number of solutions that exist. Normally, OSBI vendors develop support packages that are similar to their traditional BI counterparts. The overall goal is to provide general support that is included within the subscription fees. In other cases, support structures may be similar to traditional BI offerings. Either way, support comes in the guise of maintenance, technical support, etc. Generally, IT developers do not always require or want the additional support, but do when dealing with multiple projects.
- Training. Training comes in different levels — online, in-house, manuals, etc. Depending on the project and resources, the type of training required will be different. In some cases, organizations pay to have consultants come in-house to help develop initial applications or to work side-by-side with in-house IT developers. When looking to get solutions up and running quickly, this is probably the best way to do so effectively while learning the appropriate skillsets. However, in most cases this is not realistic. For most companies, in-class training or learning online ends up being the best way to get IT developers up to speed on the skills required.
- Documentation. OSBI vendors are well known for creating documentation on every aspect of development and making it available to developers free of charge. This documentation comes in handy when developing solutions independently and when trying to customize current offerings. In addition, this increases the ability to transfer projects between developers without having to conduct additional training. Documentation is generally kept up to date and makes it easy for those starting off or learning the intricacies of specific solutions to do so.
- Community support. This option represents the broadest way to access support without having to access formalized training programs. We've discussed community OS options, advantages, and challenges throughout this book. The reality is that support is similar in nature to collaboration. Many organizations collaborate with each other to help one another through difficulties. Alternatively, support forums can provide feedback on issues in real-time, eliminating the additional time it takes to wait for formalized support emails, etc.

Community involvement and vendor differences

In general, most OS communities are fairly similar. Access to documentation, support, forums, source code customizations, and development opportunities abound. The main differences among vendor involvement is similar to those involved in vendor development efforts. What this means is that solution providers that are in charge of their own development will be more directly involved in the community, whereas others might keep up to date and have specific resources dedicated to their community but not with the same amount of interaction. Although each vendor will differ slightly, most will be quite similar in relation to their involvement but most of the differences will coincide with the level of community commitment and product development.

Collaboration with other developers

As discussed throughout this book, many developers work with one another to develop solutions for their customers. And aside from multiple developers within the same organization, developers also collaborate across organizations to share resources in order to produce similar end results. One of the benefits of OS is the lack of proprietary restrictions and the outlook in relation to sharing ideas. This outlook enables disparate organizations to save time by pooling resources with a variety of skillsets and experience to work on customizing certain aspects of source code.

The implications of access to diverse resources and outside access to developers should speak for itself. Many companies select OS based on low costs because of a lack of budgetary resources. Consequently, access to outside resources provides these organizations with the ability to develop solutions that might otherwise be out of their reach due to limited resources − in terms of budgets, time constraints, and available resources. Because many IT projects are going on at one time, the ability to expand access to developers and collaborate on projects lets smaller organizations take part in these projects as well. The real challenge that exists is in finding the right resources and companies working on similar projects in order to collaborate on efforts. Luckily, the community provides access points to collaborative initiatives. Aside from that, companies can then break down project areas and only work on the areas that most benefit them.

In addition, larger solution providers also collaborate on projects to take advantage of their expertise. For instance, Oracle's involvement with MySQL extends its bandwidth and overall support. Other projects may include actual development efforts based on industry or niche use. In these cases, organizations can identify their area of expertise and apply it to the appropriate part of the project without extending internal resources to the max.

The ability to collaborate with developers across industries, companies, and business unit focus is something that rarely occurs with proprietary solution providers. Many organizations look at BI as a way to get broader insights into what is happening within their organization. Collaboration through OS adoption can actually widen that to include gaining broader insights into market trends and how to apply them. This can be a key consideration for businesses looking at collaborative possibilities to extend potential feature and functionality sets. In essence, collaboration for companies without the need for additional resources can still help provide insights into areas that may not have been considered within the organization.

Participating in vendor software development

The amount of participation and flexibility available actually depends on the solution selected. OS communities are similar in their broad availability of direct access to source code (at least in most cases) and interactivity. Developers can solve problems and collaborate on issues and initiatives. At the same time, some vendors use outside developers to help enhance their solution offerings. In general, there are three categories of vendor direction in relation to how solutions are developed. Each has different implications for your involvement and potential role as a developer and the type of input you may have in relation to broader application scope and software direction. The three categories are broken down as follows:

- Vendors that retain internal developers and remain the key resources for software development. Some vendors have dedicated developers on staff who are responsible for software development and actualizing the product roadmap. In these cases, customer desires will be taken into account based on the amount of interest in specific areas. But development efforts will be managed and driven by internal efforts. For instance, SpagoBI is a good example of a vendor that has an internal development team. In addition, because they focus their revenue on BI projects, their development is directly tied to the projects they are involved in. Therefore, their development efforts are managed in-house with dedicated developers who are focused on making sure their solutions best meet their client base. SpagoBI is one of the few solution providers that base their revenue on consulting projects. Therefore, its development efforts are based on customizing its OS offerings to meet customer needs.

- Vendors that use community resources to collaborate on development efforts. Many OS solution providers base their development efforts on community initiatives and identify the types of projects being collaborated on. Based on community involvement, changes posted are incorporated into new feature sets as additions to the overall product line. In some cases, this means taking projects on the community site and adding popular feature sets to the overall product offerings. This way of product development provides the highest level of interactivity and developer control over product development. In many cases, organizations collaborate on mutual projects, as do disparate vendors, to develop strategic solutions within their organizations can be worked on by multiple developers to develop similar solutions. Aside from utilizing a broader skillset, the financial and time requirements are also shared by multiple entities, making larger projects more efficient and financially beneficial and/or lucrative. Also, depending on the popularity, vendors can integrate these new modules into their broader solution offerings.

- Vendors that develop solutions on their own but that take into account the needs of key customers when enhancing their offerings and providing advancements in features and functionality. This type of development actually takes the best of both worlds into account in the sense that vendors work with internal developers to enhance their product offerings but also identify the aspects worth developing based on their customer projects. Although this doesn't differ too much from the first item in this list, in some cases this development limits itself to what commercial customers are working on. In many cases, this strategy will be good enough in relation to additional features, while in others it may fall short, with the outcome depending on the disparate interests of community versus commercial customer bases.

Upgrades, bug fixes, and the list goes on

One of the most beneficial aspects of OS involvement remains the quick times to develop and broaden product functionality. The reasons are obvious and based on the fact that so much interactivity exists in addition to multiple levels of developer involvement. What this means is that vendors are well poised to take advantage of community and developer involvement in relation to project involvement. In many cases, this means taking stock of customer priorities in relation to what best suits both vendor and customer needs. Whether developing new offerings or enhancing current product features and functions, the fact remains that OS offerings are more likely to provide upgrades, bug fixes, and new innovations on a more timely basis than their traditional counterparts.

Based on the continual community involvement, whether in development efforts or through support inquiries, OSBI vendors have access to what is happening within customer sites without having to develop elaborate support packages or training courses. The community bridges any communication difficulties by providing resources and a collaborative environment that can be used as a way to enhance the customer experience and help vendors understand what is important to their customers.

Because the BI market is constantly changing, organizations want to be able to take advantage of new features without being limited by technology limitations. The ability for vendors to do this quickly makes product adoption more likely and enables OS proponents to develop solutions that match the overall goals of OS. Basically, one of the goals of OS is to empower developers with the ability to develop the best possible solutions for their organizations without being limited by proprietary roadblocks. Access to multiple companies' BI projects helps solution providers see the BI landscape more broadly and gives them the ability to identify the most common trends and, product gaps and to create the necessary links to bring developer BI to the next level.

Bug fixes and time to solve issues represent the secondary benefits of OS community development efforts. Organizations interact with the community to solve their challenges, making it easy to identify what bugs or product limitations exist. Consequently, they can create fixes at a much quicker rate than their traditional counterparts due to their access to a broader range of clients and projects. Overall, what this means is that organizations looking for more dynamic development and a focus on continual growth that is timely and occurs more quickly than many traditional BI solutions may prefer working within an OS environment.

Looking ahead at developer requirements

Everything discussed within this chapter is really the tip of the iceberg. The details involved in building up OSBI applications are not always as simple as stated, as there are many details and in-depth steps involved in creating a functional and valuable application. But the aspects above identify what you need to know to get started. For more detailed information you can always consult detailed user guides to get you from the starting line through implementation.

Required skillsets

IT-related projects are known to have high failure rates. Some estimates are as high as 80% and obviously depend upon how failure is being defined. Looked at more broadly, failure can come in the way of missed deadlines, overstretched budgets, scope changes that cannot be met based on the chosen solution, etc. The reality is that the list is endless and can encompass any aspect related to a project that you can think of. And although it is impossible to ensure project success, having the right people with the right skillsets can actually help ensure that projects go more smoothly.

Many of the skillsets required to help build a successful BI framework will overlap whether working on a traditional BI project or whether adopting OSBI. After all, all IT-related projects require a specific level of planning and project management. Since there are a plethora of books that already exist on the subjects of project planning and project management, there is little reason to delve very deeply into these topics. Consequently, we will focus our efforts on technical and business-related skills that shouldn't be overlooked when developing an OSBI environment with the goal of ensuring project success and a strong BI framework.[1]

Let's start by looking at some of the required technical skills that should be considered. Then we will identify the business-related expertise required. It actually makes sense to develop a checklist and to ensure that you can check all of the boxes and make sure that these resources are accounted for.

Technical skills

As mentioned above, a multiple number of skills are required to complete a successful OSBI project. The reality within many companies is that for OS projects, the key resources deployed are those within the IT department. Whether managing the project, developing it, conducting testing, or gathering requirements, because of the amount of effort required to tweak BI source code, IT departments tend to provide end-to-end project management. What this means for many IT directors or CIOs is that their internal resources are required to possess a number of skills that reflect

---

[1]As a disclaimer, I am not saying that you are guaranteed success by utilizing all of the skillsets mentioned, simply that your organization is more likely to see success if you plan your BI project properly and include all the various types of resources needed to help get you there.

both IT-related and business-oriented needs and to understand both parts of the organization and how they are structured.

Many of the skills discussed may help you with other IT projects and some will be specific to OSBI. All are important when developing a project plan and making sure that individual and group tasks are performed. Wherever possible I will highlight the aspects that relate specifically to OS projects and where the skillsets can and should be applied more broadly. The only place this will be valid is within the technical skills section. Business aspects will reflect BI projects more broadly but can help provide a set of guidelines to IT staff who are tasked with managing BI projects more broadly and beyond the scope of development-related activities.

Java Programming

The most obvious skill discussed in relation to developers of OS projects is the ability to program in Java. In terms of technical skills and the ability to develop community OS offerings, this cannot be overlooked. Before businesses make the decision to select an OSBI solution, they should make sure their internal developers have the relevant skills and can read through source code and make the needed changes.

For organizations that do not possess this skillset but that want to take advantage of OSBI, here are the alternative ways to develop or acquire this skillset internally:

- Take the time to learn Java programming skills. Many skills are transferable, including those of developers. Obviously, each programming language is unique, but the more familiar programmers are with broader environments, the more likely they can learn Java to develop solutions internally. And when this is not possible, organizations dedicated to OS development need to be open to taking the time to provide education to their staff. The implications of this are twofold. Firstly, taking into account additional learning curves means increasing the project timelines and overall development times – in essence, lessening the ability to develop solutions quickly. Secondly, over time, maintenance can be managed internally, which can save future costs in relation to external resources or professional services that are no longer required.
- Hire new staff. For businesses not wanting to take time to develop extra/new skillsets internally, there is always the possibility of looking outside the organization to find a Java developer who can be used as a dedicated resource to develop BI solutions. In this case, one of the places to look is within the community itself to identify potential candidates. In some cases, it might even be possible to outsource on a per project basis, or to share developers with another organization working on a similar project.
- Go commercial. Whether or not OSBI offerings are really less expensive than newer traditional counterparts, more organizations are looking at commercial OSBI offerings as a valid alternative to traditional BI solutions. And many commercial offerings provide the ability to change source code but don't require it. This means that businesses can implement solutions in a way similar to how they would within a traditional implementation. Many companies that select commercial OSBI offerings still customize their own solutions but enjoy the added

support available. Consequently, organizations may be looking for the best of both worlds but will still require the Java skills to customize commercial offerings or to collaborate on broader projects.

- General professional services. Within OS projects the best way to develop solutions is to have the required skillsets in-house. However, if this is not the case and if hiring new resources is not possible, organizations can look to outside consultants or vendor professional services. In some of these cases, professional services can include training to enable future customization and development to take place in-house.

IT project management

In some cases organizations overlook the soft skills required to successfully manage any IT or BI project. But the reality is that to manage the tasks involved in a BI project, a project manager is needed. Because high failure rates exist, project management and following some sort of project lifecycle is a key step within any BI initiative. In larger businesses, individual IT project managers exist that may be allocated based on project type. In smaller businesses, the developers themselves may be tasked with managing the project throughout its lifecycle. Even though planning takes time away from developing solutions, gathering requirements, or testing, understanding what will be done when and who is responsible for each task makes it easier to identify and deal with issues proactively.

Projects that are no longer on track can be identified. With proper management, the whys behind the reasons can be established to identify who is responsible, how it will be handled, and what the implications are. Whether budgetary, time, or other, with proper management expectations can be set and reset as needed. In addition, many projects are shelved after much effort and many resources are placed without proper understanding of where things went wrong or how to pick up where things have been left off at a later date. Management from the start helps eliminate this or at least lessen the chances of this occurring.

Network and database optimization

Not all data warehouses or database solutions are created equally. Because performance has been optimized over the years, and with a continued focus on Big Data, there seems to be a general misconception that any database will function successfully as a data warehouse. This is not the case.[2] Targeted solutions exist that address specific business challenges. Some are suited to data storage while others address real-time analytics, and some provide the ability to simplify data complexities. The reality for OS projects is a little bit different. Although OS data warehousing solutions exist, the reality is that many developers will select general databases such as MySQL and optimize them to suit data warehouse functionality. Although a valid way to deploy BI, the fact is that this choice requires appropriate support to manage over the long term.

---

[2]It should be strongly noted that not all solutions are created equally. We've discussed this earlier in the book, but the selection of the right data warehouse for your organization can actually make or break an OSBI project based on the fact that it might not be able to perform as desired depending on the business and data requirements.

When transforming databases into functional data warehouses, specific considerations are required. This means that when looking at specific skillsets for data warehousing development and optimization, resources should have a good grasp of the following areas and how to optimize their OSBI environments:

- Data latency. Depending on required data access, considerations regarding timeliness and data refreshes should be looked at. Projects addressing one business pain may only require one type of data update, but for broader initiatives, different departmental needs may require individual latency based on differing data sets or specific metrics. Understanding the requirements in advance helps define the type of design that is required. For instance, not all data warehouse solutions are able to stream operational data in real-time. In many cases this won't be a requirement, but with the increasing trend towards operational BI, in some cases it might be. Either way, understanding data latency and the architecture that is required to manage various latency requirements relates directly to the development and implementation of a data warehouse infrastructure. The skills required for understanding the nuances between functionality and delivery are essential to ensure valid design.

- Data volumes. The amount of data and number of data sources may affect delivery times. Depending on the type of data warehouse structure, times to process millions of rows of data may differ. Columnar databases are known to help optimize analytics delivery by processing query requests differently. In addition to these considerations, resources require an understanding of how volumes over time will affect the current design. This includes the ability to support this growth over time.

- Data sources. In many cases, projects start with 5–10 data sources, but this number may grow over time. When this happens, the way in which integration processes are conducted may change and performance may suffer. In order to make sure that solutions and transitions within projects are successful, organizations require IT resources with the ability to continually optimize the environment without affecting delivery and performance.

- Analytics delivery. Combining latency requirements and analytics capabilities leads to actual delivery. In addition to the time required to access information, considerations including in-memory and data virtualization to provide on-the-fly query processing should be looked at to identify whether these analytical capabilities are required.

- SLAs and expectations. What all of the preceding factors lead to are expectations. IT project managers should address expectations at the beginning of an OSBI initiative to identify what is realistic versus what is simply a nice feature to have. In many cases, because OSBI projects are selected due to lower price points and budgetary constraints, there may be limitations in what can be provided to end users, at least in the beginning.

- Broader IT infrastructure. Usually data warehouses represent a subset of servers within the organization. Based on what already exists in-house, standards, and limitations due to integration, it is important to select and develop a data warehousing framework that works well within the current IT infrastructure. In some cases, this might mean utilizing proprietary hardware/software combinations or ensuring that adequate space is allocated within current servers to perform data warehousing functions until projects expand and require their own servers to operate.

Metrics and analytics development

In addition to having business users who understand business rules and how the processes within their organization work, it is also essential to identify how to translate these business requirements into algorithms within the structure of the OSBI solution to develop front-end analytics and metrics. In many cases, looking at source code and spreadsheet calculations can provide a good basis for new development efforts. However, without understanding the business rules behind this, most development efforts will require a large amount of rework.

Although BI applications are constantly changing to address the competitive needs of the organization, IT departments want to deliver targeted solutions to their end users. The quicker this can be done, the better business units are able to get up and running with their analytics and general BI use. By working together, IT and business units can develop solutions that take into account the relevant business rules. This, is turn, creates the ability to develop analytics and metrics that meet initial business needs without all of the rework.

Obviously, any IT developer working on an OSBI project will have the skillsets required to gather these requirements and identify additional business rules. The issue involves deciding who wants to take responsibility and be the interface with the relevant business units. Not all IT developers want to take time away from their development efforts to interview business users. Many larger organizations have dedicated business analysts to act as intermediaries between business units and IT resources. This same reality doesn't exist for many smaller organizations. In these cases, the person required for this position should be one that can bridge the gaps between business pains, general business processes, and technology delivery.

Data modeling

Although not all projects require formalized data modeling, many still do. Either way, it is an important skill to consider. For projects that do not require formalized data models or data mart design, you might still want to look at internal staff with data modeling experience as a substitute for business rules and processes experience. The reasoning behind this is that in many cases, companies with data modelers on hand have experience with these types of projects. In addition, these data modelers will most likely have the required skillsets and business knowledge discussed within the business skillset section. With this being said, it is still important to understand that not all solutions require modeling expertise. The key benefit, however, is that data modelers generally have a good understanding of the interrelationship of many data access points and the data rules that come out of general business processes.

Traditional BI solutions generally require some type of data modeling. This might include actual data mart design, if the process is not automated, or being able to map data relationships from the source systems and translate requirements to the new BI solution. Each OSBI offering will differ slightly and so will the work involved, depending on the solution choice and type of delivery (for instance, reporting versus dashboards or advanced analytics). Also of note is that within the data modeling spectrum a variety of skills might be required, either those transferred from other roles or those based on individual solution choice. And although transferable, it should be noted that these differences might also require a slight learning curve to get up to speed.

Data integration

It is important to remember that even if someone is used to developing software programs, his or her strengths may lie outside of data integration activities. Some of the skills to look for are as follows, with some of these being soft skills or desired experience:

- Flexibility to follow disparate procedures. Each solution choice may have different requirements to load and transform data, and not all ETL developers are equally well versed in diverse environments. Organizations should make sure that skills match the requirements of the solution. Although probably not an issue within an OS environment, it is important to remember that developers will have different experiences and that there should be developed to ensure that ETL procedures are handled in the same way for any given project. These procedures, however, might differ based on solution choice.
- ETL experience. Although fairly obvious, it helps if the person or people involved have knowledge and experience with ETL. If not, be prepared for a longer learning curve. Luckily, OS communities have detailed documentation to help with the process.
- Understanding the value of data quality. The importance of data quality cannot be underestimated. Initial BI implementations may be okay not looking at data quality in-depth, but as projects become more complicated and as data sources and complexity increase, quality becomes an issue. Either the resource chosen should have data quality experience or understand its value and look for ways to incorporate data quality management within the data integration process. This is not as easy as it sounds, as it takes extra time and money. Therefore, additional budget and sponsor backing may be required.

Obviously, other skills are important within data integration, and the depth and breadth required for strong data integration could take up a chapter or book of its own, but these are simply some of the general considerations to remember when selecting resources to manage or perform the processes required to load and prepare data.

Business skills

Looking at the business skillsets required as part of the project development and design are essential for anticipated project success. Many OS projects are IT-focused due to the large amount of work required related to internal development efforts and the IT skillsets required to develop and deliver applications to the business. However, without an adequate understanding of business requirements, internal politics, and the business rules that apply to data and business processes, the overall system design can only go so far.

The skills discussed below are those that will benefit any OSBI project — whether a new one or an ongoing expansion. One of the key points to remember is that these skills may be encompassed by many people or by few, may require involvement from many departments, or may represent a specific role within the organization. Either way, the business aspect of any OSBI project needs to be taken seriously. Both technical and business sides of the coin bring unique characteristics to a project. The more cohesion that exists between the two, the more likely that solutions will be developed to the appropriate specifications during the first iteration. And because of the fact that BI use is constantly changing, collaborative efforts help longer term development efforts as well.

A note about commercial offerings: In many cases, the ways in which community and commercial solutions are deployed differ. In some cases, community OS projects are developed based on budgetary constraints or current in-house expertise, with commercialization coming as part of a solution expansion. In other cases, OS ends up as a criteria within a software evaluation. For organizations looking at commercial OSBI solutions, the requirements of internal developers to create solutions may not be as much of a consideration as it is in community development because solutions are delivered in much the same way as traditional software offerings. In these cases, business sponsors and managers may be more involved in the process of defining business requirements and delivery. Even for solutions that might not require large IT development input, collaboration is still important based on the fact that as time goes on, it is likely that these solutions will be supported by in-house resources.

Business requirements

Business requirements refer to the features and functions required for the final product. For instance, a help desk requires the ability to manage calls, close rates, network issues, service levels, etc. Within sales and marketing, employees need to understand how sales break down by region, product, and the like. In addition, business units need to understand where they fall short and why. For marketers, this may mean looking at how campaigns are transforming into sales or how online reviews are affecting performance. On top of this, there are lead generation programs, social media outlets, and the age-old mailings. All of these need to be managed to identify which initiatives work best and what the outcomes are. Therefore, gathering business requirements requires knowledge of all of the areas being covered within a BI project.

Because these requirements interrelate, in many cases more than one person is required for a broader understanding of the business requirements. Sales and marketing represent a good example of how disparate departments interrelate. Marketing helps drive sales and needs to have an understanding of how sales works to develop successful campaigns. Both sales and marketing require in-depth knowledge of customer demographics and products. In terms of business requirements gathering, the level of involvement and identifying who is responsible will depend on various factors. For instance, depending on the situation one resource might be all that is required, but in many other cases many people will need to be interviewed in order to get an overall picture of how people do their jobs, what the processes are, and how tasks are divvied up among employees.

Overall, developing strong business requirements and making sure that the right requirements are gathered means learning the business, understanding which tasks need to take place and where they fit within the overall process, and knowing that sales metrics identification means not only identifying the fields where sales resides, but also requires an understanding of what everything that exists within a database means and how information interrelates to create valid and accurate metrics.

Business unit interrelationships

Selecting who will represent a department or group within an OSBI project means identifying those resources that understand the business best. This involves looking at several factors:

- Overall tasks. Understanding overall tasks means knowing what the individual role is as well as knowing how specific tasks relate to others. For example, within accounting and finance operations, each person has his or her own tasks and responsibilities, but closing at month end requires a series of steps to be finalized. And subsequent steps need to approved before the next one can start. The interrelation of these tasks becomes essential when looking at the metrics that are essential and any collaborative features that should be included. And even though this may seem simple, the reality is that not all employees know how the broader departmental tasks relate to the broader business implications. Forecasting and planning are areas that also relate to sales, products, and customer-related data, making it essential for people addressing these areas to have a broader knowledgebase.
- Business rules. These relate to the rules associated with how things work. For instance, in order to close at month end, the following eight steps need to occur. Step five may be bypassed even if the preceding step is not yet finalized. In relation to metrics, business rules help define the algorithms by looking at the calculations that are required to create the appropriate analytics. In some cases, this includes complex algorithms that are developed by IT based on the input from business, and in other cases, these business rules and calculations already exist within current spreadsheet or analytics applications.
- Business processes. The business processes put these factors together. In essence, they provide a broader view of how individual departments work and what that means for the broader organization. On a high level, this requires an understanding of how each department works at a management level and how that relates to other departments. A good example remains the interrelationship between sales and marketing and the overlap of data that is required to enable both departments to run smoothly.
- Interdepartmental collaboration. Not only is it important to understand how an individual department works, but it is also important to have input from related departments. If an organization is interested in marketing analytics, understanding the workings of sales-based data can help ensure that the proper metrics are being identified and developed. After all, each business unit will have its own intricacies, and to capture data properly it is essential to have a broader understanding of how other data is managed across the organization as it relates to the specific project.

Business sponsor

Several years ago, most BI projects were managed from IT departments, with CIOs backing most projects as part of their cost centers. As BI has become more business-focused, this level of support is continuing to shift towards business-backed initiatives. Consequently, many CFOs or other C-level executives are in charge of backing the project. Generally, this means that the budgetary allocations are from a specific department and many of the initiatives start with this department's business needs. Whether this is or isn't the case, for OSBI initiatives, having business sponsorship is an aspect that should not be overlooked.

Because OSBI (at least the community-led projects) are highly focused on IT development efforts, there are bigger risks associated with adoption and delivery. In some cases, when affected business units are not involved roll out is not accepted and employees choose to use what they currently have. This definitely shows one area of project failure that does not have to occur. In addition, although IT developers may have most of the information they require based on their ability to search through source code and have access to multiple data sets, there are always additional business rules or tweaks that are required by business units to create a more accurate picture. Creating targeted analytics applications that address these intricacies means identifying the appropriate person to do so. In many cases, this involves getting the approval of a business unit manager that will act as a business sponsor to ensure involvement within the initiative.

Business rules expertise

We have discussed the importance of business rules so will not spend too much time reviewing them. However, there are a few additional factors that should be kept in mind when looking at the expertise involved in business rules identification. Because business rules end up translating into the calculations used for defined metrics and other analytical analyses, they may be one of the most important aspects for IT developers to have. Understanding different roles and responsibilities helps IT navigate the company better, but being able to access resources who understand the math behind the business processes is valuable for metrics and analytics identification, management, development, and general testing.

In essence, business rules are the links between business requirements and how they get translated into technical requirements. The better the understanding of the rules behind the underlying data, the more likely BI development will be suited to the overall requirements of the end users. Although fairly obvious, many systems analysts feel that collecting the business requirements without gaining a broader understanding of the underlying business rules is enough. The reality is that the collection of business rules alone only provides the first glimpse into how information will be processed and analyzed. The value of business rules identification remains the ability to translate that data into strategic analytics.

Navigating the political maze

Unfortunately, most if not all organizations experience a level of politics involved in getting things done. In many large enterprises, disparate departments do not want to share information outside of their business unit irrespective of the privacy level associated with that data. In others, there is no communication whatsoever. To ensure project success, communication is essential. Although overstated and a pretty simple concept, the reality is that most projects overlook the obvious and the connections that exist between business entities. The ability to understand this and find the right resources is essential.

Politics can also exist within IT itself or as part of other departments. In addition, not everyone assigned to the project will be a willing participant. IT needs to know how to deal with difficult employees who fail to share information and who don't want to participate in the project. Knowing how to handle all of these potential issues can help further the project along as opposed to creating stumbling blocks along the way.

Another political roadblock may exist when business sponsorship exists within a single department but when the BI solution expands across the organization. In some cases, if the department backing the project is IT, then this issue may be eliminated. In other cases, business units need to share resources and identify which aspects fall under each department. This means that whoever is tasked with navigating through political issues needs to understand how each department works, who is in charge, and what the goals are. Overall, this may be the most difficult role to help manage any BI initiative − not just OS ones.

Tying it all together

Although several skillsets have been discussed in relation to OSBI initiatives, organizations will find that individual people can fill many roles, making smaller projects or fewer resources more manageable. In reality, who is involved in any given project from the business side will differ based on the type and scale of project. Expansions may be treated differently than a new OSBI initiative. Either way, businesses need to understand how all of these roles fit together to provide the project support that extends beyond IT development efforts and towards successful implementation and strategic BI adoption.

Technical benefits and challenges 17

Many developers will tell you that they prefer OS because of its flexibility and ease of development.[1] Obviously this depends on their previous development experience and expertise but, in essence, for those looking for more flexibility and general support, OS provides a positive development experience. However, even with developers' love of OS development, there are still a series of technically related benefits and challenges that exist. Therefore, a final decision should not always rest on the comfort of the developer, as a wider variety of implications exist.

In some situations, developers might not have a say in the type of offering they select. For instance, when looking at the value of BI and how to integrate its use within the organization, IT developers may be told to evaluate OS or make sure that solutions evaluated include OS whether or not the technical skills exist in-house. In these cases, companies may be restricted by budget but do not mind the time it takes to build a solution from scratch. Without the autonomy to select the solution of choice, developers might be hard-pressed to identify all of the benefits of OSBI implementations.

Up until now, we've looked at the business benefits and some of the challenges of OS to provide an idea of what businesses can expect through OSBI adoption. These factors actually provide a strong connection between business unit and IT goals and show how both can get benefits out of these solutions. But there are additional technical considerations that might seem similar but that differ and only apply to technical resources within the organization. So how do business factors differ from developer requirements in terms of overall project perspective? Some of the ways are listed as follows:

- Technical goals extend beyond simple aspects of collaboration, flexibility in customizing code, etc., towards how these benefits apply to the technical architecture. Business goals, however, focus exclusively on increasing profits with the use of information as a supporting aspect.
- Collaborating on projects means more than sharing information and ideas. Developers work on features and functions and help each other on a more detailed level.
- Building solutions on an open framework benefits both the business and IT. The benefits for IT, however, are more relevant to longer term development. Only focusing on what needs to be integrated now does not benefit longer term projects. The ability to integrate solutions more broadly has implications that apply to BI expansions over time. In many cases, business sponsors will look at the immediate benefits, so a combination of technical and business expertise and involvement will help in creating a strategy that balances both.
- Deployment times are becoming an important factor when looking at implementing BI. In many cases, time to value is reflected in how quickly organizations get BI up and running. Often, OSBI offerings are thought to provide a quicker time to value. The reality for developers, however, is a different story due to the bigger development efforts required. In some cases

---

[1]This comment is based on interviewing multiple OS developers.

actual deployment times take longer because of the development requirements of building a solution with just access to OSBI source code.

- Many IT developers like the idea of OS because of the customization available. Because there are no restrictions on changes that can be made, businesses can have more targeted and unique BI applications. Business decision makers may like open source because of the lack of software expenditure but don't always care about customization as long as they have access to the feature set they desire at the end of the process.

Expanding on the differences in technical versus business benefits and challenges

As discussed in the introduction, technical resources and business decision makers look at BI differently and will see different benefits based on their different roles. In general, end users are focused on ease of use and financial outcomes. Answering questions that include how can we increase sales? Can we optimize our processes to help increase efficiencies and consolidate data? How do we forecast better? And what about ensuring compliance and privacy?

For technologists, the questions are different. IT departments are in charge of maintaining infrastructures and managing network resources, performance, and service levels, all the while developing and supporting business applications to meet the needs of all business units within the organization. And in some cases, this extends towards partners and customers as well due to the increase in online applications and access points. Because of this, it is very important for IT to understand how disparate technologies integrate, what efforts are required, and the flexibility that exists. A good example is the upsurge of cloud offerings that are becoming commonplace within OSBI solutions. From an IT perspective, not having to add new hardware represents a benefit that may be offset by limitations of subscription models based on data storage volumes or additional time required to integrate and upload data and turn it into a usable information.

The implications of these benefits highlight the continued difficulties that exist between IT and business units. After all, not all companies are able to collaborate on IT projects and take both sides into account. When it comes to OS adoption, the reality is that technical considerations become very important due to the heavy involvement of developers, whether for actual development, deployment, or support. Consequently, OSBI is one area that requires a strong focus on technical benefits and overall requirements.

Some of the aspects discussed in the remainder of this chapter have been looked at from the perspective of the business. The reality is that many of the benefits and challenges do overlap to a certain extent, but they are looked at in a different light and have different implications.

A look at the technical benefits of OSBI adoption

Let's take a look at some of the benefits realized by developers through OSBI adoption.

Open standards and integration

Before looking at integration requirements, it is important to define open standards and what they mean in this context. Although integration affects all IT projects and still provides challenges within an OSBI project, open standards exist to make solutions fit together more quickly. Basically, many consortiums exist with the goal of increasing the ease of integration among various data sources or within disparate industries. To do so requires a centralized body that develops a set of procedures to standardize integration requirements. This is becoming more common within many aspects of software solutions and other business initiatives. And OS is no different. The key benefit, however, remains that OS projects were built with this premise in mind. For instance, Java has its own organization called JCP (Java Community Process)[2] that manages the development of Java over time. This also exists on a broader level that includes how solutions integrate with one another through APIs.

Because Java applications are developed following the guidelines and procedures provided by the community body, broader integration becomes easier based on the fact that other offerings are able to integrate with Java more easily. Obviously this is not always the case, but for organizations interested in using OS more broadly across BI, the ability to integrate multiple platforms more natively helps create end-to-end BI solutions. A good example is the partnership between Jaspersoft and Talend. Talend is the built-in ETL and data integration tool used by Jaspersoft. Organizations do not have to search out their own data integration offerings because these offerings fit together natively. Traditional offerings provide these capabilities through many APIs, but a lot of preparation is still required to transform data into the right format for integration purposes.

Hardware costs

Implementing BI usually involves additional hardware considerations. Adding new data sources means utilizing additional storage. Many companies are already tapped out because they use hardware to store information from their ERP, CRM, operational, etc., type of systems and to process all of their transactions. Optimizing these systems for operational performance differs from analytics and requires a different way of storing information. This leads to the proliferation of data warehouse optimization for advanced analytics.

Therefore, most businesses do have to consider adding a separate data warehouse or specified data storage to support a new or expanded BI initiative. This means that setting up a database that captures an additional set of this type of information will, most likely, mean new hardware that can support various types of analytics and large amounts of data. Add to this expansion over time and data warehouses can become expensive to implement and to maintain.

The key advantage of new hardware requirements in relation to OS remains the ability to select hardware based on preference as opposed to being tied to specific servers or hardware vendors. Many proprietary offerings are built to work with a subset of offerings, all of which are more expensive than non-proprietary solutions. OS is not constrained by these limitations and can be less expensive over time because of this, thereby creating more value over time based on cost savings.

Customization potential

Although solutions are becoming more robust in terms of features and functions offered out of the box, organizations still require customizations to develop targeted solutions for their business units. OS enables broader development opportunities because of the freedom of OS

[2] http://jcp.org/en/home/index

access. Since we've already discussed this at length, the only thing that remains to be said is that OS enables more IT developer-targeted development and the freedom to design solutions.

More freedom to develop personalized solutions that work with current offerings/internal infrastructure can lead to solutions that better meet the needs of organizations. It should be noted, however, that because many offerings in the broader BI market are so flexible, organizations can also look at many mainstream BI offerings to implement solutions that are tailored to suit their needs. In many cases, however, developers prefer to control how they develop and maintain offerings based on their expertise and internal IT infrastructure, which is why many developers tend to prefer the freedom associated with OS development environments.

Collaboration

Collaborative efforts strongly relate to community involvement. From a technical standpoint, developers can take advantage of the community to work with others on similar projects. This may be across industries or departments, but collaboration enables organizations to take advantage of what has already been developed by others as well as potentially saving the company time and money. The following section discusses community involvement and expands on the importance of collaboration and how it can benefit overall OSBI development.

Community members

Today many vendors develop communities to interact with their customers. In many ways, these communities mimic what OS communities were built to accomplish. OS vendors have always had communities as drivers of their solutions. Even vendors that develop their solutions internally still use community to develop offerings and enhance products and services to users. For those using these offerings, some of the benefits include the ability to find like-minded developers with different skillsets, people who can provide a broader set of eyes for feedback on solutions being developed as well as better overall ideas. In addition, many larger vendors, such as IBM and Oracle, dedicate resources to OS projects that can help quicken development times for broader solution offerings.

For internal IT developers, the benefits of taking advantage of the community can translate into quicker development times and broader access to more resources. This is particularly beneficial for smaller organizations where internal IT resources are slim. In these cases, community members can interact with each other on like aspects of projects. This, in turn, can lessen overall development times and increase the time to value.

What about commercial OS and free software trials?

Commercial OS differs from community offerings. The reality is that with the transition towards more commercial offerings, these solutions are starting to have more in common with traditional BI offerings — from costs and capabilities all the way to platform. Many OSBI vendors are looking for ways to increase profits and expand their competitive edge within the broader BI marketplace. What this means for companies is that these solutions can potentially help drive other offerings down in terms of cost, but overall, increase the number of free trials to evaluate.

Several years ago, only OSBI offerings could be evaluated cost free. With the increase in popularity of these offerings, other vendors started developing free trials to enable developers and end users alike broader access to BI and analytics without initial expenditures. Now many vendors offer free trials or limited availability of their solutions. This shows the increasing influence of OS offerings within the industry. Because of this, developers can download solutions and test integration, maintenance, development, etc., to see how everything will fit within their IT environment. In addition, this can help IT developers identify what is required for broader deployments and the resources and potential hardware that may be needed.

The issue of support and proprietary limitations

Because many developers are used to creating their own solutions or customizing ineffective in-house applications, there may be very little thought to actually changing source code or the effects of doing so. When I worked as a business analyst for a large automotive firm, one of our projects involved implementing Cognos to replace an operational reporting environment that allowed business users to create their own reports, which were self-managed. In addition to being a strain on operational transactions and performance, and wanting to centralize and control data access, one of the reasons for transitioning to BI was that the solution would no longer be supported by the vendor. With all of the changes made to the source code and based on the hundreds to thousands of reports that were created, it became very difficult and time consuming to manage these changes. Overall, even the vendor felt that the costs outweighed the benefits of maintaining the customer over time.

What all of this illustrates is that for many traditional software solutions, the flexibility to change source code does not exist. IT developers can do it, but without the support from vendors. The implications of this are quite far reaching if a solution happens to break or performance issues occur. And in some cases, it is common for vendors to provide stipulations within their support contracts that remove them of culpability and support requirements should the source code be tampered with at any level. Even though some organizations may still choose to make the changes that suit them, many others do not want to risk what will happen if their system crashes and they are unable to meet business unit SLAs.

These restrictions do not exist within community OS options. In essence, the opposite is the case. Developers are expected to come up with better ways of doing things and developing better-targeted solutions for their end users. And because of this, IT developers feel that more flexibility exists because changes and additions to source code are expected as opposed to dissuaded. In addition, building customized solutions will be supported within a community OS environment, either by the community and other experts in the field or, alternatively, through paid support.

Weighing the benefits against the challenges

Up until now we've looked at all sorts of factors that, when combined, can help organizations make informed decisions as to whether or not OS technologies and BI specifically is a valid choice for their business. The technical benefits help delve further into this analysis by providing a broader look at whether or not OS offerings best meet your organization's BI needs. Combining the business benefits and challenges with technical considerations provides a full picture of what to consider.

There is no one solution that will meet all the needs of the organization. The most important thing for companies to do is to look at the benefits and weigh them against the challenges. This is why developing an RFI (Request for Information) and requesting a POC (Proof of Concept) are so important, as pre-defined demos do not identify targeted requirements or show decision makers and IT managers how the proposed OSBI offering supports corporate data. Obviously, this applies to commercial versions of OS offerings. Community versions allow IT developers to create their own POCs and test out the offerings.

At the same time, the amount of effort placed on this initial development may necessitate further adoption. Either way, the newer level of flexibility within OS offerings, including cloud computing, commercial software offerings, and broad integration, leads to solutions that can meet the needs of a wide range of organizations. The most important thing to remember is that no one solution will meet all of the needs of the company. Therefore, you need to develop a weighting system to identify the most important factors and how each solution meets the business's needs.

In terms of financial expenditures, many organizations select OS based on a no-to-low cost of entry. This alone is a bad business decision. As you may have noticed, aside from lower hardware costs, none of the technical benefits involve lower costs. In essence, costs should be a complementary factor and not a main one.

Understanding technical challenges

Technical challenges represent unique issues when looking at BI implementations. Issues surrounding IT development and maintenance are central to the success or failure of a BI project. Furthermore, even though many solutions are business-focused in terms of requirements gathering and delivery, the bones of any solution are its data infrastructure.

In addition to the adage "garbage in, garbage out," looking at technical challenges is even more important and moves beyond the data itself. Information needs to be stored, captured, transformed, loaded, joined, and the list goes on. Hardware needs to work with software to create an infrastructure that can handle the data and usage requirements. Consequently, the only way to develop a strong BI infrastructure is through IT development effort. Within OSBI this is even more important. Community projects require more time-intensive involvement of IT departments and management over the long haul. This higher level of involvement can also lead to greater challenges that should be addressed, hopefully beforehand in a proactive manner. And if not, at least companies and IT developers should understand potential stumbling blocks to identify how to handle them.

Overall, the general technical challenges include hardware and software limitations, how to develop a successful data management structure, linking OS with proprietary offerings, and developing time to value in a way that remains valuable to corporate decision makers. The following sections delve into the general challenges organizations may face but with a small caveat. Although we can surmise ways to address these challenges, no one way will work in each situation because of differences in structures, skills, and overall BI goals. But understanding what might be faced will prepare developers for potential issues.

What types of challenges exist?

Normally when discussing BI challenges and project failures, the discussion focuses on how business units and executives are affected. For instance, project failures may translate into lack of adoption, an initiative being shelved, or the solution being designed ineffectively. Alternatively, requirements may not be met the first time around, causing multiple iterations of reports and dashboards. This, in turn, leads to longer project times, more time spent in development, and costs increasing exorbitantly. All of these issues also mean that the role of the IT developer and the ability to translate development activities into easy-to-use applications that address business challenges are not easy. In essence, many organizations are unprepared to deal with the technical challenges they face during their BI implementations because of the continued focus on business requirements gathering. And although this aspect of any software development process is important, the reality is that once these are gathered, IT developers face the additional challenges of deploying solutions that are optimized for business use. Much of this optimization comes from knowing how to make diverse information systems work together. And how this happens can be different within OSBI development, depending on the solution being used.

Some of the challenges that are faced by developers include:

- The learning curve required to transfer from traditional programming languages, such as SQL, to OS developer environments.
- Managing OS projects and source code changes while supporting multiple developers' efforts simultaneously.
- Developing a broader data management environment, irrespective of solution limitations and BI goals.
- Integrating OSBI with traditional offerings — including integrating disparate data sources or creating embedded applications.
- Potential hardware limitations.
- Understanding OSBI source code and how it differs from traditional offerings.
- Transitioning to an OS environment.
- Time to value and community OS.

Potential learning curves in relation to programming languages

When looking at OS, two types of developers exist — those who are familiar with OS and those who are used to SQL-based and other proprietary environments.[3] Within OSBI specifically, many of the solutions are based on Java source code. Java can be used with many operating systems and applications, making it easy to integrate with other solutions — whether as a standalone or embedded application. Unfortunately, at the same time development times take longer due to the fact that solutions are not finalized.

In terms of learning curves, the time to learn a new programming language, even if it is similar to others, is not always easy. For developers transitioning from proprietary software development to open environments, acquiring new skills are essential. What this leads to is the development of

---

[3]Obviously, this is a bit of a generalization. The point is that there are developers familiar with open source and open to its development, and others who are not.

new skillsets, which can be positive. On the other hand, time to value might be lower due to the time needed to become familiar with the programming environment. For organizations that are looking at OSBI as a quick time-to-value proposition, having to learn new skills and/or transfer skillsets may take time away from delivery. A challenge over and above the need to develop new skills is the development of a cost-benefit analysis to determine whether the extra time required to learn these skills (which leads to a longer deployment) will be offset by the value of managing an OSBI solution independently in the future.

The alternative to all of this for organizations without Java skills or familiarity with OS may be to select a commercial OSBI offering with professional services to get the solution up and running. Although this might provide an initial quicker implementation time, the fact remains that this is not a realistic solution for long-term maintenance. The only way to resolve this is to take the time spent by outside developers (i.e., through professional services or hired consultants) to take training and acquire the required programming language skillsets to manage the solution over time. This management includes adding new data sources, developing new analytics and reports, maintaining the data management layer, etc. In essence, this is the same issue when looking at the skillsets required in Chapter 16.

Addressing multiple developers within a single development environment

As mentioned several times, OS code enables many disparate entities to change and customize BI applications for their own use. This can be a good thing when working independently, but when collaborating on large BI projects it can create a large challenge. For instance:

- How do you make sure that everyone is working off the same source code?
- How are changes managed?
- How are community contributors told about changes while they are working on their own portion?
- How do all of these questions apply to product releases and vendor roadmaps?

All of these questions need to be addressed, whether working as a team within one organization or contributing to a broader OS project with other developers across many companies. Answering these questions actually provides good insight into and highlights the difficulties faced by OS developers. For example, let's say a university wants to expand its ad hoc reporting capabilities to include the admissions process and general student performance but does not have a large budget to do, so it might look towards OS to evaluate what solutions are available for free. Doing so, however, means that even though costs will remain low, the time required to deliver the solution may increase because of the customizations required to get the system up and running. As mentioned above, resources who understand and who have worked with Java and OS in the past are essential to the process. Otherwise, training will be required, lengthening the overall time to implementation. Once all of that is settled, however, organizations can focus on the questions above as a starting point to managing their BI project.

OSBI vendors and the communities they support are very careful about the versioning of their code to make sure that developers have access to up-to-date source code and are aware of any changes made. Within community projects this becomes essential due to the fact that multiple people may be working on the same aspects of a single solution. These developers need to know where plug-in points are and what others are working on so that changes and additions can be reused. The bottom line is that having multiple resources working within a single set of source code leads to the need to manage interactions, and entry points need to be spelled out.

Because most community OS solutions are based on this community involvement and require it, not only is there a focus on creating relevant updates but also incorporating those updates within product releases that occur regularly. Obviously, all of these aspects are positive elements of community interaction, but unless developers are aware of how to contribute to the community and how to access the right resources, extra time might be required for writing code or finding one's way around the community to figure out things out.

Developing a strong data management structure

This challenge really does exist irrespective of the type of deployment you choose. The reality, however, is that unless an organization has a mature BI environment, its focus on broader data management might not be a priority. In many cases, organizations are not aware of the importance of a broader data management initiative that goes beyond BI. For instance, depending on the information requirements for analytics, the data sources selected might only be a subset of what is required on a broader level to create a greater understanding of overall business processes and performance.

Obviously, targeted BI needs are different than the development of a large-scale or organization-wide data management program. The challenge becomes developing a balance between BI development and a broader understanding of how data interrelates and what aspects need to be managed. The areas to look at include customers (as is most common to coordinate marketing and customer experience), products, management of suppliers and partners, etc. How this links to BI bases itself on the information itself. Even though a subset of customer information is required to link to sales data, which in turn ties into supply chain, which may then reflect on internal support procedures, a circle of information access is required to maintain an accurate picture of what is happening throughout the whole supply chain and customer lifecycle.

Even though all of this sounds simple, strong data management and BI cohesion is far from simple. Talend is an example of a vendor developing MDM offerings in addition to its data integration suites to broaden access to master data management through the use of OS. The general realization that these two data intensive initiatives are not independent of one another is increasing within the market. The challenge, however, is to integrate everything into a single environment — which, based on current IT infrastructures and BI use/adoption, may not be possible in the short term. The reasons for this include:

- Lack of budget for multiple software projects that require multiple levels of data to be managed simultaneously.
- Lack of internal skillsets. This is similar to the issue above in relation to requiring specific developer skills to be able to develop, tweak, and maintain an additional offering over time.
- Overall data integration is challenging. Even with open standards, customizing solutions and adding a data management layer means that a lot of time is spent making everything work together.

Even with these roadblocks, data management cannot be overlooked. Organizations and their information assets are continuously becoming more valuable. People can no longer rely on intuition to make valid decisions. Consequently, the more data is managed across the organization, the more likely this data can be transformed into valid information to help drive business performance.

Data integration and proprietary software

Just as discussed above (within the data management section), data integration remains a large portion of any BI project. Three forms of data integration exist within any OSBI project. They are as follows:

- Using OS data integration as an extension of the OSBI solution being used.
- Traditional data integration software, such as Informatica, to integrate data within an OS environment.
- Hand-coding to create ETL code by internal developers.

Each of these types of integration will change the effort involved. But it is important to realize that each will have its individual challenges related to time to develop/customize the final product, number of supported sources, and skillsets required to manage these processes over time. Solutions such as Kettle, Talend, and CloverETL are specifically for OS and generally follow the same processes and requirements as those within other OS environments. In some cases, these offerings are embedded within other OSBI offerings to create a single approach to BI development.

The same types of processes and task requirements will exist within proprietary data integration offerings. Although more challenging in terms of integration with OS, the fact is that these solutions may be more powerful when looking at data quality and other data integration activities. When looking at hand-coding, the challenges are different. The robustness of the designed solution will be limited by the expertise of those in charge of creating the scripts to manage the data integration processes.

The real challenge, however, isn't traditional BI integration activities, because many source systems are common proprietary offerings. This makes integration easier because commonality breeds a general number of APIs or plug-ins to enable broader integration. But what happens when these integration offerings are used to transfer data to proprietary offerings? Many BI solutions today are deployed using proprietary software, such as Microsoft or SAP. In some of these cases, businesses still want to use OS as a way to integrate multiple data sets. In these cases, the challenge of integrating with these solutions can be difficult for businesses. Overall, developers need to be aware that opting for free software that enables integration may limit the robust functionality and general feature sets based on what is available within the BI solution itself. In essence, it may be important to note that free source code for data integration may or may not provide ease of use or quicker time to development. Processes might take longer, and the list of potential roadblocks goes on. Basically, integration with proprietary offerings is no easy task and requires a variety of development know-how to ensure that multiple types of solutions are covered.

Hardware and cost limitations

This challenge is also one that will apply to any project, even those extending beyond OS. The difference, however, is that OS projects are more flexible because of their open standards to enable broader integration. However, this means that the ease of integration will be dependent on what currently exists. If the organization has already used OS solutions as part of their IT infrastructure, such as their databases or other applications, etc., general hardware will more likely be used.

When looking at BI specifically, issues become more pronounced with the use of data warehouse appliances and data warehousing environments that are based on proprietary hardware. Due to broad BI deployments, many of these offerings are made to integrate with OS offerings. The challenge presents itself when looking at broader OS infrastructures and the debate between proprietary and other hardware options — for instance, Dell versus HP or the use of proprietary options in general.

When looking at this more in-depth, many businesses look towards OS to save money. The money saved tends to offset the time spent developing solutions. Companies don't always have the financial resources to develop robust data warehousing infrastructures but might have resources internally that can be used to design and maintain optimized BI environments. Not-for-profit and higher education represent two industries that tend to select OS due to the development flexibility and lack of higher software costs.

The issue with this model is the potential limitations that exist. Limiting cost of development means that many of these organizations are stuck with the IT infrastructure that exists and must work towards optimizing what exists versus developing or implementing a new offering that provides greater value. What many newer data warehousing environments offer, especially the proprietary offerings, are more agile environments. In some cases this means automated schema designs, and in others it means more flexibility maintenance over time. Flexibility in the sense of adding new data sources over time, real-time data updates, complex analytics support, and the list goes on. Within OS environments, these features might exist but may require more time and the know-how to optimize data warehousing environments. The reality is that in many cases it makes more sense to spend the money to select an optimized environment as opposed to having to tweak offerings continuously to take into account changes.

Working with OS source code

Although working with OS code and its general differentiations were covered when looking at the requirement to develop new skillsets for developers not familiar with Java-based programming languages, working with OS source code may also provide other challenges to programmers. In general, because code is provided for free and many people use it, vendors need to be careful in how they offer their code. The source code itself cannot be put together haphazardly, as developers need to know where the plug-ins are, how it's organized, etc. In essence, the code itself has to be clean.

On the flip side, this may require taking the additional time to learn the source code and how it's laid out, read documentation, and collaborate with others just to gain an understanding. And even though this leads to better knowledge in the future, initially this effort can be more time consuming. For commercial offerings this is different. In these cases, the code will be supported by the solution provider. And although quicker in terms of development times, for businesses intent on OS because of the flexibility and lack of proprietary elements, commercial adoption is beginning to mimic traditional BI offerings at a greater rate.

Transferring from traditional solutions to OS offerings

The market is slowly transitioning towards broader OS adoption. Organizations are starting to look at OS as a valid alternative to proprietary BI offerings. OSBI vendors are responding by broadening their offerings to include commercial solutions. What this means is that the OSBI landscape is shifting towards a traditional BI model. Obviously, these solutions take into account new trends such as mobile BI, agile delivery, increasing self-service, and the like. The reality, however, is that for die-hard proponents of OS, these solutions no longer follow the virtues of what OS is meant to be. Aside from SpagoBI, which bases its revenue on projects and not on software, the other OSBI offerings provide community and commercial versions with a continued push towards commercial offerings and making sure that focus on commercial availability is the main focus of new releases.

Companies looking at OS as a lower-cost alternative may not be affected by the fact that these offerings are so similar. Other businesses that like the idea of OS because of its outlook may be quickly disappointed by the fact that these solutions are becoming less and less differentiated over time. Unfortunately, this means that over time OSBI will continue to converge with the traditional BI market.

Organizations considering BI for the first time need to understand that OS is not as different as it used to be. After all, in many cases newer adopters of OSBI might not have the internal resources and, even if they do, they might not have multiple resources on hand. This can have longer term implications due to the need to transfer skillsets over time or to make changes that require additional developers in order to make these changes more quickly.

The real time to value

OSBI has two options — community access or commercial solution offerings. Either choice will have different implications in relation to the time it takes to get value out of the solution. For instance, depending on the commercial solution chosen, the end product will be very similar to traditional BI projects. Community versions, on the other hand, take longer to develop due to the source code customization. Financial savings do not always translate into ROI due to the extra time required to develop solutions from scratch.

The bottom line is that businesses expect BI offerings to provide quick time to value through broad deployments, and community OS is quite limited in this area, at least in comparison to other market offerings. The payoffs need to be weighed against the limitations to determine whether these limitations are worth it in the end — and this decision will continue to be individual to the organization, and maybe even down to the department level.

Understanding the real benefits and challenges of software development

This chapter has shown that there is an overlap between benefits and challenges, and business versus technical considerations. In reality, instead of businesses building cases based on what technical requirements exist, there should be more of a focus on the business value that these solutions provide. What organizations hope to achieve and why is just as important as the path taken to get there. But the unfortunate reality is that many companies forget this fact in favor of technical specifications. Both aspects are equally important, but the most important thing to remember is that the technical requirements and resources should be used in support of delivering business value to the organization and the various business users throughout.

Takeaways/
recommendations

Getting started: A checklist for OSBI readiness

Each section of this book should have given you pieces of a larger puzzle. Whether to select OS, the business considerations, and the technical knowledge required to get there mark the areas that are essential to making the right solution choices. For vendor-specific information, you can refer to www.osbibook.com. This site includes a breakdown of vendor offerings and where they fit within the BI market landscape. In addition, the site provides updated information about what's happening within the broader BI marketplace.

To prepare for software selection and to put all of the pieces together in terms of business and technical OSBI implementation requirements, the following checklist will help you identify the tasks and considerations involved in planning your OSBI implementation. The first step towards OSBI adoption and implementation is to identify whether or not OS is right for your business. The items listed below do not provide a traditional checklist in terms of telling you what the right choices are for your organization. The goal of this book has been to give you the tools to make the right decisions independently of marketing hype and to provide an overall understanding of the increasing importance and expansion of OS within the broader BI marketplace.

The following are the initial considerations any organization should look at when identifying whether to select OSBI and, beyond that, what factors should be considered to help ensure project success.

Familiarity with OS and current BI infrastructure		
	Considerations	**Implications**
1	Do you already have familiarity with OS?	Is there an understanding of OS within the organization? This means the realization that free software does not mean free project and an understanding of what the implications are in relation to time and money.
2	What about OSBI offerings?	Do project sponsors understand the market and what solutions exist? It is important to identify which ones fit the needs of the business. Many solutions overlap, or have a variety of components, so it is essential to identify which offerings are most likely to address business needs and deliver valuable insights.
3	What proprietary offerings exist?	The solutions that exist in-house may affect an OS implementation. Integration between data sources is not intuitive. The effort involved needs to be accounted for when planning a project.

4	What are the integration requirements in relation to proprietary limitations?	The number of data sources, how they fit, and what limitations exist are areas that need to be explored. In some cases, APIs exist, but either way additional work will probably be required.
5	Are there specific capabilities that you require for your business?	This refers to any vertical market or departmental requirements. If requirements are very specific it might make more sense to select a targeted solution and stay away from the additional development required within an OSBI environment.
6	Do you have internal resources with OS experience?	General familiarity and actual expertise in-house differs. In the first case, organizations may be familiar but do not necessarily have any expertise in relation to development. In the second case, developers exist in-house and are available to develop targeted BI applications.
7	Is your organization open to the framework associated with the OS model?	Although not essential, understanding the concepts behind OS might help determine whether its adoption suits the organization. For instance, even though price ends up being a main consideration, there are many not-for-profit businesses and government agencies that select OS due to their lack of proprietary environment.
	Bottom Line	Selecting OS requires understanding what you are getting into. This means making sure that resources are available or can be made available, project timelines are understood, and the solution limitations that may exist are known. Essentially, if you answer no to any of these questions, then more information is needed before selecting an OSBI offering.

Business considerations

Once the decision has been made, organizations can begin to identify what business requirements should be considered:

Business requirements identification		
	Considerations	**Implications**
1	What business problem(s) are you trying to solve?	Irrespective of the type of solution selected, businesses need to develop their BI programs based on a business pain being faced. What questions need to be answered? What gaps exist? These are questions that are required to help design the solution.
2	Do you already have BI in place?	This may refer back to some of the initial questions. Does something exist that can be shared or built upon?
3	Can in-house BI offerings address newer problems?	In some cases, current BI initiatives can be expanded – whether based on additional licenses, new data sources, or different applications of existing data.

4	Does collaboration exist between business and IT departments?	How disparate business units work together can be expanded to include how BI enables collaboration across departments. Some solutions enable broader collaboration than others. Consequently, this is something that should be considered, depending on how broad the planned BI usage will be.
5	Is the information already stored within a data warehouse?	Different efforts will be required when adding new data to a data warehouse. Obviously, there are also many organizations developing new data warehouses. Whether new or expanding, the data stored needs to be identified to eliminate redundancies and ensure that security and privacy are met.
6	Who is managing the data governance process?	While outside the scope of this book, it is important to understand data governance and identify who will be in charge of managing the data quality and management process over time.
	Bottom Line	At this point, it is assumed that OSBI is the solution type of choice. These business considerations are starting points and all should be considered. In essence, these are the first steps when considering an implementation. The business checklist can help get you started.

Technical considerations

Here are some general technical questions that should be addressed before embarking on an OSBI implementation:

Data warehousing and data integration		
	Considerations	**Implications**
1	What are the data warehouse requirements?	This includes latency, data sources, integration, analytics, data marts, and the list goes on. This is a key area that requires an understanding of the wider IT infrastructure within the organization.
2	How many data sources require integration?	More data sources can increase the complexities of development.
3	What data latency is required?	Although the promise of real-time data access is becoming more of a realistic possibility, the reality is that not all companies need information instantaneously. Latency requirements will affect the type of infrastructure. This also links to future expectations, as it is important to make sure that as latency needs change, the BI infrastructure can handle these requirements.
4	What APIs exist? And what requires extra building?	Depending on the data sources and overall integration requirements, APIs can make the process easier. Identifying whether these exist for the sources you want to bring into the data warehouse can help save time getting the data into the required format.

5	What about future data requirements?	It is not always easy to define what you will need in the future, but anticipating data storage requirements and usage can help you develop a solution and BI infrastructure that supports future growth, helping to save you money in the long-run and develop more effective solutions.
	Bottom Line	Make sure the IT infrastructure can support your project and that integration requirements are taken into account before starting. After all, many issues that create project roadblocks are those that occur during the integration process.

Putting all the pieces together

Whether business users or IT, the fact is that any IT project, in addition to the considerations above, will have to balance what is required versus what is desired. What this means specifically is that organizations will have a list of must-have requirements. Many of these are IT-related in terms of support for operating systems, data integration, or selected hardware. Some are more business-related and reflect the must-have business requirements for BI to be successful. For instance, specific metrics may be required for sales and marketing analytics that cannot be overlooked. Without these features, the solution will not be effective nor provide what the end user is looking for.

In general, the nice-to-haves represent the business requirements that do not fit into the required category but would be a bonus if included. Although not always easy to define, many times organizations understand what they are looking for in the sense of knowing what they hope BI will achieve or represent within their company. They cannot, however, identify the specific features and functions they require in order to achieve this. The complicated part is identifying what is required versus what is only desired.

Looking at both, it stands to reason that in many cases it may be hard to decipher the differences because during the requirements gathering period the differences are not spelled out, and business users may feel that everything is equally important. This is where many IT project managers end up using their discretion to identify what is really needed to get the solution up and running. Obviously, solutions that are more ad hoc in nature and enable broader customization at the end-user level can help solve this disconnect between what is wanted versus what is actually needed. But this is most likely not the case when dealing with community OS that is highly customized for the end user already based on previous IT development efforts.

In some cases, organizations cannot identify the specific features they require but list the metrics or reports that are essential to replicate. In these situations, it might be easier to break down the essential components of the new solution by taking a look at what currently exists, the information needed, and where the gaps are. For example, looking at a report and gaining an understanding of how employees decipher the report, analyze the data, and what steps they take once they have the information. In some cases, if the report was designed effectively, they can take action automatically. In other cases, end users export data to perform more in-depth analyses or have to search for additional information. In these situations, the new solution should include these factors as must-haves in order to make the whole process quicker and more efficient.

What all of this boils down to is that IT needs to understand the difference between both and developers need to be able to balance what is a required feature versus what is a nice-to-have or potential future feature that can be added when time permits. This is why even though this is a chapter dedicated to developers, understanding the business requirements is key to developing end-user applications that are easy to use and beneficial to the business.

Some of the reasons behind the importance of understanding these differences include:

- Increase in project success likelihood. Many project failures can be attributed to the lack of requirements translation from business to technical. What this means is that organizations try to implement everything without understanding what the most important aspects are. This is why solutions go through multiple iterations and demand more time. By understanding these general requirements, developers are more likely to get it right the first time.
- Higher adoption rates. Once end users are understood, they are more likely to actually use the solution because it provides valuable insights. In addition, because they have been asked about what their needs are and actually see their required solution(s) come to fruition, they are more likely to adopt it and use it instead of their traditional Excel or other interface.
- More cohesion between business units/end users and IT departments. Overall, all of this leads to better communication within the organization. And this in turn leads to better development over time.

The business implications are:

- More process-centric and efficient. BI can be difficult to use. By building solutions that are focused on the must-have requirements, businesses can focus on accessing the information they require without having to go back to the developer for constant reiterations. Also, because of the high level of customization capabilities, BI solutions can be tailored to match business processes or more process-centric BI applications.
- Quicker access to data. Obviously, part of gathering business requirements and determining the must-haves is gathering the data that is needed to make better decisions or understand performance. In many cases, organizations can optimize their OSBI environments to deliver relevant information in a more timely fashion. Understanding the data required and when it is required is important for providing information faster.
- Easier decision making and analytics. BI provides greater ROI and business insights. With broader access to information, business users can get what they need more quickly.

Important OS factors

Before looking at OS specifically, let's look at general factors that are required within any BI project. Then we can expand this towards what is required for OS projects specifically. Either way, the first set of factors is also essential within any BI initiative, including OS. Here are some of the must-haves in relation to important factors to look at:

- Programming language. What is the programming environment? Many BI offerings require SQL scripting abilities. Essentially, the solution that is provided out of the box may address

80% of the functionality your company requires, but the additional 20% needs customization. Some organizations choose to have outside entities perform the customization. Many businesses, however, like to control what happens in-house, making developer resources an automatic requirement. In either case, businesses need to understand what exists in-house and whether there are any gaps.

- APIs help make integration easier. BI may be one of the most important areas in terms of the importance of integrating multiple solutions into a single database, or at least moving many datasets into a series of data marts. Basically, APIs serve two functions. The first is to enable developers to use pre-made connectors so that multiple systems can communicate. The second is more practical. When APIs exist, there is a related assumption (and quite correctly) that the specific solution of interest is one that is widely used within the BI solution. For instance, when no API exists, organizations should wonder about the experience of the solution provider with that particular source system or application. Although not a reason to exclude the vendor, future support issues are an important enough factor to consider in relation to thinking long and hard about why your software selection is the best in terms of addressing your business needs.

- Data complexity. Data sources, source systems, long-term maintenance, etc. Not enough can be said about data integration requirements and managing the increasing levels of complexity that exist. How they are handled differ within any given solution. Where Pentaho has Kettle, Jaspersoft has Talend. Understanding what the differences are becomes essential to making the most out of the integration environment. In addition, complexity leads to issues related to data warehouse performance, SLA delivery, and maintenance. In many cases, even though the OS software is free, creating a supporting IT environment means adding new hardware, etc.

- Supported environments. One of the best examples of supported solutions and making sure your offering suits the requirements is Microsoft-enabled solutions. Many analytical dashboards are developed to support Microsoft. For instance, Excel- or Access-based data, or alternatively, to only work within a Windows Server environment. Although different in some respects, what both aspects have in common is the fact that offerings that do this are limited in who their customers can be, what is supported, and what can be done. For instance, if only supported within a Windows Server environment, then the solution will be limited by what is available within that server environment.

Now that we've addressed some of the general technical factors that developers cannot overlook, let's discuss some specific OSBI areas that expand beyond the items looked at above:

- Understanding Java. We've already discussed the importance of knowing or learning Java. Platforms or integration with solutions may differ, but within OSBI solution development, the overarching environment is the use of Java. Solutions are well maintained with version control. This enables collaboration between a variety of developers and companies.

- Time to develop and customize. In general, OS at the community level may be less expensive to develop, but at the same time it takes longer to develop. Therefore, considering whether the cost savings are worth the effort and extra time becomes essential, especially when vendors are pushing the ability to implement quickly, leading to quicker time to value. As price points continue to fall and as solutions become easier to implement more quickly, the benefit of free source code due to the no-to-low cost of software may lessen as an overall success factor or positive aspect of selection.

- Open standards. The ability to integrate solutions easily across multiple platforms is a definite bonus. But remember, limitations still exist as many of these solutions are only available within certain operating systems and development environments. Therefore, making everything work takes longer.

Can do with or without

In essence, this is an expansion of the evaluation of needed features versus nice to haves. But the difference is an important one — many smaller organizations or departments want to have it all. For initial OS implementations, starting with a targeted goal is essential. Within a community OS environment, the development effort can be time consuming. Getting quick time to value helps enhance adoption and use over time. Therefore, sometimes it is important to forego having everything at the start in order to have a select few applications that enable more direct access to consolidated information to get a broader view of specific departmental or business function needs. This may be in lieu of trying to capture everything and deliver it at once.

Generally, business users and managers know what they need and what process efficiency challenges they face. Consequently, developers need to develop solutions that match customer needs first. Hence, understanding the must haves versus nice to haves becomes the first step in terms of identifying what organizations can do without. Obviously, the general goal of BI is to provide end users with as much information as possible, but because OS development may take longer than other newer offerings, in order to provide quick access to BI it may be more realistic to get solutions up and running more quickly without providing everything. This means providing an initial access point to data and analytics with a game plan to provide access to everything in a subsequent delivery plan.

Another issue that arises is the need to work within both OS and traditional environments. The reality for many developers is a hybrid environment where OS lives side by side with traditional solutions. Because BI is already mature within many organizations, large amounts of money and effort have already been spent, making it difficult to continuously start from scratch. This provides an extra facet to these implementations and being able to identify what can be used and what needs to be developed. Basically, instead of reinventing the wheel, identifying what already exists and is being used successfully can help developers avoid reworking or redeveloping the same systems, lessening the possibility of redundant BI applications.

General conclusion

OSBI enables developer flexibility and a more adaptable framework in relation to many proprietary environments. At the same time, it is important to remember that the BI marketplace is slowly shifting. Free solutions exist, price points are lowering, and more diversity is available, making the proposition of OS different than it may have been a few years ago. Consequently, organizations need to look beyond the promise of free service to identify what "free" really means and how it compares to what other solution providers offer.

Index

Related Titles from Morgan Kaufmann

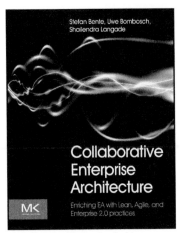

***Collaborative Enterprise Architecture:
Enriching EA with Lean, Agile, and
Enterprise 2.0 practices***

Stefan Bente, Uwe Bombosch, Shailendra
Langade

ISBN 9780124159341

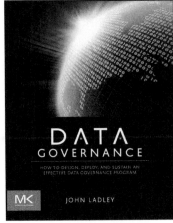

***Data Governance: How to Design,
Deploy and Sustain an Effective Data
Governance Program***

John Ladley

ISBN 9780124158290

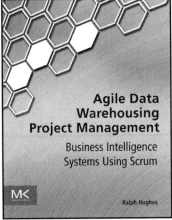

***Agile Data Warehousing Project
Management: Business Intelligence
Systems Using Scrum***

Ralph Hughes

ISBN 9780123964632

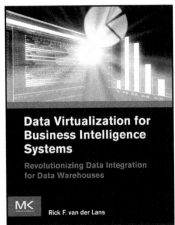

***Data Virtualization for Business
Intelligence Systems: Revolutionizing
Data Integration for Data Warehouses***

Rick van der Lans

ISBN 9780123944252

***Business Intelligence, Second Edition:
The Savvy Manager's Guide***

David Loshin

ISBN 9780123858894

Master Data Management

David Loshin

ISBN 9780123742254

mkp.com

Printed and bound by CPI Group (UK) Ltd, Croydon, CR0 4YY

08/05/2025

01864873-0001